THE VICTORIAN VISION

THE
VICTORIAN
VISION

Studies in
the Religious Novel

MARGARET M. MAISON

SHEED & WARD
NEW YORK

TO
THE MEMORY OF
J.F.T.P.

ACKNOWLEDGEMENTS

My thanks are due to Professor Kathleen Tillotson, Professor Geoffrey Bullough, Professor Samir Abdel-Hamid and Mr. Frank Nash for all their kindness and encouragement; to Dr. William Armstrong for his most helpful supervision of the Ph.D. thesis (University of London) from which this book developed; to the Editors of *English*, *The Month*, *The Aylesford Review* and *Stella Maris* for permission to use, particularly in the first and second sections of this book, material which originally appeared in their periodicals; to the late William Brown, formerly Chief Clerk of the British Museum Reading Room, for his invaluable assistance to me in my research; and, finally, to all the members of my family for their gallant patience and long-suffering.

CONTENTS

Chapter   *page*

   INTRODUCTION   I

PART 1: ORTHODOX FAITH

1: THE CHURCH OF ENGLAND

1. PRIGS, PEWS AND PENITENTS: EARLY TRACTARIAN
   FICTION   11
2. THREE SPINSTER NOVELISTS   31
3. REST IN THE CHURCH: CAUTIONARY TALES FOR
   HIGHER ANGLICANS   55
4. SURPLICED VIPERS AND SILLY WOMEN: THE PORTRAIT
   BY THE ENEMY   71
5. THE LOW CHURCH CONTRIBUTION   89
6. CHRISTIANITY MUSCULAR AND ELASTIC: THE BROAD
   CHURCH NOVELS   120

2: THE CATHOLIC CHURCH

7. GAIN AND LOSS: CONVERSIONS AND RENOUNCEMENTS   138
8. THE WICKED JESUIT AND COMPANY   169

3: THE FREE CHURCHES

9. SOME NONCONFORMIST NOVELS   183

PART 2: LOST FAITH

10. THE TRAGEDY OF UNBELIEF   209
11. TWO DISTINGUISHED DOUBTERS: MARK RUTHERFORD
   AND ROBERT ELSMERE   242
12. ESCAPE TO HAPPINESS   270

PART 3: TOWARDS UNORTHODOX FAITH

13. TOWARDS BEAUTY   287
14. TOWARDS GOODNESS   307
15. TOWARDS TRUTH   324
   CONCLUSION   339
   BIBLIOGRAPHY   347

THE VICTORIAN VISION

INTRODUCTION

INTRODUCTION

THE Victorian age saw the transformation of the religious novel from a literary outcast into a most respectable and widely fashionable form of fiction. Religious novels of that time were not, as mid-twentieth-century readers might imagine, novels merely coloured by Christian thought and feeling, interpreting characters and events from a Christian standpoint; they bore a far more distinctive label than that. Nor were they just novels about clerical life, like those of Anthony Trollope (who, from a spiritual point of view, did not penetrate very deep beneath the surplice). To the Victorian reader religious novels meant "theological romances", "Oxford Movement tales", novels of religious propaganda designed to disseminate a variety of forms of Christian belief, and assorted spiritual biographies in fiction, including converts' confessions of all kinds, from the apologies of ardent agnostics to the testimonies of Catholic "perverts".

Frequently topical and controversial in character, and usually written with a very strong moral purpose, these stories were at first highly suspect on account of their inevitable mixture of the sacred and the profane. When George Eliot in

1839 condemned religious novels as "hateful" books, "monsters that we do not know how to class", she, like the majority of serious-minded people of her day who shared her opinion, never guessed how completely these "monsters" were to conquer the reading public during the next sixty years, triumphantly breaking down all barriers of prejudice (including her own) and storming every spiritual citadel until at the end of the century reputable theologians were taking to novel-writing to get a popular hearing, cardinals, bishops and prime ministers all had best-sellers to their credit, and the romances of the faithful were quoted in a thousand pulpits. The most glorious zenith of the religious novel was indeed reached in the reign of Queen Victoria.

The history of religious fiction in England can of course be traced back far beyond the nineteenth century. The name of John Bunyan, "father of the novel", may suggest itself as a possible parent, but its ancestors can be traced even further back—to the Bible, with the stories of the Old Testament and the parables of the New, to the Grail legends, to allegory, to the long tradition of hagiography from the sixth to the thirteenth century, and to the "moral fable" type of literature throughout the ages. At the beginning of the nineteenth century an important precursor was already flourishing in the form of the tract or religious "tale", and the Evangelicals were just awakening to the immense possibilities of harnessing popular fiction to the service of religion. Stories of converted cannibals, or sinners who found a Friend, or groaning victims of Satan's snares circulated in their thousands; the popularity of tales by Hannah More or Legh Richmond was enormous, and the fame of Mrs. Sherwood's stories has lasted, transmuted into notoriety, until the present day.

But it was the Oxford Movement which really launched the religious novel on a large scale. This storm that rent the ark of the Establishment, sweeping some into safe harbour and casting others, wrecked and desolate, on every theological and philosophical shore, was responsible for a perfect *furor scribendi*; its lightnings fired the imagination of countless Victorians and from the eighteen-forties onwards we find young teenagers, middle-aged matrons, elderly governesses, statesmen, undergraduates and innumerable clerics of widely varying creeds, ages and talents all busily engaged in writing religious novels, chiefly for propaganda purposes. The union of religion and romance could no longer be frowned upon by the orthodox, and although protests against some of the more fantastic fruits of this union continued to be made throughout the century, the stalwart defenders of faith through fiction justified their literary activities with vigour. If a novel was to be about human life, then:

> . . . human life without *God*! Who will dare tell us we shall paint *that*? Authors who feel the solemnity of their calling cannot suppress the truth that is within them. Having put their hands to the plough, they may not turn aside, nor look either to the right or the left. They must go straight on, as the inward voice impels; and He who seeth their hearts will guide them aright.

Thus wrote Mrs. Craik, halfway through the century, and legions of novelists of the period would have echoed her words, convinced that for them the writing of novels was a sacred mission.

In the Church of England, Tractarian writers felt impelled to educate the public in "Church principles" through novels as well as tracts; those of Low Church persuasions turned to fiction as a divinely inspired means of attacking Tractarianism and exalting Evangelical truth in its stead, while Broad Churchmen wrote lively novels with a multitude of vigorous moral purposes, believing, like their opponents, that they were doing their duty as instruments of God. "One is guiding me and driving me", wrote Charles Kingsley, embracing authorship as a kind of crusade. In the Catholic Church converts quickly followed Newman's example in recounting their experiences in fiction, and even members of the Free Churches overcame their dislike of "the Devil's Bible" and wrote stories of Nonconformist life and faith. Those who had left the churches to interpret the teachings of Christ in a new and unorthodox way seized upon the novel as their most powerful mouthpiece. George Macdonald openly declared that, having been deprived of his pulpit by the Congregational Church, he was using the novel as a substitute medium for the propagation of his religious convictions, and Mrs. Humphry Ward, Marie Corelli and many other exponents of new creeds all reached the public in this way.

Religious stories thus developed far beyond the level of the mere pious "wholly holy, hale and wholly wholesome" type of tale. Fiction became the pulpit, the confessional and the battlefield for countless Victorians, and the novel was used by them more than any other form of art to portray the religious movements of their time, to be a vehicle for all manner of theological and ecclesiastical propaganda, to conduct debates and controversies, and to tell the world of their doubts and conflicts, their spiritual travels and phases of faith. The Victorian pilgrim of the second half of the century would find it perfectly natural to tell of his progress, and regress, through the medium of the novel.

For regress there certainly was, and it was the movement of mind towards scepticism, one of the most significant spiritual developments of the Victorian age, that proved perhaps the strongest inspiration of all to the writing of religious novels. So strong was it that in 1869 Lady Georgiana Fullerton could write:

> Now scarcely a book of any sort is published which does not take sides for or against religion . . . Even Sir Walter Scott's novels have almost ceased to charm the present generation. Stirring descriptions of historical events, glowing pictures of the pageantries of past ages, have far less interest, even for the young, than the analysis of character and revelations of a hidden life, which are often contained in the novels of the present day. Whatever treats of inward conflicts, secret perplexities, and the various trials of individual minds and hearts, necessarily commands attention at a moment when anything that can throw light on the difficulties which so many are experiencing may tend, even remotely, to their solution.

Religious novels chronicled faithfully the many skirmishes, truces, victories and defeats in those battles of belief waged in many "individual minds and hearts" in the Victorian age.

Indeed, so valuable seem these novels as powerfully revealing searchlights focused upon the Victorian spiritual scene, and as sensitive seismographic recordings of the cracks and upheavals in the accepted religious tradition, that they deserve a better fate than the neglect accorded to them by the mid-twentieth century. For, despite the advance of modern scholarship towards a reinterpretation of Victorian literature, our rich and abundant heritage of religious novels remains largely untouched. Its very abundance is probably a drawback, for the reader is presented with such an overwhelming *embarras de richesse* that he scarcely knows where to begin. Our own very different religious climate also puts these novels at a disadvantage; so many of the stories run counter to the trend of modern taste and may inspire the reader of today with little more than boredom, revulsion or irreverent amusement. But there are splendid treasures among the huge dust-heaps and even those novels most sadly lacking in literary talent or spiritual profundity still remain for us as precious clues to the understanding of the Victorian march of mind. They are worth at least a glance or two, and, using for the sake of clarity the denominational framework of Christian belief in Victorian England, this survey will attempt to give the modern reader a glimpse, swift and superficial though it may be, into some of the many religious novels that so affected his Victorian forefathers, shaking or strengthening them in their beliefs, moving them to tears or paroxysms of rage, filling them with doubt and despair or bringing them to repentance and conversion.

1

ORTHODOX FAITH

1: THE CHURCH OF ENGLAND

CHAPTER 1

PRIGS, PEWS AND PENITENTS: EARLY
TRACTARIAN FICTION

I F England escaped the horrors of a revolution in the Victorian age her National Church did not. The history of the Church of England during this time is a stirring record of warfare, struggle, persecution, agonized secession and fiercest conflict, differences of religious belief causing hostilities not merely confined to verbal clashes, lawsuits and imprisonments but extending to the level of actual physical fighting. Witness the state of St. Barnabas' Church, Pimlico, in 1851:

> During the whole of that memorable year it was held only as a beleaguered city is held by armed men against the violence of enemies who battered the doors, shouted through the windows, hissed in the aisles, and tried to storm the chancel gates.

The Anglican Church had indeed awakened from her eighteenth-century slumbers to become a real Church Militant. It was unfortunate, however, that so much of her war was internal, that the enemy was within as well as without, and that, in addition to the attacks of scientists and biblical critics, rationalists and agnostics, the hostilities of Dissent and the audacities of "papal aggression", she had to contend with innumerable battles among her own ranks. The three principal groups in the Church of England, High, Low and Broad, were frequently at daggers drawn, and controversy raged throughout most of Queen Victoria's reign, the ritualism that marked the second phase of the Oxford Movement causing even greater uproars and the growth of religious liberalism provoking the increasing wrath of its opponents as the century progressed. High attacked Low and Broad, Low and Broad attacked High, Broad attacked Low, Low attacked Broad, confusions within the parties themselves making matters worse, for each group had its moderates, its extremists and various divergences, giving every appearance of a reign of anarchy within the one Church. Here is an attempt at clerical classification made by the Rev. W. J. Conybeare in his essay on "Church Parties" (1853). He gives:

Low Church   Normal type ("Evangelical")
                      Exaggerated type ("Record-ite")
                      Stagnant type ("Low and Slow")

High Church	Normal type ("Anglican")
	Exaggerated type ("Tractarian")
	Stagnant type ("High and Dry")
Broad Church	Normal type (Subdivided into "theoretical" and "antitheoretical")
	Exaggerated type ("Concealed infidels")
	Stagnant type ("Concealed infidels").

Passions ran high, causing many broken hearts and homes, and the unhappy verdict of the Rev. Thomas Mozley, Newman's brother-in-law, gives us a vivid glimpse of the chaotic situation. He wrote in his reminiscences:

> The Church of England was one vast arena of controversy. Ten thousand popes—the lay popes ten times more arrogant, unreasonable and bitter than the clerical, and the female popes a hundred times worse than either—laid down the law and demanded instant obedience.

Any survey of the Anglican novels of this period must take into account this state of division and warfare within the Church of England, for the majority of religious stories of the time not only reflect these passionate controversies but are actually inspired by them, and innumerable "lay popes", "clerical popes" and "female popes" all took up their pens to join in the War of the Novels and to lay down their religious laws through the medium of fiction.

Early Tractarian fiction shows something of this heady mixture of idealism and aggression. Tracts for the times were followed by tales for the times and early efforts to reach the public by pious allegory were quickly ousted by "red-hot Puseyite stories" and "Oxford Movement tales", which flourished considerably in the eighteen-forties and fifties and were enthusiastically welcomed by keen Tractarians.

Today, however, even the most devout High Anglican would survey these novels with a more critical eye. Their faults are glaring. Crude in technique, clumsy in construction, they are deficient in plot, characterization and entertainment value. In general they conform to two set patterns and describe two imaginary types of lives—either the history of the chastened penitent or the life and opinions of a kind of propaganda prig. "Whether we like it or not," wrote Elizabeth Sewell, "we all by our lives preach a sermon, either of warning or example." Early Tractarian novels are chiefly concerned with these lives of warning and example. There are countless stories of those who go astray, especially in the quagmires of ignorance, Dissent, Liberalism and Socialism (all devilish snares for unwary Victorian churchmen) and who, often in the last chapter, learn the error of their ways and return to the bosom of the Church, usually only to die there. Equally plentiful are stories of men, women and children who, absorbing the truth of church doctrine, develop into founts of wisdom, model clergymen, zealous schoolmasters, exemplary farmers, dutiful wives and mothers and ideal citizens. In the first type the novel is a cautionary tale, in the second, a mere manual for instruction, a sort of glorified Church Catechism. Both, in the early years of Tractarian fiction, are brimful of sermons. Not content with letting the lives of their characters preach the messages of warning or example, the authors often burst out *in propria persona*, fulminating against Evangelicals or pews or poaching, or the dangers of rebellious intellect and private judgement.

Such prigs, penitents and "preachments" abound in the novels of the Rev. William Gresley. He and his friend, the Rev. Francis Edward Paget, another country clergyman, are, according to *Fraser's Magazine*, the "acknowledged fathers" of Tractarian fiction, and Gresley in particular holds up for us the first fictional models of Puseyite virtue and reveals the "most awful and perilous position" of those separated from Tractarian truth. In his two early novels, *Portrait of an English Churchman* (1838) and *Charles Lever* (1841), he draws his typical saint and sinner and sets the stock patterns for succeeding novelists to copy.

His English Churchman is a clergyman called Herbert who combines "deep thought" with "youthful ardour" and "practical piety". He explains his religion in detail, expounds the *via media*, condemns the ungodliness of daily newspapers and London life, gives sound advice to unsettled Oxford students—*"Shun the agreeable infidel and the accomplished profligate"*— and lashes out unmercifully at Dissenters, while advising churchmen never to lose their tempers in argument.

Herbert is the first of a long line of "new High" clerical heroes, all smug, colourless and encyclopaedic in their religious conversations. There is another in Gresley's *Bernard Leslie: or, a Tale of the Last Ten Years* (1842). (Tractarian writers frequently used alternative titles, a common practice in popular fiction of the time.) Bernard Leslie circulates an enormously long pamphlet on the dangers of Dissent, rebukes the Liberal parish doctor and reforms an eccentric curate who, with tonsure and cassock, is going a little too far in reviving the "superstitions of Romanism". (Exaggerated forms of ritualism received short shrift from Tractarian novelists of this decade.) Herbert is celibate, but Bernard Leslie gets married, the author treating the subject rather gingerly, but nevertheless defending married clergy. (It is interesting to notice how clerical writers of the period generally fight shy of marriage and its preliminaries in their novels. Paget tells us in the course of one of his stories that he "would not write an episode on love-making for any consideration" and therefore has to leave it all to "the reader's discretion and imagination". But those religious novelists brave enough to get their characters to the altar have a golden opportunity for preaching which they seldom miss.) Bernard Leslie finally restores the dilapidated parish church, thus fulfilling one of the cherished dreams of all Tractarians of that time.

Even more goody-goody are the heroes of Robert Armitage's novels. In his *Dr. Hookwell; or, the Anglo-Catholic Family* (1842)—one of the first novels to employ the new term "Anglo-Catholic"—we meet the reverend doctor, a man of "mighty intellect and superior disposition", who holds forth to an eager circle of listeners on almost every aspect of Tractarian worship. "Anglo-Catholicism", he tells them, "is not a novelty on the earth but a good old Protestant way." His opinions occupy three massive volumes—such novels as these could hardly be accused of frivolity and lack of seriousness!

A similar mine of information is Ernest Singleton, the clerical hero of Armitage's novel of that name (1848), who discourses on a bewildering variety of topics from capital punishment to the intelligence of tortoises. Unlike so many early Tractarians who, holding the "branch theory," turned eastward to the Orthodox communions, Ernest looks westward to the new world and is anxious to promote more cordial relations between the Church of England and her "daughter" Church in America. His biography is nauseatingly exemplary and the modern reader soon tires of the unbearably overemphasized moral of the importance of being Ernest.

Nor can we feel much sympathy or admiration for the model English citizen in Gresley's *Clement Walton* (1840), a paragon of insularity, who daily blesses the providence of God in supplying England with a "pure reformed Communion", "a healthy branch of the true Church". Such heroes as these, all pompous, didactic and faultless, are merely mouthpieces through which their authors voice their own prejudices and predilections. They all talk too much, either in

monologue or disputation, and, like Samuel
Wilberforce, the bishop who used to prepare
"launchers" (suitable conversational openings
calculated to lead to the discussion of some vital
matter), they are all made to introduce subjects
of talk as a mere peg on which to hang their
authors' religious opinions.

The lives of the penitents are slightly more
colourful, and in describing the temptations into
which their erring heroes are led the authors
have more scope both for narrative and for
imaginative writing, although they are somewhat hampered by early Victorian moral and
literary conventions, as Gresley's *Charles Lever*
shows. Charles is the victim of Satanic influences,
a Dissenting father and a Latitudinarian schoolmaster who teaches him "a sort of general religion". (Gresley here quotes the delightful story
of the French tutor who asked his pupils' father:
*"Mais, monsieur, quelle religion faut-il en-
seigner à vos enfants? J'en connais toutes."*) Poor
Charles inevitably becomes a Liberal, then a
Socialist and then apparently something too
dreadful to mention. "We must here draw a
veil over some portion of our hero's life", says
the author discreetly. However, after seeing a
savage mob in action, Charles becomes ill and
contrite, and finally, as a "sincere penitent" he
supports the tottering steps of his aged mother

to church for the daily prayers that the vicar, "a most zealous Church-restorer", has instituted. Charles, of course, is a mere puppet, but the book is an interesting social document, revealing and analysing as it does the various Tractarian anathemas—Dissent, Liberalism, Socialism, Chartism—and emphasizing the dire consequences of disobedience to established authority.

Liberalism and Chartism are also responsible for the downfall of Luke Sharp, in Paget's novel of that name (1845), who ends up deported and dying in the Convicts' Hospital, Norfolk Island, realizing too late that "*knowledge without religion* is POISON and DEATH." (Paget has a weakness for italics and capital letters to adorn his tales and point out his colossal morals.)

Dissent brings ruin to another foolish character, Eleanor in *Enthusiasm not Religion* by M. A. C.—(1848), an amazing novel written by a Tractarian teenager. Her heroine Eleanor finds church dull and escapes to meeting-houses, enjoying the delights of Nonconformist "enthusiasm" and the "sweet, warm, impassioned prayers" of Dissenting ministers. She soon becomes disillusioned however, especially when a friend of hers becomes "a raging maniac" through her disobedience to the Church. "Thus awfully has the Omnipotent avenged His outraged Laws", declares the young author triumphantly. (Madness was a favourite punishment for rebellious spirits in early Tractarian fiction; Ernest Singleton's friend dares to dabble in mesmerism and eventually reaches the padded cells of Hanwell Asylum, while the ungovernable Caleb in Paget's *Caleb Kniveton* (1833) ends his days as the village idiot.) Eleanor then renounces her "religious dissipations" and is "restored to Church fellowship".

There are many silly stories among the religious novels of this period, but in spite of all the false notes struck and the generally low level of literary composition these early tales have their value, not only by virtue of their interesting revelations of the political, social and economic implications of Tractarianism but also on account of their clearly-emphasized concepts of belief and behaviour and the ideals they hold up for ordinary people in search of a creed and a code. The saving of souls is after all a primary concern of these religious novelists and the fundamental question "What must I do to be saved?" is answered in detail through the medium of the narrative.

Some of the best answers are given in the novels of the Rev. William Heygate who specialized in tales of struggling penitents striving to fulfil the ideals of good churchmanship. In his *William Blake; or, the English Farmer* (1848) we see the penitent's programme: frequent Communion, daily prayers at church, private religious reading (it's not enough for a farmer just to know his catechism, we are told), regular self-examination (William "continually asked himself why he had said and done his last words and acts"), self-denial, self-sacrifice, strict obedience to the local vicar by virtue of his apostolic succession, generous almsgiving and charitable help for the poor. (The poor are frequently with us in early Tractarian fiction and their welfare is to be achieved by the paternal care and charity of the more fortunate since, as Gresley assures us in his novel *Colton Green* (1846), God has placed men "in their respective stations in order to make trial of their spirits, until the number of his elect be accomplished: the poor, in the patient endurance of their allotted toil, in soberness, obedience and faith—the rich and the influential, in the charitable provision which they afford their poor dependent brethren for knowing and doing the will of Him Who made them".) William sells his corn at a reasonably low price, even after hard winters, for to do otherwise would imply "a distrust of God's providence". He forms a night school to teach his labourers Church principles as well as the three R's and pays his men on Fridays instead of Saturdays to avoid "Saturday night drinking" and "Sunday shopping". Yet William is no Puritan and believes in enjoying himself with games, amusements and social relaxations on Sunday. (The campaign for Brighter Sundays was very strong among Tractarians, who, accusing the Puritans of turning the Sabbath into "a dismal cheerless day of austerity and gloom", advocated all manner of "festivities", "lawful enjoyments" and "innocent mirth" after morning service.) William's recreations, however, do not include shooting, for, as an act of self-denial, he has renounced his favourite sport for a year. Similarly Godfrey, the penitent undergraduate in another of Heygate's novels, gives up riding and shooting in favour of "the simplest pleasures". His gun, we are told, "lay in its case month after month".

Whereas men penitents are usually required to moderate their field sports, the women, in fiction at least, are continually being exhorted to moderate their finery. William's wife learns to dress in "a humble and retiring manner", for as the author reminds us "the great temptation and snare to young women of the present day is vanity in dress". Tractarian clergymen made great attacks on female finery. Pusey, it will be remembered, once referred in a sermon to a £60 dress that he had seen in an Oxford-Street shop window and expressed horror that "one Christian lady was to wear as one of her manifold

exterior dresses what would have removed the
gnawings of hunger of some 7,000 members of
Christ". Such dresses were not only a cause of
extravagance and vanity but were also, as Heygate noticed, impediments to devotion since they
induced ladies "not to kneel or not to go to
Church at all in bad weather". It is significant
that "Father Ignatius", that extraordinary "free-
lance" Anglican monk (described by his admiring
female biographer as one of the most "stupendous results" of the "Tractarian upheaval"),
had a special changing room fitted up near his
church where women removed the steel hoops of
their crinolines and "in the church itself every
woman looked as if she had just had the steam
roller over her".

The importance of churchgoing and receiving
frequent Communion is emphasized in almost
every story. To explain the sacramental way of
life to the uninitiated is, of course, one of the
chief aims of all early Tractarian fiction. It
continually hammers home the lessons of sacramental grace and all the prigs preach what all
the penitents come to learn—the value of the
two sacraments of the Anglican Church.

The sacrament of baptism is particularly
stressed; indeed, descriptions of christenings with
ten-page sermons attached were a commonplace
feature of Tractarian fiction long before the

famous Gorham case focused nation-wide attention on the doctrine of baptismal regeneration.
The Times of that period regarded this doctrine
as "a mass of indigestible rubbish which none
but a theological ostrich could swallow", and
novelists eventually dropped prolix explanations
of this controversial issue in favour of more exciting stories of unbaptized adults dying in agony
on desert islands. (Kind friends from the ship-
wreck, remembering the sound advice of their
local vicar at home, dip their fingers in sea-
water, perform the necessary rites and all is
well.)

Penance, of course, was not considered as a
sacrament and the practice of auricular confession was not emphasized in the fiction of the
time, being regarded by early Tractarians as a
purely voluntary affair. Lady Georgiana Fullerton however, before seceding to Rome, wrote a
fantastically melodramatic murder story called
Ellen Middleton (1844) showing the necessity
for confession. This created a *furore* and was
praised by Gladstone for its "tremendous moral".
Usually, however, it was only in later and frequently hostile novels that all the more sensational possibilities of the practice of confession
were fully exploited.

Since so many of the Tractarian doctrines
were highly controversial and liable to the wildest misunderstandings, education in Church

principles was regarded as an urgent duty, and several novelists touch on the problems of education: how to instruct ignorant Anglicans as well as how to reach the vast heathen populations of the new manufacturing districts. Some novelists even advocate sending a kind of squad of worker-priests to the industrial areas. Gresley's story *Church-Clavering* (1843) gives the fullest details of contemporary Tractarian views on schooling. Education without religion is madness, compulsory State education is a shocking and disgraceful "foreign system", Church schools should be organized through the existing diocesan and parochial systems, and the leading textbook should be the Catechism, as "there cannot be a more beautiful practical model for the instruction of children than the Church Catechism".

Education in church behaviour would appear to be another necessity for, if we are to believe the novelists, sleeping, yawning, refusing to kneel, lolling, whispering, laughing, "spitting in a filthy manner", and dashing out of church at the end like unbridled horses were all common habits of Anglican congregations of the eighteen-forties. Gresley declares that Roman Catholics and even Turks put Anglicans to shame in the matter of reverent behaviour in places of worship.

The state of the churches, of course, was partly responsible for this laxity, and the subject of church restoration inspired some of the liveliest Tractarian novels of the period. The pew was a particular grievance. J. M. Neale's paper to the Cambridge Camden Society on the history of pews, prefaced by twenty-four good reasons for getting rid of those abominations, soon fired the imaginations of the novelists. Paget, in his *St. Antholin's; or, Old Churches and New* (1841), gives us an entertaining tale on the subject. St. Antholin's is in a sadly unreformed state. An archdeacon, visiting the church, asks the churchwarden:

"Why, what in the world is this, Mr. Ouzel?"

"This, Sir, is Mrs. Clutterbuck's pew."

"Pew!" exclaimed Dr. Sharpe, "I thought it was her *bed*. Why, it is all curtains and pillows. Take care if you please, Mr. Churchwarden, that no pews are built in this fashion for the time to come. Churches are houses of prayer, not bedchambers."

Later in the story part of the church falls down and a cheapjack architect, an expert in "Gothic pigeon-houses", supervises rebuilding with "snug easy pews" and a huge stove in the centre aisle. This horror is fortunately burned down and an unknown benefactress gives six thousand pounds for a new church "on condition there are to be no pews". Paget devoted the profits from this novel to church restoration and in the following year produced another anti-pew propaganda tale, *Milford Malvoisin; or, Pews and Pew-holders*. This story, with its "wooden hero", is equally effective and contains plenty of intelligent comedy and satire—rare and refreshing qualities in early Tractarian fiction.

F. A. Paley, secretary of the Camden Society, was also moved to write a novel revealing the scandalous state of church interiors. In his book *The Church Restorers* (1844) he describes the Squire's pew thus:

> It was a very large enclosure, occupying a space fully capable of accommodating at least twenty-five persons on open seats. It was carpeted, curtained round, and furnished with a mahogany drawing-room table and a set of cane chairs. There were two easy chairs, with footstools, placed by a brazen stove on one side, which was duly furnished with fire-irons, grate and coal-scuttle. Elegant bound bibles and prayer-books lay upon the table, and costly velvet cushions with fringes and tassels lay on the ground for the use of the occupants if at any time disposed to kneel.

The altar is "a discarded dressing-table belonging to the Rectory", often used as a scaffold for whitewashing or a table for parish meetings, the pulpit is in front of the altar and close to it is a huge "black cast-iron stove, of Birmingham-gothic design". Fortunately the rector's son, an ecclesiologist, soon puts things right and restores open benches and a fixed stone altar. After reading the evidences of Paget and Paley one can well understand the Tractarians' *cri de coeur*: "Our houses of prayer are a shame and a reproach to us."

Restoration of lands to the Church is also recommended in several novels. Characters become conscience-stricken about their ill-gotten wealth derived from the robberies of the Reformation and hasten to give it back, not to the Catholics, but to the Tractarians. In J. M. Neale's *Ayton Priory* (1843) a rich colonel, realizing that his estates were originally taken from the monks at the Reformation, hands them back to the "Anglo-Catholicks" and helps with the "re-establishment" of a monastery.

The monastic aspects of Tractarian activity, and indeed the "Catholicizing" tendency of the entire movement, seemed, of course, to Protestant England to be nothing short of "rank Popery", and an account of the Romeward trend of High Anglicanism, one of the most controversial themes of Victorian religious fiction, must be reserved for a special chapter of its own. Meanwhile we shall see how some of the early Tractarian ideals are used and developed in the less theological but more domestic type of religious novels written by three Anglican ladies of the Victorian age.

CHAPTER 2

THREE SPINSTER NOVELISTS

"ELLES sont nombreuses, les spinstres lettrées du royaume uni", remarked a French critic in 1860. The Oxford Movement in particular seems to have brought forth a brood of maiden-lady novelists, of whom the best known are Miss Charlotte Yonge, Miss Elizabeth Sewell and Miss Felicia Skene. All three were devout, long-lived and literarily prolific spinsters of High Anglican persuasions who dedicated their lives to working and writing for the Church.

Miss Yonge is by far the most famous of this trio. She spent her secluded and uneventful life (almost contemporaneous with that of Queen Victoria) in Otterbourne, Hampshire, the place of her birth; she began Sunday-School teaching at the age of seven and continued it for seventy-one years and she produced nearly two hundred books, although for many years she never wrote fiction in Lent.

Her *début* as a novelist is interesting. Before she published her first story there was a family council held to decide whether or not to allow publication. "In consenting," her biographer tells us, "there was an understanding that she would not take the money herself for it, but that it would be used for some good work—it being thought unladylike to benefit by one's own writings." At first, too, she had to read every evening to her father all she had written during the day and he then made changes and criticisms. Later John Keble, her "Pope", censored her manuscripts, and under his influence she became the leading exponent of Oxford Movement principles in fiction.

In her novels we see a striking advance in Tractarian fictional technique. The crudely belligerent propaganda novel has given way to the domestic novel of manners, the interest in ecclesiastical conflict has given way to interest in individual spiritual conflict and, in *The Heir of Redclyffe* (1853), Miss Yonge's masterpiece, the portrayal of priggish virtue has given way to the portrayal of romantic virtue, involving exciting and even sensational elements.

For in *The Heir of Redclyffe* the religious, the romantic and the domestic are all most happily combined. The idea of a wild solitary figure coming from a doomed family in a grim old Gothic castle on the crags and being tamed by religious principles and cosy Victorian domestic influences was a new and attractive one, and this High Church Heathcliff, this Byron made virtuous, this new type of gentleman-saint with the passionate temper of a Brontëesque hero, the face of a Sir Galahad and the conscience of a Hurrell Froude, conquered the Victorian public and drew tears even from readers not possessed of Anglican sympathies. Like Sintram, whose "fearful spiritual wrestlings" had delighted Tractarians for many years, Guy fights to be good and fights hard, and the struggle for saintliness is decorated with all the charms of romanticism.

For Guy is striving after perfection. His quest is not for faith; he suffers from no religious doubts or uncertainties as to the nature of Church principles and the novel is exceptionally unecclesiastical in nature, churches and clergymen playing very little part in it at all. His struggle is for the control of his own pride and passion. He is the sincere penitent, battling for self-conquest just as Heygate's William Blake was, but (daring domestic touch!) he is under the spiritual guidance not of a cleric but of a comforting and comfortable middle-aged matron. It is Mrs. Edmonstone who helps him in his efforts to conquer his terrible temper and to practise forgiveness of injuries, large and small. Guy's "strife with the powers of darkness" often, in fact, takes place in the drawing-room or at the dinner-table. "Home is the element and trial of a Christian", wrote Harriett Mozley, whose books for children were forerunners of this particular type of religious fiction,[1] and few novelists can describe as well as Miss Yonge the temptations to anger within the family circle.

But Guy in his desire to overcome his failings goes farther than any previous Tractarian hero in his scrupulous self-examination and self-distrust. He is indeed a genuine self-tormentor, inspecting his tiniest faults and analysing every motive. His "habit of perverse and morbid introspection" frequently produces sudden violent storms of self-accusation: "Selfish! Selfish! Selfish! Oneself the first object. That is the root." Mrs. Edmonstone is obliged to reprove him for his exaggerations both in his attitude towards the past (it is interesting to contrast Miss Yonge with Hardy on the power of hereditary influences) and in his present strivings, and the modern reader will echo her reproach: "Self-discipline may be carried too far, Guy", for the Heir is obviously a victim of that morbid strictness of self-reform, that painful over-scrupulosity, that tormented desire for personal

---

[1] We have excluded purely juvenile fiction from this survey, although it is often very difficult to draw the line. Charlotte Yonge, in her preface to *The Daisy-Chain* (1856) describes it as "an overgrown book of a nondescript class, neither the 'tale' for the young, nor the novel for their elders, but a mixture of both", and many religious novels, especially those written by women, fall into this category.

spiritual perfection down to the smallest detail that characterized Pusey, Hurrell Froude, Christina Rossetti and many other High Church believers.

Fortunately a happy love-affair saves Guy from being too unhealthily self-absorbed, but his wedded bliss is short; Miss Yonge, for all her domestic bias, has firmly decided that her saint must have the crown of martyrdom and when Guy dies from fever, caught through nursing the unpleasant and patronizing Philip, his halo of glory is complete. Miss Yonge excels in deathbed scenes and this is one of her finest, quite untainted by any of the moralizing, sentimentality or accounts of long-drawn-out agonies that one might have expected.

Many novelists would have ended the story here but Miss Yonge, being extremely interested in moral consequences, goes on to trace the results of Guy's sacrifice in minute detail, showing how his good influence lives on in the life of his widow and indeed of the whole Edmonstone family.

As a study in self-conquest *The Heir of Redclyffe* is unequalled in religious fiction. In its story of Philip, too, it illustrates, though less ably and in the "cautionary-tale" manner, another important facet of Tractarian idealism— that of obedience. (Philip, readers will remem-

ber, goes from bad to worse after his first sinful
act in establishing a private understanding with
his cousin Laura, unbeknown to her parents.)
Miss Yonge's views on obedience, to both parental and ecclesiastical authority, were ruthlessly
strict. She remained dutiful and submissive all
her life to the severe discipline imposed on her
by stern parents. Her upbringing, as she herself
admitted, was "old-fashioned" even for the Victorian age, and she seems to us today to have
been the victim of unbearably rigid and repressive influences. But she never rebelled. "She was
always very obedient," wrote one of her cousins,
"and both her father and mother were strict
over her, which was what made us very sorry for
her sometimes." Miss Yonge, however, felt in no
need of compassion. She tells the story of how, as
a child, accustomed to a daily diet of milk and
dry crusts for both breakfast and supper, she
denounced with righteous indignation a kindly
housemaid who, out of "misplaced pity", brought
up buttered slices of bread to the nursery (with
the buttered sides turned down to escape the
nurse's eye!). Even in her old age, too, she con-
formed to the rules and prohibitions (such as
cottage-visiting) decreed by her parents sixty or
seventy years before. Rules were rules, however
harsh, and it was sheer wickedness to break
them.

This attitude is reflected throughout her fiction, and she never hesitates to punish her disobedient characters, usually in a rather childish and often ludicrous manner. In *Abbeychurch* (1844), naughty daughters who go to dangerous lectures at Mechanics' Institutes without parental consent find that dog Fido has met with a watery death in their absence; in *The Pillars of the House* (1873) Edgar, who refuses to be confirmed, gets scalped by Red Indians; and in *The Three Brides* (1876) Herbert, who doesn't take Holy Orders seriously enough and indulges in an excessive quantity of cricket and mild flirtations, fails his examinations and gets a terrible fever. (Miss Yonge usually prefers fever to consumption as a penalty for wrongdoing.) Instances, in fact, could be quoted from all her stories of the punishment of those who fail to be serious and submissive in Church and family life. Uncontrolled female intellects or emotions are particularly heavily penalized. Bertha, in *Hopes and Fears* (1860), who loathes discipline, kicks against religion and family "tyranny" and writes *billets doux* in German to an amorous cad, gets brain fever, a "shattered constitution" and "a withered, scathed countenance". In *The Clever Woman of the Family* (1865), Rachel's self-will and presumption lead her to be duped by a cunning impostor and she suffers "just

chastisement for headstrong folly and conceit".
Submission to paternal and clerical authority is
absolutely necessary, even for the cleverest
women, since, as Rachel comes to realize, "a
woman's tone of thought is commonly moulded
by the masculine intellect which, under one
form or another, becomes the master of her
soul." Large quantities of anti-feminist propaganda and a very substantial manual of all the
various sins of disobedience to authority, together with detailed accounts of punishment,
repentance and remedy, might profitably be
garnered from Miss Yonge's works. But her continual warnings to the wayward are only a part
of her lofty purpose in novel-writing. *Pro
Ecclesia Dei* is her motto and her great aim is
to educate her reader in "Church principles".
She always saw herself as "a sort of instrument
for popularizing Church views", and in novel
after novel we are taught the necessity of the
sacraments, the beneficial effect of weekday
churchgoing, the value of the Catechism, the
significance of Keble's *Christian Year* (nearly all
her good characters quote from it), the advan-
tages of auricular confession (although this is
not over-stressed) and the enormous importance
of confirmation. Weak characters become streng-
thened and stabilized through their faith and
their High Church practices. Youthful characters show great excitement and keenness over

church building. (*Abbeychurch* and *Chantry
House* (1886) give us splendid pictures of Oxford Movement Church reform.) Young men go
out as Church missionaries like knights on
medieval crusades. (One of Miss Yonge's greatest
enthusiasms was for the spread of Christianity in
heathen lands, and the huge profits of *The Heir
of Redclyffe* fitted out a missionary ship.) Young
ladies stay at home and help with parish work
and with village schools. Education must, of
course, be in the hands of the High Church
party; in *The Castle-Builders* (1854) young girls
who interest themselves in a school run by a
committee of Evangelical laymen run into serious trouble, and Rachel, in *The Clever Woman
of the Family*, who foolishly believes that "when
it comes to real practical simple teaching of uninstructed people . . . the details of party difference melt away" is made to see the error of her
ways. Nothing must be done for the welfare and
education of the poor except with the sanction
of the clergy. The *summum bonum* in fact, for
men, women and children, is "to enjoy Church
privileges to the full, and to do good works
under Church direction".

For the later developments of the Oxford
Movement Miss Yonge appears to show less
enthusiasm. Sisterhoods she approves of, especially in their nursing capacities, but none of her

men enters Anglican monasteries, and Ritualists
are usually snubbed in her later novels. She has
little patience with men who talk too much of
"colours" and "chants" and women who indulge
in "curtsies and crossings" in church. Her standards are those of Keble, who never wore vestments and whose liturgical views were sober and
cautious. Although he died in 1866 and Miss
Yonge lived thirty-five years longer, she never
swerved from his beliefs or departed from her
faithful adherence to the early phases of Oxford
Movement thought and practice.

Indeed, there is about the whole of Miss
Yonge's life and work a certain lack of development. She never seems to have completely grown
up, and there is in her novels no fulfilment of the
spiritual promise shown in her early masterpiece. Apart from this one glorious romance her
fiction preaches merely "Churchianity", institu-
tional and parochial rather than Christ-like,
young-lady-like rather than adult. As a chronicler of Oxford Movement influences on England's parish and family life she is invaluable, as
an *inspiratrix* and guide to faith she is less sure
and the modern reader will feel the truth of
Dr. Baker's condemnation: "For all her merits,
and her insight into psychological subtleties Miss
Yonge never touches profound experience or the
exalted heights of the spirit. She did not have

the necessary intellect, passion or nobility. Her religion is not mysticism, but churchgoing raised to the nth degree."

The same rather narrow qualities also characterize much of the work of Elizabeth Sewell, who, on the Isle of Wight, for nearly a century led a similarly secluded and disciplined existence, devoted to parish work, schoolteaching and writing.

Like Miss Yonge, she wrote of the religious and the domestic (indeed her early stories inspired the young Charlotte in her first efforts at novel-writing), and her books too were strictly supervised by an Anglican clergyman, her brother William, who had indoctrinated her with Tractarianism and "edited" most of her novels for her.

With a strong belief in High Church principles and a reading public of young ladies whom it became a "pecuniary necessity" to satisfy, Miss Sewell followed the conventional path of Tractarian fiction in writing large numbers of cautionary tales and exemplary biographies. Thus the life of Dora in *Amy Herbert* (1844) warns girls against pride and self-will; the life of Margaret Percival in the novel of that name (1847) warns them not to surrender to the powerful attractions of Rome; the life of Edith, in *Gertrude* (1845), cautions them not to neglect home life for Church duties, since, under Oxford Movement influences, young ladies often "rushed about to visit the poor, and were constant at daily services, whilst they were neglectful of their parents". On the other hand the lives of Amy Herbert, Ursula and Gertrude (heroines of three novels bearing those names) all remind us that we can make our lives sublime by submission to High Church authority. Her prigs and penitents, saints and sinners move in the settled world of Victorian domesticity, amid a profusion of brothers and sisters, aunts and uncles, cousins and servants, just as Miss Yonge's characters do, and they find the same trials and temptations and satisfactions from home affairs and the interplay of personality on personality in a large family. The bad ones rebel and are punished; the good ones examine their consciences, control their tongues and their tempers, interest themselves in parish work and church restoration, and generally influence their weaker brethren for the greater glory of God.

But Miss Sewell can by no means be dismissed as a kind of lesser Miss Yonge. In many ways she is the superior novelist. Less "churchy" and more introspective than her contemporary, she goes deeper into the inner life of her characters, exploring and revealing what she describes as "that busy world within—that tumultuous crowd of thoughts and feelings, which at every moment are born and die and are forgotten, but upon which God has stamped the seal of immortality."

Combining these solemn convictions with skilful powers of psychological analysis, Miss Sewell is pre-eminently the novelist of conscience. Her female characters have the tenderest consciences in all religious fiction, their self-examinations are the most analytic, their scruples the most minutely exacting. "The real difficulty of a Christian life", Miss Sewell tells us, is "the struggle against secret sins", and it is into this secret personal feminine world that she so successfully penetrates.

She herself was admirably fitted by nature to be the chronicler of conscience. As a child she suffered from morbid thoughts and all manner of strange scrupulous fancies, which at one time led her to make absurd daily confessions to her schoolteacher. On one occasion, as she relates in her autobiography, she even began to imagine that every time she thought of making a vow she had really made it and would have to keep it. "I even went so far", she says, "as to worry myself with the question whether I was not bound to kill my mother, because I thought I had made a vow that I would." (Psychologists would find Miss Sewell's autobiography a fascinating document.) She was then attacked by religious doubts

and perplexities, which caused her even greater
torments. Later she grew in faith and serenity,
her over-scrupulousness becoming balanced by
a sense of proportion and humour, but her girlhood was one of extreme "inward trouble", and
these unsettled states are recorded with fidelity
in nearly all her novels. Sensitive and passionate
young heroines torment themselves with "con-
science-crotchets", absorbed, even obsessed by
their failings for, as Miss Sewell observed in her
old age, "faults are very like diseases; one may
watch them till the contemplation becomes so
engrossing that one would be sorry to part with
them." Margaret Percival, Gertrude and her
friend Edith, Sally in *The Experience of Life*
(1852) and Myra in *A Glimpse of the World*
(1863), are all young women of this stamp.

With their over-active consciences and stern
concepts of duty goes an almost puritanical
distrust of pleasure. Gertrude hesitates to give
money to build a new church because she would
enjoy it so much: "It would give me such
pleasure, I'm afraid I may not see whether it is
my duty." Even the sweet relief of confession is
suspect—Miss Sewell shows dislike for the
"Romish" system of "a constantly repeated assur-
ance of forgiveness which should completely re-
move the burden of self-reproach". The "inward
burden" must be carried, and Miss Sewell's

heroines embrace the sufferings of religion without any of its consolations.

For the only remedy prescribed by Miss Sewell is that of absolute obedience. Even more strictly than Miss Yonge, she preaches the sermon of blind unquestioning obedience to parental and ecclesiastical authority. Obedience is the cure for all youthful discontent, the answer to all adolescent problems, the only way out of the Slough of Despond. It must be practised as a daily habit in even the most minute and trivial affairs, and it brings stability, order and tranquility to the most capricious feminine natures. It is especially useful for combating the demon of doubt. Newman's sermon on "Obedience, the Remedy for Religious Perplexity", which Miss Sewell read in 1845 and took to heart, is excellently illustrated in her works of fiction. Miss Sewell's own method of crushing doubt was "a short quick prayer and an almost physical effort to turn away from the suggestions" and her heroines follow the same procedure. Rebellious thoughts are expelled by prayer, and conflicts may thus be settled "without argument, without sympathy, without external aid but simply with the force of prayer, and the strong will to crush the very shadow of a rising doubt". "Clever" people are of course more liable than others to such conflicts, and Miss Sewell's scorn and distrust of the intellect is even greater than Miss

Yonge's; we are reminded more than once in her novels that "the highest intellect and the most consummate genius of the universe, putting aside—if one may venture so to say—the intellect of the Supreme Being, is that of Satan." The dangers of intellectual activity can only be overcome by complete mental obedience and the duty of not thinking for oneself.

Miss Sewell's best book is undoubtedly *The Experience of Life* (1852). This short novel is a neglected treasure of High Church fiction— heavily autobiographical and distinguished by the marks of profound Christian experience. It is a spinster's apology, the story of "the uneventful life of an old maid, condemned to poverty, and in a great measure to loneliness". Its heroine, Sally, is clearly a self-portrait, and Miss Sewell's vivid descriptions of Sally's phases of faith form an interesting psychological document and throw light on the various spiritual influences at work on middle-class youth of the eighteen-forties and fifties.

After a tormented and unsettled girlhood Sally resigns herself to spinsterdom, learning from her wise old Aunt Sarah that "to be an old maid is to be able to live to God and work for your fellow creatures in an especial manner". She grows wiser and happier with the advancing years—"happiest of all at sixty. It is better to be travelling towards age than away from youth", she says. Old age brings no terrors, nor does loneliness, for she finds her real home and true fellowship in the Church, where she is continually fortified by the "calming and strengthening" services. The power of religion to mould a wayward girl into a high-principled and splendidly self-disciplined woman is a favourite theme of Miss Sewell's; it finds its most effective expression in this book. "Nothing I have written has ever been as really popular as *The Experience of Life*", wrote Miss Sewell in her autobiography. Its popularity is well-deserved, and even those who cannot share Miss Sewell's extremist views on obedience and intellectual submission can yet appreciate *The Experience of Life* as a most readable novel, a penetrating study of character and a valuable piece of confessional literature.

With both Miss Yonge and Miss Sewell the stricter and more sober aspects of Tractarian life and worship are emphasized; their perpetual insistence on obedience and discipline tends to make the system appear somewhat repressive, and both novelists breathe an atmosphere that is slightly drab and insular. Apart from a few romantic flights of fancy, their attitude to their faith is one of didactic narrowness and almost schoolmarmish seriousness. The colourful and more emotional approaches to religion—the mystic, the passionate, the ecstatic, the aesthetic —are not for them.

It is perhaps fortunate, therefore, that, as a happy corrective, we have the more vivid and ardent expression of Oxford Movement beliefs in the personality and novels of Miss Felicia Skene. Miss Skene was also a long lived Anglican spinster but her exuberant unconventional character, her French education and her extensive experience of foreign travel (including seven years' residence in Greece) make her as different from Miss Yonge and Miss Sewell as a phoenix from a pair of sparrows.

Miss Skene's parents were intimate friends of Sir Walter Scott and her mother was the only woman to whom the secret of authorship of the Waverley Novels was confided. It is interesting to notice that historians recognize Scott's novels as paving the way for the Oxford Revival; Newman himself acknowledged the debt, and the opponents of Tractarianism often laid all the blame on Sir Walter's stories. "Whence did the pedants get the Popish nonsense with which they have corrupted youth?" demanded George Borrow indignantly, and, in his view, the answer was not far to seek: "Why, from the same quarter from which they got the Jacobite nonsense with which they have inoculated those lads who were not inoculated with it before—Scott's novels." It is well-known that Miss Yonge's admiration for *Guy Mannering* influenced *The Heir of Redclyffe*, and upon Miss Skene the influence was even more direct and powerful. Her "favourite and much-loved Sir Walter" was a frequent visitor to the Skenes' house; he took her, as a little child, on his knee and told her tales; then she in return would tell him fantastic little romances of her own and they would exchange wild stories about "fairies and hobgoblins".

It was these strange "hobgoblin" elements rather than any medieval paraphernalia from Scott's fiction which attracted Miss Skene most, and it is not surprising that her first effort at a religious story contains plenty of "Gothic" romance and oriental elements. *Use and Abuse* (1849) is an unusual example of a religious novel that is in fact a tale of terror. But Miss Skene goes farther than Scott in her appetite for horrors; she revels in the fantastic and the gruesome; she splashes purple passages everywhere; she indulges freely in italics, exclamations and rhetorical questions, and the result is one of the most extraordinary and perfervid tales of all religious fiction. Her heroine is the usual virtuous Anglican girl, "accustomed most rigidly to examine and sound the secret springs of her own actions", but her experiences are unlike any that befall young ladies in the novels of Miss Sewell or Miss Yonge. Carried off by her infidel lover to a Turkish tower, forced to view the decaying horrors of a charnel-house, embraced and almost hurled over a precipice by her ardent pursuer, she lives in a melodramatic atmosphere of frenzies, suicides, corpses, moaning maniacs, and ghastly deathbeds where all the time breasts heave, hands are wrung and characters fall groaning and senseless to the ground. This is indeed an exotic blossom of early Tractarian fiction!

But Scott's inspiration soon gave way to another force, vital, it seems, to all the High Church spinster novelists of the age—the influence of a zealous clergyman. In the late eighteen-forties Miss Skene met the Reverend Thomas Chamberlain of Oxford, a most vigorous Tractarian, who, for his controversial views, was frequently pursued along the High "with abuse and stones". He worked valiantly in a poor parish, helping the needy, introducing daily services, establishing sisterhoods and founding "The Englishman's Library", which published many High Church novels. Moreover, his strength and force of character fascinated women, and Miss Skene was soon under the spell. She promptly moved to Oxford (where she remained for nearly fifty years until her death), and became his penitent and passionately devoted parishioner.

It was during this initial period of enchantment that Miss Skene produced two of her most fervently religious works. She wrote of her inner life in *The Divine Master* (1852), a book in the form of a dialogue between master and pupil and radiant with mysticism. In its purity and ardour of devotion it occasionally recalls Thomas a Kempis and in the body of the devotional literature of the Oxford Movement it deserves greater recognition than it has hitherto received.

But when she endeavoured to translate her mystic ardours into fiction she was less successful, and her story *St. Albans; or The Prisoners of Hope* (1853), although perhaps the only novel we have that is really permeated with the romantic mysticism of early Oxford Movement ideals, is nevertheless a disappointment. Everything is wildly over-dramatized and Miss Skene's imagination, as usual, runs away with her. The story tells of how a pious but uninstructed young girl, Maude, under the influence of a noble clergyman, Mr. Chesterfield (an idealized portrait of Mr. Chamberlain), becomes an enthusiastic churchwoman, devoted to ecstatic sacramental worship and good works. As well as the glowing accounts of Maude's beatific progress we are treated to the familiar cautionary tale warning us against Mechanics' Institutes and Liberals, the undoing of Maude's brother Henry, who wilfully throws off all authority, divine and human, and is punished accordingly. Maude, however, wisely learns never to trust her own judgement and always goes for advice to one who has received "none other than GOD the HOLY GHOST in sacramental gift".

Miss Skene herself, however, did not follow her heroine's example in passionate and lifelong submission to her spiritual director. Shortly after writing *St. Albans* she broke away from overwhelming clerical influences, and her biographer tells us that "in after years she regretted having surrendered too much of her religious liberty and independence". She stopped going to confession, resisted Mr. Chamberlain's efforts to make her join his sisterhood and become Mother Superior, and although she frequently wore the severe black dress with big loose sleeves that the sisters wore she took "special pleasure in wearing a little bit of bright colour in every bonnet as a flag of independence". Ignoring the comment of her cousin, Bishop Forbes, "I like whole sisters, I don't like half ones", she pursued her own path to sanctity and concerned herself more and more with practical social work, which included nursing (she trained a corps of nurses for the Crimean War and earned the gratitude of Florence Nightingale), teaching, prison-visiting and rescuing fallen women. (The door of her house was always open throughout the night, so that any "unfortunate" might come in and find help.)

Her later novels reflect this change in her attitude and her characters, instead of being idealized clergy and adoring female parishioners, are now prostitutes, prisoners, would-be suicides, tramps and drunkards. *Hidden Depths* (1866) deals boldly with the evils of prostitution and pleads for the reform of the too austere and unsympathetic Penitentiaries. Miss Skene's forthrightness and her indignation at "the difference of treatment accorded by the world to the erring man, and the erring woman" led many Victorians to regard her novel as "a most distressing book", but to us today it is a valuable social document, based on Miss Skene's personal knowledge and experience of prostitutes.

Through the Shadows (1884) is concerned with problems of suicide and *crimes passionnels*; *The Lesters* (1887) is a "temperance story", full of the horrors arising from addiction to drink, and *Scenes from a Silent World* (1889) contains thrilling tales told by prisoners (some of which were actually related to Miss Skene by the inmates of the many gaols that she visited). All these novels suffer, of course, from Miss Skene's dramatic exaggerations—characters are full of ecstasies, agonies, "intolerable longings", and "maddening spiritual hungers"—and from her fondness for inhumanly perfect heroines who spend whole nights on mountain-tops praying for the sinners. (These High Anglican female saints are really tough, in contrast to the conventional delicate heroines of popular Victorian fiction.) But in spite of such hazes of romantic idealism her novels do contain touches of vivid realism and interesting glimpses of High Church contact with life in the raw.

Indeed Miss Skene, for all her flamboyant eccentricity and melodramatic style, makes a genuine contribution to High Church fiction. She widens its rather narrow associations and goes beyond the prosaic world of gentlemanly vicars and middle-class Victorian households, soaring into the more romantic realms of mysticism and exotic sensationalism and descending to the haunts of low life, far removed from the comfortable and respectable bourgeois spheres in which Miss Yonge and Miss Sewell move. As their worlds are different, so is the colouring of their faith; all three write fiction exclusively to promote Oxford Movement ideals and practices but whereas Miss Yonge and Miss Sewell emphasize conscience, self-examination, obedience and submission of the will, Miss Skene extols fervent emotion, passionate philanthropism and the more ecstatic states of sacramental enthusiasm.

CHAPTER 3

REST IN THE CHURCH: CAUTIONARY TALES FOR HIGHER ANGLICANS

NEWMAN'S conversion to Catholicism in 1845 had a profoundly far-reaching effect on the Tractarian novel. The Church of England reeled under the blow and when its members recovered from this and from the many other blows inflicted by their seceding brethren they immediately set to work to show in fiction that Tractarianism was not "incipient Popery" and that Canterbury was emphatically not a junction for Rome and should never be used as such. *"We have no more right to desert our Church than to abandon our father and mother"*, declared Gresley in firm italics in a novel of 1845 and from that year onwards flowed a steady stream of fiction written to warn "border-line" Anglicans of the dangers of going over to Rome. These propaganda novels mark the beginning of the age of anxiety in Tractarian fiction and strike the new note of doubt, troubled indecision and even pessimism that was to enter more and more into the religious novel as the century progressed.

It was Miss Sewell's brother William who really launched the anti-Roman cautionary tale for High Anglicans. Unfortunately, however, his *Hawkstone* (1845) is written in the tradition of crude and ignorant melodrama associated with the vast outpourings of anti-Popery fiction that flooded England throughout the century with tales of wicked Jesuits, renegade nuns and all the sensational fantasies of Mrs. Sherwood. (These "horrific" specimens will be dealt with in another chapter.) Although we are told that thousands of troubled spirits, after Newman's secession, read *Hawkstone* for consolation, it really is a very silly book. The hero has bloodcurdling adventures on the Continent and triumphs over an evil Jesuit who is finally punished by being eaten alive in a vault full of rats. The description of his end is one of the most horrible pieces of writing in all fiction. It would in fact be hard to find a religious novel more violent and venomous than this work of a Victorian Oxford don, and it is a striking reflection on England's ignorance of Catholicism that so many Anglicans, after Newman's departure, could find satisfaction and "the seeds of truth" in this piece of hysterical and nasty-minded nonsense.

Cheap vilification of the enemy was one form of deterrent, but for sensitive spirits who had once embraced the *credo in Newmannum* and were now suffering from disillusion, shock and perplexity, a rather more serious and thoughtful approach was required. It was William's sister, the scrupulous Elizabeth, who produced a far more valuable contribution to the fictional biography of the Rome-haunted Anglican. Unlike William, Elizabeth Sewell showed great sympathy for the Catholic Church and her brother must have grown extremely alarmed when, influenced by Newman, she showed distinct Romeward tendencies and local papers even reported that she had seceded. She never did, however, and eventually found peace and happiness in the Church of England, as *The Experience of Life* shows. But *Margaret Percival* (1847) records her period of spiritual uncertainty and gives Miss Sewell's answer to the problem of "going over".

Her heroine Margaret, like Tancred and Lothair in Disraeli's novels, is a young, gifted and discontented Anglican, "self-willed and visionary", to whom churchgoing seems "a burden upon rather than an assistance to, the spirit of piety". On a Continental holiday she first comes in contact with Catholicism and meets a charming Italian Countess. (Miss Sewell describes well the part that may be played by the personal influence in conversion and knows too how "a naturally imaginative and ardent disposition will instinctively cling to the beautiful vision of past ages".) Margaret draws very near to Rome with her faith in the Church of England almost completely destroyed. This state of losing faith in one Church while not yet gaining complete faith in another can give rise to the keenest spiritual agony, as Newman found, and it is interesting to notice that this novel, appearing a year before *Loss and Gain*, describes with similar insight the sufferings of one beginning to despair of the Church of England. Margaret's condition is pitiable:

> It was miserable to doubt, most miserable; it took from her every comfort in religion; it made her hasty and moody; it depressed her spirits day by day, and broke her rest at night, until it sometimes seemed almost impossible to bear her present state of existence for another hour.

But Miss Sewell's remedy, as we might expect, is to stifle all doubts mercilessly and shut eyes and ears to any unsettling influences. The English clergyman, Mr. Sutherland, tells Margaret that by submitting to Rome she would be a traitor to the Church of her baptism and that it is her duty to stay in the Anglican Communion and crush her doubts, if necessary even making "a physical effort against them". This Margaret does and eventually wins through and settles down again in the Church of England.

This novel had considerable influence in America, where a New England writer produced a sequel to it, mentioning in the preface that "a host of English books, called 'Religious Novels' have been transplanted into this country" and describing the admiration of American girls for Margaret Percival. They looked upon her as "a heroine who has *conquered*", and were accordingly grateful to her. "For instance", says one of them, "I thank Jane Eyre for having conquered as I would thank a real martyr for having lived and suffered." Although today we might consider Margaret Percival's methods of spiritual warfare somewhat unsatisfactory, yet we must appreciate the reality of her plight and recognize that the religious situations of the time provided ample material for a genuinely tragic conflict in fiction as well as fact.

Even worse conflicts and even more extraordinary solutions appear in the life and writings of Elizabeth Harris. Her two novels *From Oxford to Rome* (1847) and *Rest in the Church* (1848) both describe the spiritual lives of Puseyite clergymen who, after agonies of indecision, go over to Rome and end by finding they have made "a great mistake".

But the mistake appears to the author to be irrevocable. Miss Harris herself was converted from Anglicanism to Catholicism in 1846, then regretted her step, but felt it her duty to stay in the Catholic Church and warn others not to come in! This incredible and muddle-headed position, ramblingly but passionately expressed in her novels, drew, as might have been expected, the severest censure from critics and reviewers. *Fraser's Magazine* accused her of an "inconsistent and immoral attitude" and an "unfixed, unbalanced and distempered mind", Newman wrote *Loss and Gain* as an answer to her, while Gladstone in *The Quarterly Review* spent thirty-four pages castigating her, with reminders that "a vow is conditional upon continued conviction" and that "such of our misdeeds as are capable of being undone, it is our duty to undo, and that with promptitude."

It is obvious from her novels that Miss Harris was the victim of what Frederick Oakeley called a "form of innocent delusion under which some minds laboured, which far exceeded any other in its almost incredible absurdity", the idea of hoping to set up "a Union between the Catholic Church and the Establishment". It was of course the dream of many Tractarians of the time: Gresley in his novel *Frank's First Trip to the Continent* (1845) devoted a whole chapter of the story to the serious consideration of the prospects of union and "friendly intercommunion" with Rome, but, as Gresley himself said of the Tractarians' approach, "we offer to shake hands, and get a good rap on the knuckles". Miss Harris, however, had not merely offered to shake hands but had actually embraced the Catholic faith in full hopes of such a union, and her novels reveal all the unhappiness attendant on the smashing of this most cherished piece of Tractarian castle-building. The anguish that her characters experience in awakening from their "Utopian dream" is quite overwhelming, particularly as they cling, Jephthah-like, to their rash vows. Their heads are weak but their emotions are strong, and both Miss Harris's novels, although abominably muddled in plot and in reasoning, do give us a convincing picture of sheer spiritual misery, hopeless disappointment and utter "wretchedness, remorse and woe".

The attraction of Rome for High Anglicans, especially young ones, and their various phases of enchantment and disillusion are shown far more effectively in fiction by Disraeli. To read Disraeli after Miss Harris is like enjoying *sauce piquante* after a lukewarm stew.

Yet, perhaps because of these very piquant qualities, Disraeli's gifts as a religious novelist have often been underestimated. Certainly any reader of his stories seeking a religious message soon becomes bewildered by all the gay flippancies and absurdities, the bright air of insincerity and unreality, and, dazzled but disappointed, may well feel that he has been given a stone

instead of bread—a brilliant, precious stone, it
is true, a gem of the Orient, but hardly satisfying to a spiritual demand. Miss Harris at least
cries *de profundis* but Disraeli sparkles with continually flashing, perhaps flashy, wit and cynicism. Yet underneath this effervescent surface
there are occasional depths of religious thought
and feeling to be found, and Disraeli often darts
from the shallow to the profound, from the false
and tawdry to the true and inspiring.

Like Miss Harris and Miss Sewell, Disraeli
passed through a phase of great sympathy with
Rome, and some of his early works, especially
Sybil (1845), are considerably influenced by a
kind of "sentiment of regret for pre-Reformation
Christianity". Especially did he see the powerful
but often quite superficial attraction of Catholicism for the artistic temperament. His "psychological autobiography" *Contarini Fleming* (1832)
tells of a young man, a typically Disraelian
hero, rich, imaginative, restless and unhappy,
coming by chance in his solitary wanderings,
upon a Catholic church. He enters. The
priest in "flaming vestments", the "tall, white
candles", the "musical silver bell", the atmosphere "redolent of perfumes and adorned with
flowers" and a "magical picture" of Mary Magdalene, full of "ecstatic melancholy", enchant
him completely.

I gazed upon this pictured form with fasci-
nation. I came forward, and placed myself
near the altar. At that moment the organ burst
forth, as if heaven were opening; clouds of
incense rose and wreathed round the rich and
vaulted roof; the priest advanced, and revealed a God, which I fell down and wor-
shipped. From that moment I became a
Catholic.

Needless to say, the seed has not taken root
and the next moment we find Contarini rejoicing in Voltaire, founding revolutionary societies
and, after his wife's death, dedicating himself to
the infernal gods and attempting suicide. But
for an account of the temporary, dizzying, de-
lighting effects of the enchantments of Catholicism on impressionable youth this description of
Contarini's conversion could hardly be bettered.

Contarini Fleming seems to provide Disraeli's
answer to the problem of "going over"—it appears merely as a passing phase of adolescence
and one soon grows out of it into other things.
Lothair (1870), written nearly half a century
later, suggests the same attitude. Lothair, young,
aristocratic and Anglican, follows the usual
career of the hero in so many of these religious
novels; he has exciting adventures on the Continent, he falls in love, his beliefs being influenced by the ladies concerned, and he finally

returns to England and to the Church of his
baptism. We are treated to splendid descriptions
of his first contacts with Catholicism, and later,
to some brilliant and merciless satire on "the
intrigues of ultramontane proselytisers". Lothair
has dramatic disillusionments—he differs from
Miss Sewell's and Miss Harris's characters in
quitting Catholicism with repugnance at being
the dupe of dishonest and crafty perverters;
moreover, his final Anglican position is somewhat unorthodox, with stronger sympathies for
Jerusalem than for Canterbury ("all Disraeli's
heroes who want spiritual comfort are sent to
Jerusalem", complained J. A. Froude), and the
end of the story peters out rather feebly. The
"religion" that Lothair was seeking "was really
a wife", wrote Bret Harte in his wicked parody
Lothaw. But the author's perception of the
powerful attractions of Catholicism, combined
with his exceptional psychological skill in the
portrayal of sensitive young men in fiction,
makes *Lothair* a subtle and intelligent, even if
over-sophisticated, example of the anti-Roman
cautionary tale for Anglicans.

The most famous religious novel of the Victorian age dealing with the soul's escape from
Catholicism to Anglicanism was written by one
who possessed less sympathy with Catholic ideals
than Miss Sewell, Miss Harris or Disraeli. *John*

Inglesant (1880) is in essence a cautionary tale to warn us against Roman "fanaticism and superstition" as opposed to Anglican "culture" and to show us the life of a young man and his "gallant struggle for freedom" from the snares of Rome. Its author, J. H. Shorthouse, was a Birmingham vitriol manufacturer but, despite his private views on Catholicism, there is nothing vitriolic about his masterpiece.

Indeed, it is a welcome change to find an Anglican novel in which an attempt is made to treat the claims of Rome philosophically and not satirically, emotionally or hysterically. Shorthouse's philosophy, too, is charming, and instead of amusing or disgusting us, the book enchants. There can be no doubt that *John Inglesant* casts a spell over us. Its exquisite style, its symbolism, aesthetic sensitivity and mystic fervour give it an indescribable fragrance of otherworldly beauty and have misled more than one critic into echoing Paul Elmer More's praise of it as " the one great religious novel of the English language". Even the discovery that it is a tissue of plagiarisms[1] cannot detract from the haunting beauty of the story.

But, basking in its richly perfumed atmosphere of loveliness and mystic supernaturalism,

---

[1] See W. K. Fleming's revealing article "Some Truths about 'John Inglesant'" in *The Quarterly Review* for July, 1925.

the reader inclines to forget the basic truth that
the author's purpose is to show that "God prefers culture to fanaticism". Shorthouse contrasts
Catholicism with Anglicanism. On the one side
he sees obedience, servitude, ignorance, fanaticism, and on the other culture, intellect, freedom, tolerance. John Inglesant's life is intended
to be the escape story of a man "handicapped"
by being trained from childhood by the Jesuits
to obedience and devotion, the emancipation
of one attached to what Shorthouse condemns as
a false system of belief involving the mainten-
ance of dogma "no matter at what sacrifice of the
individual conscience or reason". Such a theme
might have made a great novel of spiritual biography, especially as Shorthouse sees in the
Roman and Anglican claims not merely a clash
between Churches but "a conflict within man's
own nature—nay, between the noblest parts of
man's nature arrayed against each other. On the
one side obedience and faith, on the other, freedom and the reason".

Yet the actual result, particularly in the work-
ing-out of the leading character, is sadly
disappointing. Inglesant is indeed a feeble figure.
Like Lothair, he is portrayed as a rich, aristocratic, beauty-loving, God-seeking young man,
like Lothair he has dramatic adventures on the
Continent, like Lothair he is influenced by the

religious views of various young women, like
Lothair he listens to different characters who are
more or less mouthpieces for different forms of
faith, and like Lothair too he finally returns to
England and to the bosom of the Anglican
Church. But here the resemblance ceases. No
flash either of humour or of profound spiritual
illumination lights up the drabness of Shorthouse's hero. Leslie Stephen called Lothair a
"passive bucket", but it is Inglesant who merits
the title far more than Lothair. He is even more
pathetically susceptible than Lothair or Margaret Percival to the element of personal influences in religion and he is instructed by teacher
after teacher: Nicholas Ferrar and Hobbes,
Quakers and Jesuits, Benedictines and Philosophical Deists, Molinos and the Quietists. Lord
Acton's criticism of Inglesant's spiritual development is worth mentioning. He writes:

> The three channels by which God speaks to
> the soul are excluded. Inglesant will do any-
> thing but read the Bible. He has never studied
> to distinguish the voice of the Church, the
> constancy of her teaching, the line of least
> resistance, the law that regulates her move-
> ments. Conscience is a word that does not
> occur during the first hundred pages of reli-
> gious training ... We repeatedly find that he
> knows not right from wrong, and is not scared

by sin . . . He is as destitute of conviction as he is free from vice. His one security is Direction. He passes from hand to hand, and successive teachers impress him for a time, but impart no principle.

In particular, Inglesant's final change from Catholicism to Anglicanism is very poorly handled. Shorthouse was most anxious to show that Inglesant's troubled spirit had at last found repose. "I intended the last chapter to represent John Inglesant as having attained to an atmosphere of complete rest and peace", he wrote. "If this is not done my object is not attained." It is not done, and Inglesant's change from Roman dissatisfaction to Anglican content leaves the reader completely unconvinced. To quote Lord Acton again:

> Mysticism and High Church Anglicanism are so highly favoured that the hero, when the Jesuit relaxes his grasp, acquiesces in both. At Rome he is a hearty Molinosist. Driven from Rome he is a hearty Anglican. Perhaps Malebranche or Fénelon might have facilitated the transition from Petrucci to Norris and Nelson and Ken. But there is no transition. The passage is made by the help of no subtler agency than a Newhaven smack. The thing is unexplained, inartistic, inorganic.

This feeble, almost "phoney" nature of the hero and his beliefs forms a serious defect in the spiritual quality of the story. Whatever its merits as a "philosophical romance" or a historical tale, *John Inglesant* as a religious novel, and particularly as one with the avowed purpose of warning Anglicans against Rome, fails and fails badly. It lacks any ring of authentic experience and has all the crudities of the mouthpiece and oracular types of characterization found in early Tractarian novels without any of the compensating clarity of their "good sterling principle", for Inglesant's final form of Anglicanism would never have satisfied Paget or Gresley. True, times had changed, and just as in High Church theology *Lux Mundi* (1889) showed "a sharp development, if not a sheer departure", from the teaching of the *Tracts*, so in many of these later High Church novels a kind of *fin-de-siècle* cloudiness was beginning to obscure the clear-cut principles that had inspired the religious fiction of earlier decades. But even allowing for this we find Shorthouse's faith—in life as well as letters —to be very odd indeed, and in *John Inglesant* he is clearly so delightfully absorbed in fitting together his superb mosaic of historical borrowings and in working out his own personal brand of religion (which we shall discuss in a later chapter) that he fails to create a living character in his hero or to give him the happy release that he intended. Shorthouse casts a temporary spell but he does not permanently convince. He enchants but he does not enlighten, and his continued insistence on Anglican freedom and "culture" (never clearly defined) seems at times dangerously like a plea for Anglican eccentricity.

Thus do the "Warning Voices" speak to us from the pages of High Anglican fiction, and amid the chorus we can distinguish William Sewell's rabid denunciations, Disraeli's cynical chuckles, Shorthouse's mellifluous utterances and the more poignant *cris de coeur* of Miss Sewell and Miss Harris, all endeavouring to deter churchmen from Catholicism, to stop perplexed pilgrims from taking Newman's path to Rome and to help the many truly wretched victims of Oxford Movement confusion to find settled happiness in their own communion, peace in Anglicanism and "rest in the Church".

CHAPTER 4

SURPLICED VIPERS AND SILLY WOMEN: THE PORTRAIT BY THE ENEMY

NO survey of Oxford Movement fiction would be complete without a brief glimpse of the portrait by the enemy. Material is not lacking: Trollope and Thackeray, George Borrow, Charlotte Brontë and many other novelists have left us plenty of unflattering pictures of the new High Church clergy, and we can gaze upon a wonderful collection of coxcombs, effeminate aesthetes, hypocrites, humbugs, sensual seducers and "surpliced vipers" of all kinds. It is not our purpose, however, to explore the whole of this vast and entertaining rogues' gallery, but we must, rather, limit ourselves to examining the hostile portraits that appear in the religious novels themselves. Attacks come most frequently from the Evangelical camp, although the agnostics deal some vigorous slashes in their fiction and Broad Church novelists clearly enjoy ridiculing the faith and followers of the "fancy parsons".

Hostile novels of the eighteen-forties and the early eighteen-fifties, especially those written by Low Church authors, show a tendency to portray

High Church clergymen as poor unsuspecting victims led into Tractarian error but brought back to the right path in the end, thus twisting the cautionary tale to fit their own particular brand of religious propaganda. Mr. Walton, in the Rev. C. B. Tayler's *Margaret* (1844) and Mr. Pennycross, in the Rev. W. F. Wilkinson's *The Parish Rescued* (1845), are both "amiable" men who eventually give up the "heresy of Tractarianism" with all its "tricks and playthings" and return to Evangelical sanity. Philip, in Anne Howard's *Ridley Seldon* (1845) is another of these "backsliding children" who follow the "new schism", and after endless theological arguments, repent in the last chapter. Some of these misguided men go right over to Rome before they see sense and it is implied in most of the Protestant novels of the period that the Oxford Movement is part of a Jesuit plot to convert England to Romanism. "Puseyism is a wolf in sheep's clothing, an enemy in the midst of the camp of God; offering itself to the desires of the unrenewed heart, it draws into its snares unsuspecting victims by the glare of its external forms." Thus speaks a character in *Alfred Lennox; or, Puseyism Unveiled* (1851).

Besides the eternal "Popery" complaints (which usually include violent attacks on the practices of celibacy and confession within the

Church of England, of which we shall speak later), these early novels also continually accuse the High Church party of turning religion into "a mere musical and theatrical entertainment". Objections to crosses and candles, flowers, music and ornamental altar-cloths in church occur again and again. Crucifixes are a particular source of annoyance and unfavourable comment in the more Protestant novels of this period. In *Alfred Lennox* the hero's father is dying a beautiful Evangelical death when his

> ... expression changed as he perceived a small crucifix in Alfred's hands, and agony for the first time was painted on his countenance. With a wonderful effort he raised himself, and exclaimed before any one knew the cause of his emotion, "Take it away, Alfred, take it away! put not your trust in graven images; make no likeness of your God!"

In this novel (which incidentally follows other hostile novels of the day in borrowing the label *A Tale for the Times* from enemy fiction), Evangelical young ladies swoon with horror at a picture of the suffering Saviour.

Surplices, too, are condemned as part of this religion of externals and "fripperies"—"continual work for the washerwomen", complains one Low Church novelist—and the clergy are

frequently rebuked for paying too much attention to clothes. Newman, in his *Loss and Gain*
(1848), agrees with the Protestant novelists (and
also with *Punch*) in attributing to his High
Churchman a love of dressing up in peculiar
clerical clothes and vestments. Later, of course,
the full sartorial glories of ritualism and religious aestheticism—lace, perfume, "man-milli-
nery" and so on—come to provoke even greater
outbursts of wrath and ridicule.

Pride and vanity indeed, cry the enemy, and
the Rev. S. Jenner, in his novel *Steepleton*
(1847), attempts to analyse the attractions of
Puseyism for young men, and tells us in italics
that "*the love of pre-eminence*", the desire for
power, dignity and authority, is "the first feature
of the High Church party as contrasted with the
Low".

Other accusations include an absurd emphasis
on baptismal regeneration and a wicked neglect
of the Bible. "Men and women of England, clasp
your Bibles to your hearts," cries the anonymous
author of *Alfred Lennox*, "and dread the approach of any one who would take from you this
charter of your liberties—this volume of inspiration!" A tendency to excesses and to worldliness
is also criticized ("Fasting one day—the next at
all the abominations of the theatre. What a sick-
ening mixture!" exclaims one Evangelical

character in disgust), and an apparent tolerance, if not an encouragement, of such practices as theatre-going, drinking and card-playing brings down heavy torrents of Evangelical wrath and repeated claims in novels that High Churchmen are attempting to import that abomination of abominations, the "Continental Sunday", into England. Politically, too, their enemies accuse them of conducting a "shallow flirtation with the lower orders", and "Young England" is soundly castigated by the Rev. W. F. Wilkinson in his novels several years before Charles Kingsley joins battle.

It is interesting to notice that all these early novelists credit their opponents with sincerity, and, while preaching vehemently—and often very longwindedly—against the Satanic poison of the Tractarian system, they are sufficiently charitable to portray their chief Tractarian characters as essentially good but mistaken people (often just impressionable young curates) rather than as deliberate evil-doers. "Why, the Puseyites are a set of foolish young men, just come from college (where some who ought to be wiser, have turned their heads)", says a character in Anne Howard's *Mary Spencer* (1844). At this period opponents and advocates alike agree as to the sincerity and industry of the Oxford Movement clergy, even though these Protestant novels

of the time maintain that the sincerity and industry are sadly misplaced and the innocent
victims and "foolish young men" are unconscious instruments of the devil and tools of the
Jesuits.

By far the most amusing and intelligent of all
these "unsuspecting victim" tales belongs to the
eighteen-fifties. Dr. Davies's *Philip Paternoster,
a Tractarian Love Story* appeared in 1858,
caused a scandal and got its author, an "ex-
Puseyite" clergyman, into serious trouble with
the Bishop of London. It is a delightful book.
Philip is a "Puseyite puppy", a "hyper-Trac-
tarian", who brings "Anglo-Catholic follies" into
the parish and goes in for fasts, tonsures and the
whole ecclesiastical bag of tricks. He rigs up a
private oratory in the curates' cottage, joins
"The Society of the Blessed Bones" and becomes
a favourite with the middle-aged nuns in the
Anglican sisterhood. The author satirizes most
wittily all the extravagances of the "ultra set".
His lighthearted approach fails him, however,
when he comes to the subject of the confessional
and he bursts out in impassioned fury warning
his readers that "it would be a fatal day for
England if ever England's wives and daughters
were led to deem the confessional a more sacred
place than home." But he quickly recovers his
good humour, and at the end of the novel provides us with a recipe "to cure young gentlemen

of the Anglo-Catholic disease", part of the cure consisting of contact with attractive young ladies, together with a reminder that "all this kind of thing is tabooed to a celibate clergy"!

Later the theme of the unwise Tractarian becomes exploited by writers of both sensational and domestic fiction, and sufferers from "the Anglo-Catholic disease", instead of being the subjects of heavy and argumentative theological novels, or witty satirical tales, either become characters in long family chronicles where homes and hearts are broken by members getting "too High", or else develop into heroes of the most fantastically melodramatic stories, full of conflict, passion, terror and tragedy. Sometimes the two types of story are combined, as in Miss Worboise's *Overdale* (1869) where the religious conflict has a domestic setting and many sensational features, including a Jesuit who "comes and goes like a shadow". Miss Worboise's poor clergyman, pushed Higher and Higher by his clerical friend (who is of course a disguised Jesuit), suffers agonies of spirit and a terrible "cloister-and-hearth" conflict. His agonizing struggle to renounce his wife and children is accompanied by terrible self-torments and passionate arguments among the other characters about the sacredness of marriage and the wickedness of celibacy. Miss Worboise's extremely confused ideas about clerical celibacy are equalled only by her fantastic notions about confession. Her High Church young lady, Rosamund, is summoned to confession late at night by a brief note from the clergyman. She is panic-stricken at the thought of a "clandestine appointment with a man in a lonely church at almost midnight hours", but the "habit of obedience" is strong within her and she goes. Once there she has to "lay bare" the "most secret workings" of her soul, and the clergyman asks her all sorts of questions about her recent romance with a young man, "questions which no mother would have asked—strange questions, of which she could not clearly see the import, but which drove the blood from her heart and coloured her cheeks with burning blushes".

At the end of this extraordinary *tête-à-tête* the clergyman says:

"Hark! That is midnight striking. Meet me here again at the same time this day week."

"May it not be at an earlier hour?" she faltered.

"It may not," was the stern reply; "it is a complete, an unquestioning obedience which our Holy Church requires. Though the flesh may shrink, let not the spirit waver. Be here at the time appointed."

Rosamund is eventually extricated from all this (sensible young men are the usual doughty knights rescuing these damsels from Puseyite distress) and the poor clerical hero, who has toppled right over into Rome, also manages to right himself, but by this time "his form was bent and wasted to emaciation, his face was haggard, and his hair whitened as if the snows of four score winters had passed over it." *"I have not been writing fiction"*, insists Miss Worboise at the end of this amazing novel. "The same story is being told daily in every county of England. Facts similar to those I have narrated have recurred—are still recurring; and examples will multiply so long as the errors of Ritualism, the great heresy and schism of the nineteenth century, prevail among us."

It was, of course, these Anglican practices of celibacy and confession that aroused the greatest hostility of all as the century progressed, and afforded the best opportunities for highly sensational fiction with considerable sex interest. As Dr. Baker wrote, "A novelist setting out to show the effects of belief in celibacy of the clergy, in a world where the clergyman was often the most eligible matrimonial prospect in the community, had tapped a mine of excitement that would enrich even a mediocre talent." The practice of auricular confession, too, was full of dramatic possibilities that the novelists were not slow to exploit. John Bull did not take kindly to the idea of confession, regarding it as a form of sneaking and fraught with terrible dangers for the British female. The nation-wide storm caused in 1877 by *The Priest in Absolution*, a High Church manual on confessing young women, was characteristic; Protestant England was scandalized, the Home Secretary declared that proceedings could be brought against it as obscene literature, and one parson demanded capital punishment for any Anglican clergyman who heard confessions! The boiling wrath of public indignation against the confessional system was for ever bubbling over into popular fiction and the husband-wife-priest triangle received its full share of attention in the novel. If we are to believe contemporary novelists, the cry that "these ritualistic parsons have some kind of spell over women" was frequently a husband's complaint in the second half of the nineteenth century, and we hear much in hostile fiction about "spiritual flirtation" and "spiritual philandering" and even find a vicar classed as a "spiritual cicisbeo" (by Charles Kingsley), or as one possessing a "spiritual harem" (Mrs. Lynn Linton) and powers of "spiritual seduction" (Robert Buchanan).

For the conception of the High Churchman as the innocent victim of Puseyite error soon gave way in fiction to the conception of the High

Churchman as the unpleasant and unscrupulous Ritualist, and we have some very nasty types drawn for us by the religious novelists. In an Evangelical novel of 1851, *Allerton and Dreux* by Jean Ingelow (better known for her poetry than for her fiction), the very High Church clergyman, Mr. Newby, is a horrible creature, shifty, underhand and spiteful. It is heavily emphasized that he is no gentleman—a butcher's son, in fact—and has "a nervous sensibility about his low origin". This inferiority complex prompts him to all kinds of malicious acts, and one moment he is professing celibacy and the next moment running after rich heiresses. Mr. Morgan, the High Church vicar in the Rev. W. Conybeare's witty Broad Church novel *Perversion* (1856), also leads the ladies up the garden. When he first came to the parish we are told that he "loudly advocated the celibacy of the clergy; which invested him with a romantic prestige of cenobitical austerity, and inspired dreams of the triumph that might be won by her who should convince him of his mistake". Later however he proposes to a rich widow after "a personal inspection of her husband's will at Doctors' Commons", and they are married "in the fullest pomp of ritual", the bridegroom even wearing his surplice for the ceremony!

Sensational stories, most of them very crude

and trashy, continue to be written throughout the century on the subject of the Anglican "spiritual director" and his misbehaviour with female parishioners. One of the most striking of these tales is Robert Buchanan's *Foxglove Manor* (1884), which shows the Ritualist as a complete villain, corrupted absolutely by the practices of his religion. Buchanan advances the theory that the appeal to the senses, so prominent in Ritualist services, combined with the authority delegated to his person, can be fatally conducive to sensuality in the clergyman himself. In his story the Rev. Charles Sankey, at first filled with "religious amorousness, a soft sensuous delight in female sympathy and female beauty", becomes thoroughly vicious and hypocritical. He seduces one of the girls of his parish and on learning that she is pregnant and demanding marriage says calmly, "I shall always be glad to give you such assistance as a clergyman can give." (His punishment, by the way, which is meted out to him in the closing sentence of the story, is to enter the Church of Rome—that "cesspool" into which so many of the "surpliced vipers" are cast by the indignant novelists, with no chance to repent and return, as in the more lenient anti-Tractarian novels of the forties.)

Other Ritualist villains are found in M. L. Lord's *An Obstinate Parish* (1899), where the young clergyman is indeed a "horrid serpent". His flirtations with local girls under the pretext of recruiting them for sisterhoods bring scandal to the parish and earn him a ducking in the village pond. Another horror comes in Sir Walter Besant's *In Deacon's Orders* (1895), where we meet a deacon whose faith is all emotion and play-acting, "all religiosity without the least tincture of religion", and who is a cad, a thief, a forger, a lover of female attentions and, as might be expected, an enthusiastic reader of French novels.

The subtlest and most scathing study of an unpleasant High Church cleric is in *Red Pottage* (1899) written by Mary Cholmondeley, herself a clergy daughter. Her picture of Mr. Gresley— petty, spiteful, presumptuous and ignorant—is a brilliant piece of character-drawing. The author emphasizes the pride and "the arrogance which a belief in Apostolic Succession seems to induce in natures like Mr. Gresley's"—an echo of the complaints voiced in fiction fifty years back against Tractarian "love of pre-eminence". She also criticizes the low standard of parish magazines and asks, "Is it Utopian to hope that a day will dawn when it will be perceived even by clerical editors that Apostolic Succession does not invariably confer literary talent?"

These studies in clerical beastliness provide

some very good reading but undoubtedly the most entertaining stories of all are those in which interest is centred on the female victims, the "silly women", who worship at the feet of the local clergy and make complete fools of themselves. Oxford Movement revivals gave plenty of scope for such female activities. As a satiric novelist wrote in 1858:

> This faith is peculiarly suited to young ladies, for it encourages and utilizes their accomplishments, sets them upon embroidering altar cloths, illuminating prayer books, elaborating surplices, practising church music, carving credence tables, and a hundred and one other innocent diversions, which it invests with the prestige of a religious duty.

Hostile novels contain much ridiculing of these diversions, but their main quarrel is of course with the practice of female submission to a clerical authority. They share the view of Charlotte Brontë who in her first novel attacked the "tame, trained subjection" of a girl to "some despotic confessor", and they condemn as foolish and perilous self-surrender that obedience so earnestly enjoined by Miss Yonge and Miss Sewell. Whereas the High Church novelists emphasize the strengthening and developing of the female character through submission to authority, their opponents show the ruin of women through their stupid entrustment of themselves and their secrets to a man outside the family circle, and their senseless delight in what Mrs. Lynn Linton calls "a new direction, a new influence, a new love if you will, which the conscience approves and which neither the husband nor society can condemn".

This "new love", which, to quote Mrs. Lynn Linton again, mingles "religion and romance . . . in one sweet dangerous cup", furnished abundant material for Victorian sensation novels. Mrs. Trollope, in *The Vicar of Wrexhill* (1837), had shown Evangelical excitation and the influence of an Evangelical clergyman as the undoing of a woman, but Evangelicalism, with all its "enthusiasm", obviously could not hold its own for long against the Oxford Movement as a provider of religious intoxication for foolish women of all ages.

An anonymous novel *Trevor; or the new St. Francis* (1847) gives us the first good study of the High Church female victim in fiction and describes how Mrs. Arden, placing herself under the spiritual guidance of the local curate, is led "into a strain of devotion which unfitted her for her duties as a wife and mother". This novel treats us to some unexpectedly good analyses of the psychological state of an unsatisfied middle-aged woman, the appeal of a certain kind of religion in such a case, and the dangerous confusion possible in the female mind between love of God and love of his representative. Mrs. Arden's ecstasies, too, are well described and her approach to what William James would have called a "theopathic condition", a spiritual elevation beyond the realms of practical usefulness, reminiscent of St. Margaret Mary Alacoque and other female mystics.

A similar story of female folly is told by F. W. Robinson in his novel *High Church* (1860). This is the tale of Ada Chester, who, infatuated by the religion of her "pet preacher", "gave up her husband for Puseyism". The full details of Ada's progress towards spiritual drunkenness are vividly described, including accounts of her confessions, when, weeping and excited, she tells the curate every secret detail of her life, "sacred as it should have been to God and her husband", as the author sternly remarks. (The author follows the usual practice in these tales of taking sides with the husband against the wife and the priest, and inserts his own comments on female susceptibility and religious bigotry.) Finally the clergyman is conveniently murdered and Ada is reconciled to her husband. Here again we are shown a form of feminine worship that is less spiritual ardour than spiritual intoxication, devotion to the Almighty being inextricably entwined with devotion to the individual appointed by him for spiritual direction. The individual gone, the excess of fervour quickly departs and the worshipper returns to normal.

One of the best fictional studies of this intoxication was made by the agnostic Mrs. Lynn Linton in her novel *Under Which Lord?* (1879), dealing, as the title suggests, with the husband-wife-priest triangle. Although this novel is cheaply sensational in parts, it is redeemed by some flashes of excellent satire and by a penetrating study of the wife, Hermione, who, like Mrs. Arden, is a middle-aged woman longing for "passion, romance and mental exaltation". Hermione is soon worshipping at the feet of Launcelot Lascelles, the handsome and "perilously fascinating" new Ritualist vicar. Hermione is not the only one whose spiritual zeal gets out of hand under Mr. Lascelles' direction; the young girl Teresa, growing ecstatic in passionate adoration of her Saviour through her "beloved Superior", has all manner of hysterical trances; Hermione's own daughter becomes a nun, and even Aunt Catherine starts having visions. All this intense activity, this "spiritual camping out in high latitudes", ceases abruptly when the beloved superior drops his convictions of celibacy (the fact that High Church clerical celibacy was purely a voluntary affair helped considerably with the *dénouement* in this type of fiction), and marries a plain little woman with "small ferret eyes" and "an insignificant nose". Hermione's wrath knows no bounds, and she realizes that she is utterly ruined, having sacrificed "love, home, happiness, her husband and her child" for the excitement of a false and transitory religious exaltation. Although this is a most entertaining story it is also a clearly-emphasized cautionary tale, warning readers against the cruelty of superstition, the "inhuman blindness" of fanaticism and the dangers of unquestioning obedience to ecclesiastical authority, so passionately hated and opposed by the enemies of the High Church party.

CHAPTER 5

THE LOW CHURCH CONTRIBUTION

THE Low Church novel, an older and more abundant species of fiction than the High Church variety, flourished exceedingly in the Victorian age.

Evangelicalism in the Church of England had already enjoyed a long and fruitful association with fiction before Queen Victoria ascended the throne. Although some of the stricter Evangelicals held that fiction was to be avoided altogether, the majority of them enjoyed a good tract, and Evangelical writers were not slow to perceive the enormous possibilities of fiction as the handmaid of religion. Indeed, the longer type of Evangelical tract, known as the "tale", was in fact the forerunner of the Victorian religious novel. Rowland Hill's *Village Dialogues* (1810), Legh Richmond's *The Dairyman's Daughter* (1810), and dozens of Hannah More's tales were still being widely read in the first decades of the Victorian age and Mrs. Sherwood's famous *History of the Fairchild Family* (1818) was so popular that two sequels to it were produced in the eighteen-forties. In serial fiction too, Evangelicals held the religious field and counteracted the "penny dreadfuls" by at least half-a-dozen pious periodicals containing "healthful moral stories" calculated to encourage conversion, virtue, thrift and self-help among the working classes.

With this numerical superiority one might also expect a superiority of merit, for Evangelicalism, possessing a greater emphasis on the personal, a stronger insistence on the depravity of human nature and yet an ardently passionate philanthropy, suggests wonderful potentialities for fiction. With none of the Tractarian reserve in religious matters, no preoccupation with sacraments or ceremonial, but with a deep and searching sense of sin, a recognition of the importance of states of feeling and of the reality of the inner life, the Evangelical novelist might be considered well-equipped for the portrayal of a deep spirituality, for penetrating accounts of repentance and conversion, for tales of missionary zeal (did not the Evangelicals boast a most romantic and inspiring figure in the famous Henry Martyn?) and for studies in philanthropic virtue and that saintliness in daily life which, in spite of the gibes of Thackeray and others, was generally considered characteristic of the Evangelicals.

Yet the results in the Victorian age are disappointing. Low Church novels, declared

George Eliot in 1856, differ from High Church novels in being "a little less supercilious, and a great deal more ignorant, a little less correct in their syntax, and a great deal more vulgar". "Low" indeed seems the applicable epithet, and in reading the many Evangelical novels of the period one is struck by their trashy nature and the worst elements of Victorian Evangelicalism that seem to come to the fore—excesses of emotional gush and sentimentality, the introduction of the cheaply sensational and the luridly spectacular, a certain narrowness and negativity, a lack of good taste, self-control and discipline.

In story after story the same message is hammered home with relentless monotony: no drinking, no theatre-going, no novel-reading, no card-playing, no Popery (the anti-Roman sentiments of many Evangelical novelists were heightened by the Oxford Movement into raging obsessions), and the reader is continually exhorted to pray, repent, study the Bible and have God for a Friend (usually with a capital F). The emphasis is on conversion rather than baptism, and any such conversion, the stories almost always imply, brings worldly prosperity as well as spiritual well-being. Love and death are the commonest themes, love being treated with far less squeamishness than in the High Church novels, for

Evangelical writers, possibly following the lead of Hannah More, had little timidity in mingling "romance" with religion, and as for death, no Evangelical writer could resist a good wallow in a deathbed scene, particularly if the victim were of tender years. One must in fairness realize that the rate of infant mortality in those days was appallingly high, and lest Mrs. Sherwood's fictional accounts of juvenile deathbeds seem unnatural and exaggerated it is as well to remember that she herself lost five children in infancy —not a rare occurrence in those days. But even so the Evangelical treatment of such things seems slightly morbid—the poems on such subjects as "Baby's Shroud" and articles offering Advice to Bereaved Mothers (a common feature of the Evangelical penny weeklies) appear to modern readers somewhat morbid and sentimental, while the Evangelical novelists' fondness for the horrors of the condemned cell seems, even in this age, revoltingly macabre. The average Evangelical hero is even more priggish than his Tractarian counterpart and usually more concerned with prohibitions than with the more positive aspects of his faith.

We need examine only a few choice specimens in order to see the differences between the leading characters of High and Low Church fiction. An early novel *Truth Without Fiction*, written in

1837 by an anonymous country rector, shows us two Oxford students, flowers of the Evangelical faith. As well as their Bibles, they keep diaries full of holy resolutions to be read in moments of temptation, and their activities include throwing packs of cards into the fire and rescuing actresses from the evils of the playhouse. The theatre is vigorously attacked: even a performance of *Hamlet* is frowned upon, and characters are praised in these terms: "He has never gone to the theatre, nor touched a card, nor witnessed a dance." We hear much throughout the story of the lust of the flesh, the lust of the eyes and the pride of life, and the cure prescribed is prayer and "regular perusal of the Word of God". The novel is dedicated to Victoria, then Princess (the book was published a few months before her accession), who is described as exemplifying "female wisdom and virtue". Queen Victoria, of course, was of Low Church convictions all her life, but nevertheless she took pleasure in all the operas, plays and balls that this author so strongly condemns.

Other narrow-mindedly pious heroes appear in the popular stories of "Charlotte Elizabeth" (Mrs. Phelan, afterwards Tonna). She was one of the first to use the religious novel for the double purpose of exalting Evangelical virtue and combating Tractarian vice. Much of her

work is pre-Victorian, but from start to finish
her religious novels bear the tract-like characteristics of much spiritual earnestness and little
literary art. They show a recurrent pattern of
Evangelical prig rescuing Tractarian child or
worldly profligate. In such stories as *Falsehood
and Truth* (1841), *Conformity* (1841) and
Judah's Lion (1843) her unbearably virtuous
heroes go round with Bibles in their pockets,
instructing the ignorant and unbelieving. There
are plenty of deathbeds, corpses and conversions
(Jews as well as Tractarians are saved) and every-
body indulges in much weeping (from joy as
well as sorrow) and an enormous quantity of
religious discussion, which is frequently shown
as a family affair, even the youngest on their
parents' laps joining in. "What is a latitudinarian, Mamma?" asks little Sarah in *Falsehood
and Truth*, and these stories provide us with
plenty of studies in juvenile religious conflict, for
the Oxford Movement, so it seems, caught some
of its victims very young and these are some of
the earliest examples of Victorian novels dealing
with the "unsettled" minds of little children in
religious matters.

"Charlotte Elizabeth" died in 1844, but there
were other zealots to carry on her work, and in
the same year there appeared the lives of three
typical Evangelical saints of fiction, the leading

characters of the Rev. C. B. Tayler's *Margaret*, Lady Catherine Long's *Sir Roland Ashton* and Ann Howard's *Mary Spencer*. Margaret is one of the most boring and insipid propaganda heroines ever portrayed in a novel. Having escaped from the "perilous" teachings of a High Church vicar and the "dangerous" literature of Gresley and Paget, she is converted by a genuine Evangelical pastor, and, devoted to her Bible, quickly becomes a "shining example of every loveliest grace of Christian character". She gets up at five every morning, and although impoverished and dwelling in a humble cottage she manages to contract a socially successful marriage, for her pious charms attract the great Lord Claude Duneden, and virtue is rewarded by worldly success, with the author preaching a long sermon on the religious significance of marriage and its degradation in popular novels of the day.

In *Sir Roland Ashton* the love interest is not merely incidental but central to the story and the whole novel is drenched in sentimentality. Sir Roland is another unutterable prig who goes through life preaching against Puseyite error, avoiding theatres, "Satan's most approved workshops", rescuing drunkards and making several conversions, especially on deathbeds, always "drawing from his pocket a small Bible" for these occasions. He is in love with Lady Constance, and before departing to the Continent arranges to meet her "every night, at midnight, before the throne of God". This exciting suggestion of a spiritual tryst is a typical Evangelical contribution to the novel. Lady Constance however, belying her name, falls in love with Sir Roland's brother, and we are shown in great detail the agonies of Sir Roland's renunciation and his final emergence from the struggle, calm and satisfied, with God for his Friend. This sickly mixture of religion and romance, with its unsuccessful attempt to ally the Bible with the silver fork and sweeten the pill of Evangelical doctrine with the sugar of high life, is more calculated to nauseate than to convert, and certainly serves to drive the reader into the company of "many most excellent people who do not approve of religious sentiments being brought forward through the medium of fiction", to whom the author refers in her preface.

Mary Spencer is another impossibly virtuous type who finds that reading the Bible can always assuage "her pangs of loneliness and bitter bereavement". While all around her either die or fall victims to Tractarianism, Mary stands firm for her faith. Here there is no love interest but rather hate interest, Mary's most passionate feelings being reserved for Romanist "seducers and evil men". In fact, during the controversial forties at least, the hate interest in Evangelical novels is often dangerously in excess of the love interest, and there are far too many examples of unsuccessful efforts to record in fiction the spiritual lives of characters who are paragons of virtue and anti-Catholic fanatics at the same time. Writers such as the Rev. W. F. Wilkinson, the Rev. S. Jenner and several other clerical novelists produce not a few such monstrous characters in their fiction. In addition, Wilkinson's characters fume and rage against "the infection of the Evangelical body with High Church sentiments", and Jenner's characters wax quite rabid against Evangelical clergy who "by coquetting with the Delilah of High Churchism become shorn of their strength". Contemporary reviewers slated such novels as being "rude and unfair beyond all human decency", and certainly the heroes of this stamp—to say nothing of the heroines—show an appalling lack of charity in their dealings with their fellow-Christians.

Indeed, there are probably only two genuinely *likable* heroes in all the Evangelical fiction of this period. One is Felix in Anne Flinders' *Felix de Lisle* (1840), a "noble savage" type, brought up on a lonely island by an atheistic father. Felix, a delightful and simple soul (one is reminded of Voltaire's *Candide*), comes to Europe

and examines all religions there, his quest for
faith being successfully concluded by the discovery of a Bible and the existence of a Friend
"that sticketh closer than a brother". His conversion is an intellectual one in contrast to the
usual emotional and moral ("conviction of sin")
conversions portrayed by Evangelicals, and he is
refreshingly free from smugness. The only other
really pleasant and attractive hero is the Low
Church curate Dreux in Jean Ingelow's *Allerton
and Dreux* (1851) who converts the High Church
vicar Allerton. Here both sides of the controversy are set forward fairly by the author, and
both protagonists are portrayed as good men,
possessing humility and charity.

So much for the heroes and saints. What of
the sinners? Tales of Evangelical sinners are
more common in the form of tracts than novels,
and we have in the tracts innumerable stories of
the descent from virtue to vice, from purity to
profligacy (this word, slightly indelicate but
permissible in popular Victorian fiction, is conveniently and frequently used to cover a multitude of sins). Lengthy descriptions of the agonies
of repentance and equally long-drawn-out deathbed scenes are a commonplace, for the Evangelical story-tellers punished even more horribly and
heavily than their High Church contemporaries
and an exaggerated and morbid sense of sin and

its consequences frequently reveals itself in their writings.

One of the most impressive novels of this kind is the Rev. C. B. Tayler's *Mark Wilton* (1848). This is a most vivid cautionary tale, told in the first person by a "poor broken-hearted wretch" wishing to warn young people and to exhibit "the process by which the young and inexperienced may gradually and almost insensibly be initiated into the common everyday vices of a guilty world". It tells of the downfall of Mark Wilton, a merchant's clerk, and how, under the influences of dissolute companions, he tells his first lie. From then onwards it is but a step— *facilis descensus Averni*—to gambling, theatregoing, reading indecent French novels and running into excesses of debt and drunkenness. Desmond, one of the vilest of Mark's friends, initiates him into the mysteries of "dissipation" (another convenient word) but finally reaches the condemned cell at Newgate, and a visit to him there, combined with the sight of another former associate hanging dead in chains, has a sobering effect on Mark, and he begins to reform. Too late, alas, for a "short and dry cough" indicates that his end is near, and the author, unable to resist the final deathbed scene, changes abruptly from the first person to the third and

describes the death of the now broken and contrite Mark, uttering in the presence of an Evangelical clergyman his last words, words of faith—
"Come, Lord Jesus—come—come!"

A balance sheet is then included so that we can
calculate all the wages of sin in detail:

THE BALANCE SHEET

The Single Crime.		Character.
		Credit.
		Health.
		Fortune.
	"God be merciful to me, a sinner". "Having forgiven you all trespasses, blotting out the handwriting that was against us, which was contrary to us, and took it out of the way, nailing it to his Cross." Coloss. ii., 13, 14.	Respect.
		Confidence.
		Friends.
		Peace of Mind.
		Hope.
		Mortal Life.
		Heaven.

This is a convincing and well-told story, although it suffers from both certain crudities and certain restraints. Evangelical fictional efforts to "unveil the naked deformity of vice" in the nineteenth century were considerably hampered by the conventions of the time. The author shrinks from describing Mark's sexual irregularities and makes him silent on the subject. "I give no details of this portion of my life", Mark is obliged to say, since, he continues, it might "offend the delicacy of my youthful reader". But the author resembles Mrs. Sherwood and the traditional Evangelical cautionary tale-tellers in having a horrible weakness for the gibbet. One rather boggles at Desmond's speech in the condemned cell—"this throat . . . will be clutched in the hangman's grasp, and throttled by the hangman's rope; and I shall hang dangling, a swollen and bloated carcass, until I am *dead, dead, dead!* Take, O take the warning, dear, dear Mark . . . You see what want of principle, and love of self, and the licence of the pleasures of the world have brought me to." All this seems as distasteful as it is unnatural, and the illustration, in the first edition, of a corpse in chains, is, even to the twentieth-century eye, quite shocking, and likely to offend the delicacy of any modern reader, youthful or otherwise.

The best-known of all young Evangelical

characters who take the downward path is of course Eric, who little by little ruins his whole life in the famous novel by Dean Farrar (1858). Who can forget young Eric at his Evangelical public school, swearing, cribbing, lying, stealing, cigar-smoking and indulging in "the disgraceful and deadly habit of tippling"? Beer and brandy do their worst and Eric is soon sinking deep in unfathomable floods of moral turpitude and iniquity, until he dies young, wasted and repentant, and the reader is completely exhausted by all the sobbings, sermons and exhortations. "The lacrimosity is, I know, too much", admitted the author, and although this novel caused conversions and actually rescued a Bishop's son from an evil life, it was ridiculed even by contemporary critics, and can hardly be considered seriously or sympathetically by any modern reader.

But the downward path is not only for the young: the middle-aged may well succumb and in Lady Scott's *The Old Grey Church* (1856) the heroine's father, a banker, cannot resist temptation and commits the crime of forgery. This unfortunate man, the author tells us, "was by birth, education and manners quite what is termed *a gentleman*; but the horrid trade in which he was engaged—that of money-making— had by degrees hardened and even *vulgarized* both his mind and feelings". This sinner, as we might expect, is hanged at Newgate, after a last-minute repentance and conversion when, we are told, "his prison-house became to him a passage,—an entrance into the gates of heaven." This story also boasts a very coy heroine, always blushing and swooning, and a smug clerical hero named Eustace who sternly rejects anything savouring of worldliness, from opera tickets to frivolous fiancées, and ends up as a missionary in India (that country being the favourite missionary field for the Evangelicals).

It was this novel that inspired George Eliot's scathing article, "Silly Novels by Lady Novelists" in *The Westminster Review* for October 1856. George Eliot has much to say about this type of "Evangelical travesty of the fashionable novel", this kind of "genteel tract", a "sort of medicinal sweetmeat for Low Church young ladies". "The inability," she writes, "of a lady novelist to describe actual life and her fellow men is in inverse proportion to her confident eloquence about God and the other world, and the means by which she usually chooses to conduct you to true ideas of the invisible is a totally false picture of the visible."

Very shortly after this George Eliot herself began writing fiction for the first time, and, doubtless feeling that Evangelicalism had been very badly served, particularly by the women novelists, she produced her own splendid contribution to the Low Church tale. *Scenes of Clerical Life* (1858) gives us three excellently drawn portraits of Evangelical clergy. Although, of course, by this time George Eliot had travelled far from the Low Church convictions of her girlhood, her lasting sympathy with certain Evangelical ideals is apparent, and in the *Scenes* she shows us the sterling qualities of the Establishment's Evangelicalism, and, probably deliberately, makes her tales a striking contrast to previous Low Church stories.

Thus, instead of portraying the usual priggishly and repellently perfect clerical heroes she shows us three very ordinary and unspectacular specimens. Their lack of distinction is emphasized throughout. Amos Barton is "palpably and unmistakably commonplace" and even his faults are "middling". Mr. Gilfil preaches very ordinary sermons and does not "shine in the more spiritual functions of his office", whilst Mr. Tryan possesses "an ordinary whiskerless blond" face and nothing remarkable whatsoever in his character and habits. But it is through mediocrities such as these that God's work is done, for, as George Eliot reminds us:

The blessed work of helping the world forward happily does not wait to be done by perfect men; and I should imagine that neither Luther nor John Bunyan, for example, would have satisfied the modern demand for an ideal hero, who believes nothing but what is true, feels nothing but what is exalted, and does nothing but what is graceful. The real heroes of God's making are quite different: they have their natural heritage of love and conscience, which they drew in with their mother's milk; they know one or two of those deep spiritual truths which are only to be won by long wrestling with their own sins and their own sorrows; they have earned faith and strength so far as they have done genuine work, but the rest is dry; barren theory, blank prejudice, vague hearsay.

Everyday characters and an atmosphere of homely realism as opposed to priggishness in a setting of "high life" or macabre sensationalism —this is the keynote of George Eliot's story-telling in the *Scenes*. She deals neither in impossibly perfect virtue nor in hopelessly depraved vice. Even her portrait of the coarse, brutal drunkard Dempster is toned down somewhat. "The real Dempster was far more disgusting than mine", she wrote in a letter, and went on to say that in this story "everything is softened from the fact, so far as art is permitted to soften and yet to remain essentially true."

She thus avoids the two extremes of absurd artificiality and ghastly crudity, the Scylla and Charybdis that wrecked the majority of Evangelical novels of the period. And how well she describes her homely scenes—the domestic struggles of Amos Barton and his wife with their six children, Janet's husband and his mother having a walk round the garden, Mrs. Jerome at the tea-table in her parlour, the very drinking of a cup of tea.

And just as she replaces exaggerated virtue and vices by simple ordinariness, so too she replaces bigotry by sympathy and breadth of understanding. The tolerance of the author, the absence of sectarian preaching and tirades against other Church parties—all this is most welcome and refreshing in religious stories of this age. Gentle humour takes the place of narrow partisan zeal: the weaknesses of Evangelicals as well as their strength are revealed, and we smile at their old maids who write religious novels and show a marked "susceptibility towards the clerical sex", at the insatiable Evangelical hunger for tracts and their unpopularity amongst the many who regard their doctrines as "hypocritical cant", smacking too repulsively of Dissent. There is not a single attack on Puseyism in the whole book. It is human beings rather than "isms" that interest George

Eliot, and she puts in a much-needed plea for understanding and charity in religious matters:

> While we are coldly discussing a man's career, sneering at his mistakes, blaming his rashness, and labelling his opinions—"Evangelical and narrow", or "Latitudinarian and Pantheistic", or "Anglican and supercilious" —that man, in his solitude, is perhaps shedding hot tears because his sacrifice is a hard one, because strength and patience are failing him to speak the difficult word, and do the difficult deed.

It is this human interest that gives particular greatness to the third story in the *Scenes*, the tale of *Janet's Repentance*. It is a story of temptation, of an unhappy wife who, married to a drunkard, herself takes to drink but is saved by a clergyman who later dies of consumption. A story typical of the Evangelical tracts and tales of the period (so concerned with drink, depravity, temptation, conversion and consumptives' deathbeds)—but in treatment how very different! George Eliot can convey more convincingly than any of her contemporaries the subtle agonies of mental and spiritual suffering and their effect on the female personality. Janet is a typical Eliot creation, noble and frustrated, the forerunner of a Maggie or a Dorothea. Miserable, childless, victim of her husband's brutal hatred and feeling no balm of divine pity, she is brought to the brink of despair, reproaching God angrily for his neglect. Her *via dolorosa,* from her first "initiation into sorrow" to her final dramatic expulsion from home, is brilliantly shown in all its misery. If George Eliot had written no other story but this we should have recognized in the description of Janet's God-forsaken anguish alone the touch of a master hand.

Janet's progress towards faith and happiness also receives a different presentation in the hands of George Eliot. It has something of the classic Puritan conversion in it, for Janet becomes convinced of her own sinfulness rather than her husband's, but the main ingredient in it is the influence of Mr. Tryan, the clergyman. Readers may feel that there is just a little too much personal hero-worship about Janet's faith, just as there is about Romola's—these two unsatisfied and disillusioned wives seem to adore the human representatives of their religion perhaps a shade too devoutly. But George Eliot attempts to justify her use of personality as the dominant factor in conversion by an impassioned piece of panegyric:

> Blessed influence of one true loving soul on another! Not calculable by algebra, not deducible by logic, but mysterious, effectual,

mighty as the hidden process by which the tiny seed is quickened, and bursts forth into tall stem and broad leaf, and glowing tasselled flower. Ideas are often poor ghosts; our sun-filled eyes cannot discern them; they pass athwart us in thin vapour, and cannot make themselves felt. But sometimes they are made flesh; they breathe on us with warm breath, they touch us with soft responsive hands, they look at us with sad sincere eyes, and speak to us in appealing tones; they are clothed in a living human soul, with all its conflicts, its faith and its love. Then their presence is a power, then they shake us like a passion, and we are drawn after them with gentle compulsion, as flame is drawn to flame.

It is through such human contacts, George Eliot tells us, and through "the act of confiding in human sympathy" that the soul is prepared for "that stronger leap by which faith grasps the idea of the Divine sympathy". Certainly many people, especially women, have their first real spiritual awakening through the influence of some noble soul. Browning realized the same truth when he made Pompilia say about a priest:

> Through such souls alone
> God stooping shows sufficient of His light
> For us i' the dark to rise by. And I rise.

Although religious critics might complain that George Eliot's converts were too dependent on a human rather than on a divine Saviour, thus encouraging "a sentimental view of the new birth", as one clerical critic expressed it, there can be no doubt that her accounts of conversions through personal influences and relationships make for good fiction (infinitely superior to previous stilted accounts of sudden conversions through picking up a Bible) and the stage is now set for the psychological novel in all its richness and subtlety.

But unfortunately the Evangelical tale never again reached such a high level (ironic that its best expression should come from the pen of an unbeliever), and from the mid-eighteen-fifties onwards Evangelical writers busied themselves with sensational rather than psychological fiction and produced some very trashy tales of murders, hangings, elopements, shipwrecks, deathbeds full of unutterable agony, and dozens of wildly improbable conversions, all conveniently attributed to divine grace. In vain did the Pure Literature Society (founded in 1854 with three archbishops and sixteen bishops on the committee) rail against contemporary taste—the rising tide of sensationalism was too powerful to control. In 1863 the Religious Tract Society felt itself bound to lay down "the essential rules for healthful fiction", insisting that it should be *moral* (not investing vice with interest), *natural* (not exaggerating its characters) and *unexciting* (not arousing the passions). But the rules were frequently broken by Evangelicals and although writers like Miss Fanny Mayne (a stalwart denouncer of sensationalism and champion of "a purified penny press") kept within the prescribed limits and wrote about good working-class heroines who cooked their fathers' dinners and did needlework for ladies and clung tenaciously to their Bibles, such stories did not please the public nearly as much as the more eventful and exciting ones.

Hence the secret of Miss Worboise's popularity. Emma Jane Worboise (Mrs. Guyton) was a zealous Low Church writer who produced nearly fifty novels in which religious, domestic and sensational elements are all judiciously blended. She tells her stories well, and her portrayals of domestic life are not without psychological skill; indeed, she has left us several quite penetrating studies of the husband-wife relationship (she is particularly clever at showing the little rift within the lute) and such novels as *The Wife's Trials* (1858), *Married Life* (1863) and *Husbands and Wives* (1873) deserve to be rescued from the oblivion into which they have now fallen.

Miss Worboise's main interest however is in

showing how people are brought to God and she specializes in studies of conversion. But her characters are always converted after some highly dramatic event, some bereavement or great shock or tragic calamity. It is no doubt a well-attested truth that God does draw many souls to him through profoundly shattering experiences of this kind, but the frequency with which Miss Worboise employs this method of making converts in her novels would suggest that in her conception of the divine plan she attached an exaggerated importance to shock-tactics. Possibly, too, she felt that the slower and less spectacular methods of becoming a Christian were not suitable material for novels, for in the interests of entertainment many mid-Victorian religious novelists exceeded all reasonable speed limits for their pilgrims' progress, and only a few isolated writers such as Newman dared to ignore popular taste and show in fiction a conversion of an agonizingly slow and gradual variety, an almost crawling progress towards the light. Miss Worboise, and her readers, preferred St. Paul's road to Newman's, and rejected conversions characterized by slow, almost imperceptible growth in favour of conversions characterized by the sudden shock and the blinding flash—this in itself perhaps a typical Evangelical tendency.

Nearly all Miss Worboise's pilgrims thus have

the most sensational adventures. A typical novel, *Millicent Kendrick* (1862), shows a girl's quest for faith and how she found *"true religion"*, but she found many other extraordinary things as well and the story has all the trappings of romantic mystery: eerie haunted mansions, long-lost wills, women with veiled pasts praying in ruined chapels and, for full measure, at least half-a-dozen deaths from consumption. Similarly, in using a favourite theme of mid-Victorian religious fiction—that of a pious girl converting her unbelieving lover—Miss Worboise, in *Canonbury Holt* (1872), gives the unbelieving lover an incredible and exaggerated Heathcliff-cum-Rochester manner and endows him with a former wife, believed dead, who dramatically appears in the guise of a governess. (In minor Victorian fiction governesses who are disguised wives are nearly as common as clergymen who are disguised Jesuits.) In the end the pious girl makes friends with her lover's wife, who suddenly and conveniently dies, bequeathing her husband to the long-suffering heroine. The rate of sudden deaths in Miss Worboise's novels is probably the highest in all Victorian fiction—no mean claim. Nor does the rate decline in her later novels; her characters are still falling off precipices in the eighteen-eighties. (Her rate of sudden births too is exceptionally high. We read that a female character is taken ill, and the next minute "on her arm", we are informed, "was laid the tiny blossom whose little life had so nearly cost her her own". But it must be admitted that George Eliot and Charlotte Yonge were also guilty of producing babies without warning in their novels—due no doubt to Victorian conventions of reticence on this subject.)

If Miss Worboise deserves to be remembered as one who killed off more characters unexpectedly than any other religious novelist, she also merits our attention as the one novelist who defended the Rev. William Carus Wilson, the notorious "black-marble clergyman" of Charlotte Brontë's *Jane Eyre*. Miss Worboise attended the same Clergy Daughters' School as the Brontë sisters, and in her semi-autobiographical novel *Thorneycroft Hall* (1863) she is at great pains to speak highly of the school and particularly of its founder Carus Wilson, whom she describes as her "second father" and the kindest man she ever knew.

Carus Wilson himself edited a number of Evangelical periodicals and wrote several stories for children. Readers of *Jane Eyre* who think that Charlotte Brontë exaggerated his teachings on sin and damnation should glance through the pages of *The Children's Friend* or *The Teachers'*

Visitor. Indeed the whole subject of nineteenth-century instruction to children through Evangelical tracts and tales is a deeply interesting one. The modern reader marvels at the vividness of these tales, their stern rigidity and narrow-mindedness, their continual emphasis on punishment and above all their extreme—often worldwide—popularity. Mrs. Sherwood's stories for children enjoyed an enormous circulation, and the famous *History of Little Henry and His Bearer* (1816) was even translated into Chinese; the little tales of A.L.O.E. (Charlotte Tucker), on sale for less than a farthing each, flooded India in their thousands, and Mrs. Mortimer's *Peep of Day* (1833) was translated into thirty-seven languages. It is clear that the Evangelical religious novel, concentrating as it did on adult conversion rather than juvenile delinquency and interesting itself more in a Friend for adults than a hell for miserable young sinners, was not nearly as popular as the Evangelical tract or children's tale that dealt so morbidly and horrifically with the wickedness of sin and the torments of damnation.

So far the harvest of novels reaped from practising Evangelicals, though large in quantity, is poor in quality, but as the century advances less rigid and more attractive forms of Evangelicalism begin to show themselves, with great advantage, in the religious novel. This is particularly noticeable in the work of two women novelists, Miss Sarah Smith and Mrs. Elizabeth Charles.

"Hesba Stretton" (Miss Sarah Smith) made her name with a typical Evangelical tale *Jessica's First Prayer* (1866), which tells us of how the little daughter of a wicked actress (who pawns everything for gin) is rescued by a kindly coffee-stall owner. This sold a million and a half copies and followed in the Sherwood-Mortimer tradition of fantastic popularity at home and translations into dozens of foreign languages abroad.

But Miss Stretton's later works, particularly her novels, are an improvement on this. Although all her stories have a definite moral (usually on the evils of money—debts, thefts, wills, forged cheques and misers' hoards are a common feature of her novels), it is not too obtrusively pointed, and she has a pleasant style of writing and a kind of "pathetic simplicity" in her work that is particularly appealing. One of her best novels is *The King's Servants* (1873), the story of an elderly workhouse couple, which is, curiously enough, popular in present-day Russia. Although she never touches either great heights or great depths in her novels, they rise above the unsympathetic elements of Victorian Evangelicalism and reach a level of admirable Christian simplicity. Humility, charity, kind hearts and simple faith—the virtues shine out brightly from the pages of her novels and render them pleasurable to readers in ages and countries far different from her own.

If Miss Stretton is the Evangelical dove, Mrs. Charles is its eagle. A powerful writer, superior in literary talent, intelligence, scholarship and breadth of vision, she has left us some outstandingly good novels. Her most famous and popular book, *Chronicles of the Schönberg-Cotta Family* (1862), tells of the life and career of Martin Luther in a kind of domestic novel. The story is told in diary form by members of a family friendly with Luther from his boyhood upwards. It is an extremely well-written and readable book, based on considerable research, and it well deserves its high reputation. A pity that it is so little read today, for a more intelligent and interesting study of the Protestant reformer was never made in any novel.

Mrs. Charles excels in historical novels, covering the Early Christian period with a series of most stirring stories: *The Victory of the Vanquished* (1871), *Conquering and to Conquer* (1876), *Lapsed but not Lost* (1877), all dealing with the early martyrs and as vigorous and inspiring as their titles suggest. (The "Early Christian novel" was a most popular literary *genre* in the Victorian age, and writers of all shades of religious opinion, from Catholics to agnostics, tried their hands at it. Even the author of the much-ridiculed *Eric or Little by Little* redeemed his reputation as a novelist over thirty years later by producing two very good Early Christian novels—*Darkness and Dawn* (1891), a tale of persecution under Nero, and *Gathering Clouds* (1895), a study of St. John Chrysostom and his times, both, like Mrs. Charles's novels, revealing great scholarly erudition and a broad and mellowed Evangelical outlook.)

But Mrs. Charles ranges through the centuries with an apparently effortless ease and is as much at home describing the agonies of primitive martyrs as she is in writing the diaries of twelfth-century abbots or describing the career of David Livingstone or General Gordon. She has given us novels about Joan of Arc, Bunyan, Fox, Baxter, and the Wesleys—all well-told tales against a vivid and accurate historical background. Many of her novels take the form of a kind of family log-book; she is very fond of the diary method, some of her chapters even consisting of excerpts from a character's "moan-book"! (The revival of the "moan-book" might well find favour in mid-twentieth-century England.) Mrs. Charles can portray Catholic heroes and heroines as successfully as the most Protestant and Puritan ones, and her books show an amazing breadth of sympathy as well as of scholarship.

It is this cultured and catholic outlook that sets Mrs. Charles apart from the majority of Evangelical story-tellers of the time. Many of the stricter Evangelicals in the Church of England would have dismissed her as "Low gone Broad" (she was in fact a friend of Stanley, Kingsley and Jowett), and she is expressing her own beliefs when she makes a character in *The Bertram Family* (1876) say:

It is our deep conviction that whilst the Anglican Church, unburdened with claims to infallibility or supremacy, and heir of all the Christian ages, may be the widest, freest and most fruitful Communion in Christendom, she may, if by our narrow-heartedness we degrade her gifts for all men into exclusive privileges apart from all, become to us a mere insulated prison.

Mrs. Charles's novels, like those of George Eliot and Hesba Stretton, escape the "narrow-heartedness" that characterizes so much Evangelical fiction of the time. They are thus not typical, perhaps not even orthodox, but they open up a brave new world and supply fresh life and healthy vitality to counteract the morbid, sentimental and too narrowly didactic tendencies characteristic of so many Evangelical novels of the Victorian age.

CHAPTER 6

CHRISTIANITY MUSCULAR AND
ELASTIC: THE
BROAD CHURCH NOVELS

FTER the grim "narrow-heartedness" of so
much Low Church fiction it is a relief to
turn to the Broad Church novel, where
the atmosphere is considerably brighter. Intelligence and humour, gaiety and gusto—qualities
conspicuously absent in so many religious novels
—now come upon the scene; we are entertained
rather than exhorted, we can relax and we can
be amused.

The number of such novels is of course comparatively small. Broad Churchmen, called
liberal by their friends and latitudinarian by
their enemies, were not a consciously organized
party in the Victorian age; they grew in power
and breadth as the century advanced, but they
had no organ in the periodical press and little
unanimity and clarity as to the exact nature of
their beliefs. In general they represented the
"anti-dogmatic principle and its developments"
that Newman battled against, and although some
of them were, in the words of D. C. Somervell,
"so Broad that their Churchmanship was visible

to very few except themselves", they were all united in their stand for greater charity, tolerance and understanding among Christians. Their novels thus escape that sectarian virulence that damages so much religious fiction of the time.

Some of their characters, however, do not altogether escape from the priggishness of the age. We see, for example, a typical Liberal propaganda prig in Mr. Oswald of M. M. Howard's *Brampton Rectory* (1849)—a virtuous but revolting bore, stuffed full of quotations from Stanley, Bunsen and Arnold (the book is dedicated to the "honoured memory" of the great Dr. Arnold) and overflowing with the dull sermons that mar so many of the controversial novels of the eighteen-forties. Dr. Grant in *Compton Merivale* (1850), by the same author, is a similarly didactic lay figure, a friend of Mechanics' Institutes, in favour of the union of Church and State, anxious to hold out the olive branch to Dissenters, and completely static and perfect in his own spiritual condition.

Broad Church sinners, on the other hand, are generally those who have fallen into the snares of sectarianism and their lives are often humorously related cautionary tales against narrow-mindedness in religion. F. W. Robinson wrote of such sinners in his novels, endowed with titles

that are refreshingly brief and to the point—
High Church (1860), *No Church* (1861), *Church
and Chapel* (1863), *Beyond the Church* (1866).
The last one is probably his best and certainly
his most amusing. He pokes sly fun at old High-
and-dry Rectors, pious spinsters and Puseyites
with their "little holy jokes" and "little holy
books, such as the life of St. Ulularius, who lined
his mattress with darning needles and sang
hymns without ceasing, or a monograph of St.
Parcelblinda, who always screamed when a man
approached, and never kissed her father after
her third year". His account, too, of a typical
church bazaar, with the Dean invoking "the
Divine blessing upon the pin-cushions and pen-
wipers" is highly entertaining. The satire in this
story is without bitterness, and it is pleasant to
find an author so good-tempered in dealing with
such flamingly controversial subjects.

Ridicule is indeed a weapon that Broad
Church novelists use with considerable success,
and it is not surprising that the most amusing
religious novel of the century should come from
a Liberal pen. The Rev. W. J. Conybeare's *Perversion* (1856) is a neglected masterpiece of
humorous fiction. (Lest the title might appear
misleading, it should be noticed that the word
"perversion" in popular Victorian usage had a
religious and not a sexual significance, and to

pervert or " 'vert" meant to apostatize.) This book is written with the excellent purpose of showing how "the inconsistency, extravagance or hypocrisy of those who call themselves Christians" has the effect of driving the young into infidelity, and it tells the story of a young man's quest for faith and his wanderings in the mazes of ecclesiastic conflict and labyrinths of scepticism that characterize the mid-Victorian spiritual scene. Charles Bampton, the hero, learns Pantheism from his German tutor Shrecklich, then Evangelicalism from a pious humbug, Mr. Moony, then Tractarianism from a Puseyite maiden. The young couple sing Gregorian chants together, but when she jilts him he discards his rosary in disgust and "the enthusiasm and romance of his ecclesiolatry" die away. After many adventures he is at last converted to Christianity by a clergyman who solves his doubts by letter in forty pages, and recommends a broad and practical brand of religion involving no "theoretic narrowness" but several Arnoldian doctrines of hard work and helpfulness. Conybeare's clerical portraits, his descriptions of the free-thinkers' club at Oxford, and, *mirabile dictu*, life among the Mormons in America, are some of the funniest pieces of writing in all religious fiction. Nor does the spiritual biography suffer from these lighter touches—Conybeare's sense of humour helps rather than hinders him in the portrayal of a bewildered young man in search of a religion; the whole book is remarkably free from prudishness and preaching, and Charles's search for faith is treated with zest, adventurousness and manly realism.

These were also the distinguishing qualities of the novels written by another Broad Church country clergyman, Charles Kingsley, Rector of Eversley. Kingsley too brought gusts of fresh air into the religious novel—indeed, so vigorous and breezy are these gusts that the spiritual element is often almost entirely blown away, and we are left with magnificent adventure stories and only scanty accounts of the inner life. Kingsley was a man with a message who regarded his novel-writing as a divinely-inspired vocation, but his genius for descriptions of exciting physical events exceeded his powers of portraying the adventures of the soul, and although in his own day his novels caused conversions, and brought faith and its consolations to many, the modern reader may well find the spiritual content of his novels a little shallow and schoolboyish.

Today we read *Yeast* (1851) for its superb descriptions of fishing and hunting rather than for its accounts of the hero's struggles for faith (ending in the rather nebulous conclusion of serving "Jesus Christ—THE MAN"); we read

Hypatia (1853) for the splendid pictures of Rome ageing hideously that form a triumph of the historical imagination, for those gorgeous pagan scenes that Kingsley describes with such relish, and for the masterly account of the death of Hypatia herself rather than details of the colourless hero's search for truth and the author's intended message of warning that was the whole *raison d'être* of the book. We read *Westward Ho!* (1855) for the joy of the adventures and not for information on the spiritual progress of the characters, and we read *Two Years Ago* (1857) for nautical rather than eschatological illumination. Similarly, *Hereward the Wake* (1866) holds us by the mighty deeds of the hero, and we are far more interested in learning how he was outlawed and slew bears and performed saga-like feats than in learning how he lost the grace of God. Kingsley's gifts as a novelist are better suited to describing a man's fall from his horse than his fall from grace, and many of his best-known characters seem distinguished more by a thirst for blood than a hunger for God.

Yet, while admitting these exaggerations in the "wolf-vein", we see that Kingsley does make an interesting contribution to the religious novel. The preacher of "muscular Christianity" and the stalwart opponent of all forms of asceticism, he endeavours to show in his novels how spiritual welfare can be greatly assisted by vigorous physical activity and by encouraging rather than crushing the natural appetites and passions. True Christianity, according to Kingsley, involves an appreciation of the great importance and value of animal spirits and physical strength, and a hearty enjoyment of all the pursuits and accomplishments which are connected with them. His views are in agreement with the clerical writer who proclaimed in *The Christian World* that bodily exercise is "at once a religious duty and a means of grace".

Thus in his novels he shows us men and women developing spiritually through being toughened physically. Philammon, in *Hypatia*, who at the beginning of the story is a rather soft young monk in a deplorable state of cloistered ignorance (having never seen a woman), becomes a great Christian and a model Abbot only after he has had amazing adventures in the world, has fought hippopotamuses and Goths, has witnessed riots, murders, fires, has had hairbreadth escapes from death, has loved and lost and has scandalized his fellow monks by his astonishing confession: "Tell my brethren that I pray nightly for two women: both of them young; both of them beautiful; both of them beloved by me more than I love my soul; and tell them, moreover, that one of the two was a harlot, and the other a heathen." Thus has Philammon's spiritual education been completed. Pious schoolmistresses too have to be shocked and battered out of their inadequate conceptions of Christianity into a higher, finer faith, and in *Two Years Ago* Grace Hervey learns from the grim horrors of an outbreak of cholera "how much of the unheroic element" is still left in her, and how narrow and untenable are her views on the doctrine of eternal damnation. True to the principles of Broad Church tolerance, Kingsley makes both Philammon and Grace Hervey have their creeds widened as well as their spiritual and physical powers developed through a more extensive acquaintance with life in the raw.

But although for Kingsley, a period of contact with the shocking and the sordid may assist in the heroifying of certain souls, yet in general it is one of his most vigorously emphasized doctrines that the soul suffers from continual exposure to bad physical conditions. Hence it is the duty of a parson to press for social, political and economic reforms, and problems of wages and sewers are as much his business as those of sacraments and prayers. Thus might Kingsley answer any critic likely to accuse him of preferring sanitation to meditation.

Bodily welfare being thus indissolubly linked with spiritual welfare, physical ills and evils cannot, in Kingsley's view, be cured by purely physical means—a lesson that Alton Locke learns to his cost. *Alton Locke* (1850), that interesting novel based on the life of Thomas Cooper, the Chartist poet whom Kingsley himself converted, shows how the hero, alienated from religion by the grim Calvinism of his mother, burns with longing to save his fellow workmen from their wretched sufferings in filthy hovels and sweat-shops. He finds, however, that all his efforts fail and eventually he learns that it is Jesus of Nazareth who is the only true "People's Friend" and that nothing but Christianity can cure economic and political diseases. The souls of the lower orders, we are told over and over again, are in danger because of the vileness of their living and working conditions, and both Alton Locke and the hero of *Yeast* come through their experience of "the condition-of-the-poor question" to their first real understanding of the Christian religion.

This emphasis on one particular aspect of the faith—Christianity in its role of physician to the social ills of the Victorian working classes—gives a certain narrowness to Kingsley's notions of spirituality. His characters look outwards and downwards rather than inwards and upwards; indeed, one leaves his novels with the confused impression that the highest spiritual development can take place only through an intense and belligerent humanitarianism or else a welter of hectic and sanguinary bodily activity, wherein animal strength, spirits and courage are being tried and tested to the uttermost. Yet, inadequate as Kingsley's spiritual creations tend to be, in their strength and healthy virility they form a suitable corrective to some of the more mawkish and young-ladyish features of Oxford Movement novels as well as to some of the morbid excesses of much Evangelical fiction.

Kingsley also showed deep concern with Christianity as the one and only answer to the scientific as well as social problems of the age, although this does not reveal itself quite so strikingly in his novels. To reconcile religion with science (too often implacable foes in the nineteenth century) was a Herculean task and Kingsley tackled it with his usual gusto. An enthusiastic amateur naturalist and geologist, a self-confessed "convert to Darwin's views", he was in touch with many of the leading scientists of his day and enjoyed "working out points of Natural Theology, by the strange light of Huxley, Darwin and Lyell". (Three mass-murderers of orthodox belief, according to most of the religious novelists.) *The Water Babies* (1863) was indeed a sort of adaptation for children of Darwin's theory of the natural selection of species, with a moral and religious application,

although its continued fame rests on its merits
as a children's fairy tale rather than its
curiosities and subtleties as a fascinating piece
of Christianized Darwinism.

Kingsley had a sure touch where juvenile
literature was concerned. It was he who enthused
vigorously to the publisher, Daniel Macmillan,
about a first novel that his barrister friend
Thomas Hughes had written and submitted. "As
sure as eggs are eggs," wrote Kingsley excitedly,
"the book will pay both of you well." His
prophecy was correct, for the book *Tom Brown's
Schooldays* proved to be not only a best-seller
of 1857 but a classic of its kind. New editions
still appear—it has even been televised—and
although few today share in its hero-worship of
Dr. Arnold, readers and viewers can still enjoy
thoroughly the lively schoolboy adventures and
the glorification of the robust, vigorous, manly,
sporting type as opposed to the gambling bully
or the "mammy-sick" milksop. Like Kingsley's
works, it has gained immortality through its
virility and adventurousness rather than through
its spiritual content or religious message. *Tom
Brown at Oxford* (1861), a less vivacious and
more long-winded sequel, shows the same sterling qualities in its hero.

"Manliness" of course was the great virtue.
The "tough guy" was indeed a favourite hero in

the popular fiction of the eighteen-fifties. The Crimean War had stimulated interest in stories of heroic action and strenuous adventure, and the Old Norse sagas, becoming more widely known in this decade, whetted the public's appetite for tales of lusty warriors. The upper and middle classes too were becoming increasingly concerned with matters of physical exercise and athletics, and a companion best-seller to Tom Brown in 1857 was *Guy Livingstone* (by George Lawrence, also an Old Rugbeian), a novel which boasts a thrillingly ultra-masculine hero, magnificent in size and sinew. Guy Livingstone, however, and his many fictional successors led very "fast" lives and were dazzling but wicked in their "muscular blackguardism"; it was for the Broad Church novelists to reconcile muscles with morals, gusto with the Gospel and fitness with faith.

Sometimes indeed the reconciliation went a little too far. Dr. Davies (himself a Broad Church clergyman) gives us, in his novel *Broad Church* (1875), a very comic picture of an ultra-hearty muscular Christian curate whose morning devotions include an ice-cold tub and a ten-mile spurt. He leaps hedges and fences, more "like an escaped lunatic than a reverend minister of the Gospel", stays at pubs and smokes "like a volcano". (Broad Churchmen rarely viewed tobacco or alcohol with disfavour, and this particular curate, even when at college, could "drink or smoke his juvenile rivals under the table as easily as he could punch their heads".) He also sings roaring songs and possesses an enormous appetite ("to eat like a Muscular Christian" had by this time become a byword) and an outspoken loathing of all humbug and anything that could be called "sissy", including elaborate vestments and jewellery—"I hate jewels and would rather have warts on my hand than a ring." This unconventional cleric is so dangerously like one of the "fast" heroes of the *Guy Livingstone* school that some of his parishioners even suggest making him head of a new "Fast Church". As for his theological opinions, they are as broad as his shoulders; his one great maxim is "In all things charity" and ecclesiastically he maintains a "Happy Family" atmosphere with beliefs "adjusted to the requirements of the age", and no "jarring sectaries" to denounce each other.

As the century advanced the "Happy Family" of Broad Churchmen grew much bigger and quite amazingly diverse. The Broad Church in fact became a congenial refuge for perplexed agnostics (D. C. Somervell even places the poet Clough "on the outermost frontiers of Broad Churchmanship"), theists such as George Macdonald, regretful unbelievers such as Matthew

Arnold and enthusiastic Modernists such as Mrs. Humphry Ward. One remembers that even Thomas Hardy keenly supported the Broad Church proposals for "rationalizing" the Church of England. Some of the faiths that came to dwell harmoniously together under the extremely generous and comprehensive *aegis* of the Broad Church can hardly be called Christian in any orthodox sense, and the religious novels inspired by these later developments of Liberalism will be discussed in another chapter. The tolerance for which earlier novelists campaigned stood in danger of being carried too far, and the Broad Church showed signs of encouraging beliefs such as those held by John Pickard Owen in *The Fair Haven* (1873), who was convinced that "all ideals gain by a certain amount of vagueness, which allows the beholder to fill in the details according to his spiritual needs," and that "no ideal can be truly universal and permanent unless it has an elasticity which will allow of this process in the minds of those who contemplate it", or by Dr. Jenkinson in *The New Republic* (1877), who outdid the broadest Anglican by declaring that "Christianity . . . really embraces all religions, even any honest denial of itself." Conybeare's definition of "exaggerated Broad" Anglicans as "concealed infidels" becomes only too evident as the years pass.

Since extreme "elasticity" of belief, together with a tendency to humour and satire, shows itself very strongly in the Broad Church novels, it is perhaps only fitting that we should conclude this survey with a brief reference to two novels by an author who professed himself "a member of the more advanced wing of the English Broad Church", novels in which the heroes, after many spiritual vicissitudes, both become practising Broad Churchmen, the earlier novel being considered by many as a valuable piece of Broad Church propaganda, Canon Ainger even going so far as to send copies to friends whom he particularly wished to convert from infidelity.

The author in question is of course Samuel Butler, whose powers of satire in spiritual matters make him a unique figure among Victorian novelists and who never hesitated to mock, *inter alia*, that section of the Church to which he professed allegiance. The story of John Pickard Owen in *The Fair Haven* is extremely amusing. This young man in search of a faith, after many changes and conversions, all humorously recounted (had Butler read Conybeare, we wonder?), at last becomes a Broad Churchman, broad "in the true sense of being able to believe in the naturalness, legitimacy and truth *qua* Christianity even of those doctrines which seem to stand most widely and irreconcileably asunder".

He plans to be "the interpreter of Christianity to the Rationalist and of Rationalism to the Christian", but in his noble efforts to resolve these discords he falls into religious melancholy and dies. This story, rich in irony and satire, proved an excellent literary hoax, for it was taken as a serious defence of Anglican orthodoxy by many reviewers and readers, including the unfortunate Canon Ainger.

Several of the incidents in the life of John Pickard Owen which affect his spiritual development are similar to those in the life of Ernest Pontifex, the hero of *The Way of All Flesh* (published in 1903, written between 1872 and 1884). This novel, Butler's masterpiece, falls more naturally into the category of fiction of lost faith, and will be discussed as such in a later chapter. But if Ernest's life is the story of lost orthodoxy it is also a pungent satire on the heroes of religious novels in general and Broad Church novels in particular. Ernest, like a typical hero of a Broad Church propaganda novel, reacts sharply from narrow, bigoted forms of Christianity. Like Alton Locke and Charles Bampton, he finds Evangelicals repulsive and full of humbug. Like Charles Bampton, too, he becomes disgusted with High Church exponents. Indeed, *The Way of All Flesh* as a spiritual biography might gain considerably by detailed comparison with *Perversion*. But whereas Charles' freethinking,

which follows his experience of so much fraud
and trickery among Anglicans, is only a temporary phase in his spiritual development,
Ernest's scepticism, resulting from the same
causes, never leaves him, and he develops along
lines which would have considerably shocked the
later Charles. Ernest preaches the desirability of
wealth, bachelordom and orphanhood; he denies
the "niceness" of the poor, recommends tepidity
in all spiritual matters and takes Communion
once a year "as a sop to Nemesis lest he should
again feel strongly on any subject". His life, in
fact, represents the passing from naïve and gull-
ible faith to intelligent, cynical and sophisticated unbelief, and is certainly the most brilliant
example in all Victorian fiction of a spiritual
journey from traditional orthodoxy to the "concealed infidelity" of the "exaggerated Broad".

Butler's novel, negative and insincere as it
may be in the quality of its spiritual conclusions,
yet possesses robust vitality, realism and splendid entertainment value. Indeed, most Broad
Church novels share, though in a lesser degree,
in these qualities, and today we can still appreciate their vigour and masculinity. (Unlike the
High Church party, the Broad Church had few
female novelists.) If fiction reveals certain spiritual shortcomings in liberal Anglicanism it reveals also a cultured wit, a civilized tolerance

and a delightful *joie-de-vivre*, and the modern reader may find it a congenial and refreshing change to turn to such religious novels, full of virility rather than sentimentality, humour rather than hatred, and enthusiasm for the practical reforms of the "Social Movement" rather than interest in the theological complexities of the Oxford Movement.

2: THE CATHOLIC CHURCH

CHAPTER 7

GAIN AND LOSS:
CONVERSIONS AND RENOUNCEMENTS

THE Catholic contribution to the religious novel is also a minor one, but of considerable interest. The small and despised body of Catholics in England, although emancipated in 1829, increased by Irish immigration and conversions from the Oxford Movement in the eighteen-forties and restored to its orbit in the ecclesiastical firmament in the eighteen-fifties, did not make any really substantial mark on English fiction until the last decades of Queen Victoria's reign, and the glories of Rome's second spring were slow to show themselves in the novel. It is the portrait by the enemy that only too often appears in Victorian fiction, "No Popery" being so much more popular a theme than "Popery".

But the Catholic novels we do possess shed significant light on the Oxford Movement and on the sufferings of those who passed from Canterbury to Rome. For suffering was indeed the keynote of these conversions. Newman, in his *Apologia*, speaks of that unhappy period when

he was on his "deathbed" as regards member-
ship of the Church of England. The metaphor is
an apt one, and we know that the deathbeds of so
many Victorian Anglicans, far from being peace-
ful and painless, were beds of anguish, full of
tragedy, torment and spiritual suffering of the
keenest kind. Rejected by their families,
mourned by their friends and abused by their
enemies, these "perverts" frequently ended their
Anglican days in great loneliness and distress,
and only after enduring the most grievous conflicts and sorrows did they finally pass over to
the other side.

Detailed accounts of such "deaths" are recorded in much fiction of the period and give
to the religious novel a new power and depth of
autobiographical sincerity that even the best
hostile stories or propaganda tales are unable to
convey. The name of Newman suggests itself
at once here, for Newman, besides being the
central figure of the Catholic revival in England,
was also a novelist. With *Loss and Gain* (1848)
and *Callista* (1856), he contributed to the two
most popular types of religious fiction in the
mid-nineteenth century: the contemporary
"quest for faith" story and the historical romance. *Loss and Gain*, the story of the conversion of an Oxford student (written as a kind of
answer to Elizabeth Harris' muddle-headed

novel *From Oxford to Rome*), is especially revealing, for here Newman, availing himself of
the greater freedom that fiction and anonymity
can bestow, gives us not only the intellectual
but the emotional elements in his conversion—
all still fresh in his memory.

Charles Reding, the hero of the novel, is
clearly a self-portrait—a soul "naturally timid
and retiring, over-sensitive and, though lively
and cheerful, yet not without a tinge of melancholy in his character". He possesses a large
number of Newman's traits, including an early
inclination towards celibacy, a deep attachment
to Oxford, a love of Gregorian music, a slight
superstitious vein and a strong craving for truth
and certitude. Like Newman, too, he is matured
by family bereavement and finally received into
the Catholic Church by a Passionist Father.

Many of the principal features of his conversion are very similar to Newman's, for he
shares his author's fate in being condemned to
the miseries of a dreary and lingering Anglican
deathbed. The painful slowness of the whole
process is emphasized throughout. Conversion
never comes to Charles in a single sudden blinding flash of glorious illumination; he arrives at
his goal, as Newman did, by a gradual, tedious,
inch-by-inch crawling process towards the light.
The actual length of time for the conversion

period is shortened in the interests of the narrative, but we frequently see fiction giving place to pure autobiography in Newman's descriptions of Charles's mounting disillusionment in the Church of England, his dissatisfaction with "those odious Articles", his unsettlement of mind amid the uprooting storms of theological argument raging at Oxford, the continual "depression of spirits", the gradual, almost imperceptible shaping of ideas, the slow, unconscious ripening. "Growing towards the Church", Newman sometimes calls it, and this novel shows us that the growing pains involved were at times almost intolerable.

In this story, too, Newman points out that the pains of interior spiritual conflict are not the only burden that such Romeward-bound Anglicans have to bear. Separation from much-loved people and places is yet another part of the sacrifice demanded of them. Charles, like Newman, deeply filial and loving, the pride and hope of his family, their "only stay" after the father's death, finds that his change is a "crushing blow", especially to his mother, and the parting between mother and son is one of the finest scenes of the book. We recall that Newman's own mother had in fact died before his final conversion, but not before she, and indeed the whole family, had felt that John was getting too "high" for them, and at the time of his conversion the rest of the family, although diverging widely in their own beliefs, were yet unanimous in their disapproval of the step he had taken. Indeed, his sister Harriett never spoke to him again. Newman had thus tasted to the full those bitter draughts of family disagreement over religious matters, but, far from using these tragic scenes of family warfare as an argument against leaving the Church of one's baptism, as Miss Harris, Miss Sewell, Miss Worboise and so many other contemporary Anglican novelists do, Newman maintains on the contrary that such suffering is part of the price one pays for securing the truth, and, as a Catholic tells Charles, although "it is a sort of martyrdom" to break "the dearest and closest ties", yet "they who do so have a martyr's reward".

Parting from beloved places was almost another kind of martyrdom, and Charles's enforced departure from his university is one of the saddest events attendant on his conversion. Newman's love of Oxford shows itself throughout the story, and if the modern reader finds it a little mawkish to hear of Charles passionately embracing the willows near the Isis and plucking their leaves as a memento, he must remember the deep fervour of Newman's attachment to Oxford and the very real agony of his parting. (He never returned there until he was an old man, thirty years later.) Loss of Oxford was one of the worst losses he had to count in reckoning his loss and gain.

Having described all these losses in such detail, Newman still has to convince us that the gain outweighs them all. This he does in the concluding chapter when Charles is finally received into the Catholic Church and finds peace and serenity of mind, "like the stillness which almost sensibly affects the ears when a bell that has long been tolling stops, or when a vessel, after much tossing at sea, finds itself in harbour". The weary voyager, sad and sick from all the confused storms and fogs of Anglican controversy, has at last reached *terra firma*.

But this novel is not merely a younger and more emotional companion to the *Apologia*: it is a brilliantly amusing piece of writing, sparkling with wit and gaiety. In a most unexpected way the lighter touch everywhere redeems the sombre atmosphere of the "deathbed", and we are treated to a feast of witty conversation and clever satire on Oxford life and religious eccentricities. Some contemporary reviewers noticed this with rather shocked disapproval and *Frazer's Magazine* declared that "a book of this kind, a book of jokes and gossip, of eating and drinking, of smartnesses, levities and most probable personalities—appears as a somewhat undignified vehicle for the opinions of one who has

long been revered as a prophet and a saint."
But the modern reader, so accustomed to that
subtle sweet mournful figure of the Newman
legend, finds it a pleasant surprise to look back
on the Newman of three years' conversion standing and see such clear evidences of jollity, zest
and merriment in his temperament. His sense
of fun sometimes suggests Disraeli's treatment
of religious themes, but whereas Disraeli's religious sincerity was on the whole questionable,
no-one today could question the deep sincerity
of Newman's conversion, and indeed of his entire
spiritual life, and he thus has the distinction of
being the only eminent Victorian who could
write a confessional novel of spiritual biography
in high spirits as well as high seriousness: a
unique and delightful achievement.

In *Callista* we see yet another facet of Newman's genius: his outstanding ability as a historical novelist. *Callista* gives us a magnificent portrait of the third century in Proconsular Africa,
as well as another fascinating piece of autobiography. The convert this time is a young
pagan Greek girl, who is, like Newman, a person
of "ardent affections, and keen sensibilities, and
high aspirations"—Newman was able to express
much of his feminine sensibility in this character—and the chief stages in her spiritual growth
bear no little resemblance to Newman's own. She

passes through the same phase of mingled attraction and repulsion with regard to the Catholic Church. When she expresses her belief that "Christianity seems to be too beautiful to be anything else than a dream . . . its *maxims* are too beautiful to be believed; and then, on the other hand, its *dogmas* are too dismal, too shocking, too odious to be believed", we hear the echo of Newman's cry from Palermo in 1833:

> Oh that thy creed were sound!
> For thou dost soothe the heart, thou Church of Rome.

Her arrival too at that desolate "midway region of enquiry" parallels Newman's own stage in the struggle, for "to see that heathenism is false, to see that Christianity is true, are two acts, and involve two processes." Substitute "Anglicanism" for "heathenism" and "Catholicism" for "Christianity", and we have Newman's own position of 1843. Here again the excruciatingly painful slowness of the journey is emphasized, for this midway region, Newman tells us, "as surely takes time to pass over, except there be some almost miraculous interference, as it takes time to walk from place to place. You see a person coming towards you, and you say, impatiently, 'Why don't you come faster?—Why are you not here already?' Why?—because it takes time." And during this time Callista is in "a state of mind utterly forlorn"; she is "weary, disappointed, fastidious, hungry". The pain of this transition period is even more strongly stressed in *Callista* than in *Loss and Gain*.

Estrangement from family and friends are likewise involved in Callista's change of faith. Her nearest and dearest are all opposed to the step she has taken, not only because of its unpromising outlook for the future, but also on account of the havoc it has caused her physically. Callista, like Hypatia in Kingsley's novel, combines great intelligence with noble physical beauty and possesses both pride of intellect and pride of looks. But whereas Hypatia keeps her glorious beauty to the end, Callista's looks change after her conversion, and Newman spares us no detail in showing us this pride in her appearance, this feminine vanity, being utterly humbled by belief in Christ. Indeed throughout the book the sin of pride is scourged mercilessly; Juba, the arrogant sceptic, is punished by madness (later changed by the miraculous intervention of Callista to imbecility); the priest Caecilius is delighted when he visits Callista in prison and notes the disappearance of her previous haughty beauty, "that majesty of mien which was once hers, a gift so beautiful, so unsuitable to fallen man", and the author too rejoices that his heroine "had lost every vestige of what the world worships under the titles of proper pride and self-respect. Callista was living, not in the thought of herself, but of Another". Here again we see the autobiographical touch, as we think of Newman's own losses in the struggle and his shrunken appearance that so shocked his doctor in 1844. Indeed the meditations of Agellius on Callista's martyrdom might well be applied to Newman himselr. Here was

> ... a soul full of gifts, full of greatness, full of intellect ... yet this choicest, rarest specimen of Almighty skill, the Almighty had pitilessly shattered, in order that it might inherit a higher, an eternal perfection. O mystery of mysteries, that heaven should not possibly be obtained without such a grinding down and a breaking up of our original nature! O mysterious, that principle in us, whatever it is, and however it came there, which is so antagonist to God, which has so spoilt what seems good, that all must be undone, and must begin anew! "An enemy hath done this"; and, knowing as much as this, and no more, we must leave the awful mystery to that day when all things shall be made light.

No other novelist who passed from Anglicanism to Catholicism succeeded in plumbing the depths of the convert's suffering quite as well as Newman did, but many wrote of their experiences with a convincing vividness and sincerity. The unhappiness of the disillusioned Anglican is shown in several tales by Mrs. Gertrude Parsons, a convert and popular novelist of the day. Her *Thornberry Abbey* (1846) describes the conversion of the heroine and her clergyman fiancé to Catholicism. The story is full of religious discussions; everyone indulges in long conversations on Church topics, and a baby's christening is the scene for a heated argument among the relatives about baptismal regeneration. (The Catholic teaching on this extremely controversial matter had been well threshed out in fiction before the Gorham Case arose and harvested a distinguished crop of converts.) This novel, like *Loss and Gain*, stresses the "depressing and exhausting" effects of too much theological argument and the misery and misunderstanding that such a conversion inevitably causes in the sphere of human relationships.

But depression and exhaustion from overdoses of theology are not confined to the heroes and heroines of these novels: the reader often suffers too, particularly the modern reader. Who, for example, could really be enthralled by the sort of conversation that takes place in Miss E. C. Agnew's conversion novels?

> When he [the priest] informed her [Lilia] that the same Divine Being, of whose perfections they had discoursed on the preceding evening, would, in the three persons of His essential unity, descend on her soul in Baptism, Lilia immediately inquired, "By particles, or emanation?"

However thickly coated with the jam of "romance", the pill of theology in this type of novel is usually too unwieldy to swallow. Miss Agnew liked to turn her heroes into priests and her heroines into nuns, but her propaganda for the religious life was far too feeble and unconvincing to combat the strong and scandalous tradition of "wicked Jesuit" and "nunnery-tale" books in England at that time.

However, in A. H. Edgar's *John Bull and the Papists* (1846), the story of the conversion of an Anglican rector, the arguments for joining the Catholic Church are a little more attractive, and in Lady Georgiana Fullerton's novel *Mrs. Gerald's Niece* (1869), they are set forth in a very readable and entertaining manner. Like Mr. and Mrs. Parsons, Lady Georgiana and her husband were converts from High Anglicanism, and Lady Georgiana, a truly saintly character (Newman wrote of his "reverence and admiration" for her life), devoted herself to work among the poor and the writing of books to raise money for her charities. *Mrs. Gerald's Niece* was one of her most popular and influential works of fiction, and caused many conversions, including, it is said, that of the Marquis of Ripon. The story tells of the progress of Edgar, a High Church clergyman, and his wife Ita, towards Rome. Edgar is at first wildly enthusiastic for "Catholicism without Popery" and Lady Georgiana gives an excellent account of the revolutionary effect of the Oxford Movement on the young mind. But Edgar, of course, finds that to many of his friends the idea of a Catholic Anglican Church is "dreadfully puzzling", and discovers that, when abroad with his wife in Italy, they can convince neither priest nor peasant that they belong to the Catholic Church. (One is reminded of Thomas Mozley, Newman's brother-in-law, describing his visit to a French convent where he naïvely told the nuns "that I was a priest and that lady with me was my wife". He reports that the nuns "shrugged their shoulders, exclaimed *Mon Dieu!* uplifted their hands and exchanged glances with one another. Our visit proved unwelcome and fruitless.")

The position is rendered even more awkward by the fact that the only other Anglican clergyman in the district is an ultra-Protestant. (The same situation in Brittany is used by Lady Gertrude Douglas to hasten the conversion of her

High Church heroine in *Linked Lives* (1876).)
"What, are there two religions in one church?"
ask the Italians, and an old peasant woman tells
them flatly: "Those who do not acknowledge the
Pope are not Catholics." Spirited arguments
follow; Ita's faith in the Church of England is
now destroyed, but her husband stubbornly
resists all attempts to shake his convictions and
the conflicts begin in earnest. Ita tries vainly to
stifle her doubts and to "shut out" conviction,
and clearly the author knows well the agonies
of such resistance movements:

> What desperate battles have thus been
> secretly fought in support of the Anglican
> theory, within the depths of many a soul,
> whose whole freight of earthly joys and weal
> has been embarked on that sinking vessel!
> How it has played the devil's advocate against
> itself, and with what almost conscious evasions
> silenced the cry of awakened conscience. Let
> those who have never known any measure
> of this strange suffering deal gently with
> others who are writhing under its pangs.

After much heart-searching Ita becomes a
Catholic and is temporarily estranged from her
husband, but he finally follows her into the
Church and the story has a happy ending.
Similar sufferings are endured by converts in

the novels of E. H. Dering, an Anglican clergyman's son who became a Catholic in 1865 at the
age of thirty-eight. He was received into the
Church by Newman himself, who, knowing Dering and "aware of the mental struggles" that
his friend had undergone, made a special journey to Kent to perform the reception. In his
novels *Florence Danby* (1868), dedicated to
Newman, *Sherborne* (1875) and *The Ban of
Maplethorpe* (1894), he stresses the great difficulties of converts in tearing themselves away
from the Church of England: "You can't think
how hard it is to get out of what one was taught
by one's Mother." He has much to say about the
disabilities of English Catholics in public life,
and his accounts of the anguish of the Victorian
convert in having to break through the enormous barriers of tradition, environment, education and feeling give his novels a high value as
spiritual autobiography, and such studies of
"reluctant converts", as we may style them, are
psychologically of the greatest interest as well
as being extremely effective as Catholic propaganda.

Several writers of such "deathbed" fiction follow Newman's example in giving comic relief
to a tragic situation and introducing satire in
their novels. A most amusing conversion novel
comes from the pen of that witty convert and

editor of *Punch*, Sir F. C. Burnand, whose novel *My Time and What I've Done With It* (1874) contains a wickedly satirical picture of life in a High Church seminary. Indeed, satire in the Catholic novel reached admirable heights with such writers as Thomas de Longueville, whose *Life of a Prig* (1885) and other novels satirize the Church of England mercilessly and win praise even from *The Church Times* for their "smart hits" and "very excellent fooling", and Edmund Randolph, the son of a Cambridge convert, whose dazzlingly entertaining novel *Mostly Fools* (1886) hits a number of targets, including Downside and Cardinal Manning's pet project, the Catholic University College in Kensington. Randolph's death at the age of thirty-nine robbed England of an unusually brilliant Catholic novelist.

Not quite so dazzlingly entertaining were stories of conversions from other creeds and from unbelief. However, Canon Sheehan's book *The Triumph of Failure* (1899) is a good chronicle of a young unbeliever's progress towards the light. The tales of "Iota" (Mrs. Kathleen Caffyn) tell of conversions from Dissent, and in *The Flower of Asia* (1901) by "Cyril" (Canon Dennehy) the heroine is a Hindu girl and only becomes a Catholic after examining the claims of Brahmanism, Buddhism, Islam and Anglicanism. There are several very bad novels by women writers showing the conquest of scepticism by Catholicism. The presence of a fabulously wealthy Catholic lover usually assists the conversion process considerably, as in M. C. Bishop's *Elizabeth Eden* (1878), where a silly little unbelieving widow finds faith—and many other things—through the love of a Catholic millionaire; Cardinals attend her wedding and the Pope himself takes a kindly and—to the modern reader—completely inexplicable interest in her.

Less widely controversial and more stuffily and conventionally "Victorian" in character are the stories of moral rather than intellectual conversions to Catholicism. Here women novelists indulged in much sentimental romance and Cecilia M. Caddell, Agnes Stewart and Mrs. Parsons all wrote rather tract-like tales of repentant sinners, stories abounding in angelic heroines, wicked squires and juvenile deathbeds. The Mary-Magdalene type of conversion, too, received its attention in Catholic novels. The story of the "fallen woman" and her punishment was a favourite theme of mid- and late-Victorian fiction, and novels that punished the most sold the best, as the success of *East Lynne* showed. Catholic writers attempted to emphasize the spiritual issues, but the results, in such stories as Miss Caddell's *Home and the Homeless* (1858) and *Never Forgotten* (1871) and J. C.

Heywood's *How Will It End?* (1872), are utterly rubbishy. Such tales as these merit the tart comments of *The Month* in 1874, when a reviewer felt compelled to remind readers that:

> A bad novel is a bad novel, even though the love-making goes on between the devout Bridget and the patriotic Phelim, and though the villain of the story be an agent of Dublin Castle or a redshirted Garibaldian. Trash is trash, in whatever form it presents itself, and Catholic trash is the worst of all.

After this salutary statement the Mary Magdalenes of Catholic fiction improved somewhat, until Canon Barry produced a really splendid one in his novel *The New Antigone* (1887). This fallen woman, the seducer rather than the seduced (she airs her advanced views on free love before her astonished and embarrassed suitor), later repents and becomes a nun, and the story is told with lively intelligence and refreshing originality. Indeed the three Canons (Barry, Sheehan and Dennehy) did much to raise the standard of the moral conversion tale, lifting it out of the sloppy rut of feeble piety where so many women novelists were content to preserve it in all its sentimentality.

Newman's *Loss and Gain* thus has no real rival in the field of conversion stories, and the same may be said of his *Callista* in the field of historical fiction, although Catholics wrote many religious novels with historical settings and *Callista* has several good successors and one distinguished predecessor.

Fabiola (1854), appearing two years before *Callista*, inaugurated the Catholic Popular Library and was Cardinal Wiseman's contribution to the Early Christian novel, already flourishing and fashionable in the Victorian age. Indeed, so common did these "thrillers" about Early Christian martyrs become that one critic referred to them as a "literary nuisance". But it was far from common for cardinals to produce such stories, and Wiseman's comment in this connection is illuminating. To a friend he wrote:

> When it was first announced that I had written a "romance" there was terrible commotion among my cardinalatial brethren. Now, however, from the Pope downwards I have nothing but thanks and compliments, and all Rome is placarded with it, my name in large type. I consider this a perfect revolution, a great triumph of the "spirit of the age" or "progress" over forms and etiquettes.

Fabiola is a lively story, with a detailed account of the conversion of the haughty and sophisticated heroine (she is even prouder than Hypatia and Callista) and some impressive descriptions of various well-known martyrdoms, chronological and geographical accuracy, as the author admitted, being sacrificed for this purpose. Although much less spiritually profound than *Callista* it was a far more popular novel— in fact a real best-seller, having no less than seven translations in Italian alone, translations into almost every other European language, and high praise from the Archbishop of Milan as "the first good book that had the success of a bad one".

After this great impetus provided by *Fabiola* and *Callista*, Catholic historical fiction developed by leaps and bounds. Contemporary events in Italy, with the continual conflicts between the Pope and the rebels, inspired ultramontane writers such as William McCabe to seek for historical parallels, drawn for us in such novels as *Bertha, A Romance of the Dark Ages* (1851), *Florine, Princess of Burgundy* (1855), and *Adelaide, Queen of Italy* (1856). (The very common use of female names as titles for historical novels served no doubt as a bait to attract women readers.) But the "martyrological" novels remained the most popular of all, especially when spiced with plenty of sensationalism. After exploiting the early ages of the Church Catholic writers turned to the Elizabethan period, which they also found prolific in gore and glory. As C. M. Caddell wrote:

> So rich indeed is the private history of the Catholic families of England in all the materials for a "sensation novel"—in hairbreadth escapes, in daring rescues, in lifelong imprisonments and heroic deaths—that it is wonderful that it should so long have escaped the prying eyes of the novelist in search of adventures "too strange not to be true" for his embryo romance.

Mrs. Ogden Meeker's *Fortune's Football* (1864), Lady Georgiana Fullerton's *Constance Sherwood* (1865) and C. M. Caddell's *Wild Times* (1872), are all very adventurous and exciting novels of sixteenth-century Catholic life in England. The first two give us a good account of Jesuit martyrdoms at that time—a welcome corrective to the usual anti-Jesuit propaganda of Protestant fiction and the caricatures of Kingsley in *Westward Ho!*[1]

The agonies of martyrdom did indeed haunt the imagination of Catholic writers throughout the Victorian age and inspired a new type of religious novel, neither controversial nor historical—the spiritual biography of the contemporary Catholic soul in anguish, revealing stories

[1] See the following chapter.

of the most excruciating sufferings and the conquest of them by faith. Julia Kavanagh, Mrs.
Parsons and M. E. Francis all wrote novels to
show "the way in which Catholics can suffer".
The renouncement of earthly affection proved a
popular theme, and tales of a conflict between
passion and principle, describing a kind of
heroine-lover-faith triangle, were in great demand throughout the century. Catholic novelists
wrote of the pains that could arise from attach-
ments to non-Catholics, and the subtle agonies
of a mixed marriage, which one lady novelist
went so far as to describe as "a martyrdom unseen, unacknowledged, neither comprehended
nor believed—a martyrdom than which no pain
could be more acute, and of which it was impossible to complain". These modern martyrdoms
with a strong sex interest produced many very
passionate and popular stories. Such novels as
Lady Georgiana Fullerton's *Grantley Manor*
(1847) and Michael Denham's *The Massingers:
or the Evils of Mixed Marriages* (1862) spare us
none of the anguish of this kind of suffering and
pave the way for Mrs. Wilfrid Ward's fine novel
One Poor Scruple (1899), one of the most subtly
penetrating and psychologically skilful studies of
this struggle within a woman's soul.

Sometimes the chief sufferer in these triangles
is a man. Tales of cloister-and-hearth conflicts

were, of course, often best sellers, but these were generally written by non-Catholics hostile to the rule of clerical celibacy in the Catholic Church. Charles Reade's own magnificent novel *The Cloister and the Hearth* (1861) is an example of this (Charles Reade suffered himself, as a Fellow of Magdalen, from being bound to a law of celibacy), and many lesser writers wrote melodramatic and often ridiculous tales of suffering celibates. Catholic novelists, however, concerned themselves more with men in love with women barred to them by marriage or a different faith. Canon Barry's *The Two Standards* (1898) has a Catholic hero in love with a married woman, and Dorothea Gerard's *Orthodox* (1888) is a most forceful, emotional and dramatic story of an Austrian army officer who loves a beautiful Jewess, but renounces her and enters a monastery. Usually, however, the Catholic reading public preferred a renouncing heroine, and the minor fiction of the faithful provides plenty of instances of saintly young women dying gracefully on couches with their formerly unbelieving lovers (converted now, but, alas, too late!) rushing from the ends of the earth for forgiveness and a last embrace.

Curiously enough, one of the most deeply sensitive and analytical studies of a Catholic heroine torn by a passion-and-faith conflict was written by a man, and one who had ceased to profess the Catholic faith. George Moore's *Evelyn Innes* (1898) and its sequel *Sister Teresa* (1901) give a subtle and delicate rendering of this drama. His story has much in common with earlier Catholic novels on this theme, but he shows superior psychological insight and greater frankness in treatment of sex. His heroine is highly-sexed and he tells us so; she is interested chiefly in "sexual emotion" and the author's thesis seems to be that "it is by denial of the sexual instinct that we become religious". The unscrupulous lover is a somewhat conventionally-drawn character, but Evelyn herself, her conflicts, her surrender and her renouncement, are excellently portrayed, and although George Moore afterwards condemned the story as aphrodisiacal and worthless, it remains as a valuable study of a Catholic girl's conquest of passion by faith, wherein a genuine and sympathetic interest in Catholic ideals, in the life of the spirit and in the psychology of sex replace the obsessive interest in melodrama that dominated earlier and cruder novels on this theme.

The inspiration of these two uncharacteristic books of George Moore was almost certainly his unsuccessful love for a fellow-novelist, Mrs. Craigie, who on her side suffered personally from such conflicts in her own life and made them the

Leitmotiv of her stories. Pearl Mary-Theresa Craigie, who wrote under the pseudonym of "John Oliver Hobbes", was the most brilliant and gifted of all Victorian Catholic novelists. A wit, a divorced woman and a convert from Nonconformity, this unusual genius writes with a flippancy and sophisticated cynicism that may suggest the atmosphere of the "nineties", but unlike her Catholic contemporaries such as Henry Harland, whose charming novel *The Cardinal's Snuff Box* (1900) is merely an exquisite piece of frivolity, Mrs. Craigie reveals exceptional depths of thought and feeling beneath the sparkling surface.

Most of her novels tell of unhappy marriages (her own, contracted when she was nineteen, lasted only four years) and the troubles arising from love for someone else's partner. The main problem that she presents in all her stories (was it also perhaps the greatest problem in her own life?) is this—should one boldly seize or heroically renounce forbidden fruit? Over and over again this problem occurs in her fiction, and the answers worked out are not always the same. In *Some Emotions and a Moral* (1891) Cynthia has the strength to renounce her married lover; she realizes that sometimes "a woman can best show her love for a man by leaving him". In *The Sinner's Comedy* (1892) Sacheverell, in love with the unhappily-married Anne, renounces her and she dies. Sacheverell is ever afterwards tormented by the thought that, had he defied convention and lived with Anne, she would certainly have recovered her health and strength. In *The Gods, Some Mortals and Lord Wickenham* (1895), Dr. Warre is married to a snobbish little vixen, and, limp from her hysterical scene-making, crawls to a Catholic church for consolation. He is in love with an Italian girl, but even when his wife elopes with another man he does not wish to have the scandal of divorce, nor does he consider himself free to marry again. He, like Anne, dies from his unhappy marriage. In *The Serious Wooing* (1901), Rosabel has been married at nineteen to an imbecile peer (Mrs. Craigie should have limited the number of her heroines with husbands in lunatic asylums—there are far too many of them) but is in love with a Socialist reformer and elopes with him. Here the author's sympathies appear on the side of those who break unwanted ties and courageously seek their own happiness. In *The Herb-Moon* (1896) Rose, another heroine with a lunatic husband, languishes in misery for years before her husband dies and sets her free to marry the man she loves.

Sometimes Mrs. Craigie twists her eternal triangles into shapes of overstrained complexity and in such novels as *Love and the Soul Hunters*

(1902) the tangle of people all in love with people who are in love with other people is too complicated to unravel at the first reading. Sometimes, too, the frivolous frothy style that Mrs. Craigie uses so well tends to obscure the deeper meaning. Like Disraeli (whom she admired and of whom she drew two portraits—one from life and one idealized—in *Robert Orange*), Mrs. Craigie occasionally seems too flippant for the religious novel. But this is a false estimate; beneath the sparkling gauds the sackcloth is only too obvious. Like Newman and Lady Georgiana Fullerton, Mrs. Craigie regarded novel-writing as a very serious occupation. "Of course people read a novel carelessly," she wrote, "for amusement when they are tired of their own environment and seek a change. But the novelist is none the less bound to write his unconsidered trifles with the same pains and thought he would bestow on a Philosophical Treatise—with this reservation, that his pains and thought must not be too apparent."

It is, however, apparent to any but the most superficial reader that the treatment of this main problem—to renounce or not to renounce—cost Mrs. Craigie considerable pains and thought, in literature if not in life, and the conflict between passion and faith in the Catholic novel finds its greatest expression in Mrs. Craigie's *The School for Saints* (1897) and its sequel *Robert Orange* (1900), the latter being generally acclaimed as the finest Catholic novel of the Victorian age.

The hero Robert and the heroine Brigit are both noble and virtuous beings. (Robert is an idealized and Catholicized Disraeli.) These "two charming Christians" are clearly destined for each other, the barrier, however, being Brigit's husband, for she has been married at sixteen to a political adventurer, a "velvet buffoon", a "goldfish with a soul". The apparent death of this creature leaves Brigit and Robert free to marry, but on their honeymoon they hear that he is still alive. Here is Mrs. Craigie's account of Brigit at this point:

> Every feature quivered under the invisible cutting hand of cruel experience. In those sharp moments of introspection she had gained such a knowledge of suffering that a fire seemed to have consumed her vision of life, reducing it to a frightful desert of eternal woe and unavailing sacrifice. Partially stunned and partially blinded by misery she felt the awful helplessness and pain of what is sometimes called the second birth, a crisis in all development when the first true realization comes that the soul is a stranger, a rebel, strong as eternity, weak as the flesh, free as the illimitable air.

The inevitable renouncement takes place, described brilliantly and poignantly by the author. Some of Mrs. Craigie's descriptions of the sufferings of believers and idealists are particularly fine. Take this passage, for example, in which she writes of Robert's feelings when, long after parting, he sees Brigit on the stage. (She has become an actress.) Mrs. Craigie writes:

> Sometimes the soul speaks first, sometimes the senses first influence a life, but the turn, soon or late, must inevitably come for each, and the man or woman, sick of materialism, who begins to suspect that the unseen world and its beauty is an inheritance more lasting and more to be desired than all the vindictive joys of the prison-house, has no such bitterness as the idealist who finds himself brought into thrilling touch with the physical loveliness, the actual enchantment, the undeniable delight of certain things in life. The questions, "What have I missed? What have I lost? What birthright have I renounced?" are bound to make themselves heard. They beat upon the heart like hail upon the sand—and fall buried in the scars they cause. Things of the flesh may and do become dead sea fruit, but things of the spirit often become stale and meaningless also. What is more weary than a tired mind? What

joys and labours are more exhausting than those of the intellect, and the intellect only? Does an idle week in summer ever beget more lassitude or such disgust of life as a month—alone with books—in a library? Dissatisfaction and satiety, melancholy and fatigue show as plainly in the pages of a Kempis as they do in Schopenhauer, as they do in Lucretius, as they do in St. Bernard, as they do in Montaigne, in Marcus Aurelius, in Dante, in St. Teresa.

The final twist of the knife for Brigit comes when her legal husband dies and she and Robert are now really free to marry, but Robert, not knowing this new turn of events, is on the brink of entering the priesthood. Brigit, learning this, renounces him a second time and thus the story closes.

In these two novels Mrs. Craigie has told a story of tremendous moral and spiritual force, a tale of tragic grief and frustration redeemed and ennobled by the Catholic faith. Like Newman in *Loss and Gain*, she has spiced her story with piquant wit; the clever "jokes and gossip" are not absent. Like Newman, too, she has searched the depths of the human heart and the heroic heights of sacrifice and martyrdom; like Newman once more, and like so many Catholic novelists of the Victorian age, she has shown in her writings a profound awareness of pain and suffering, a realization and a conviction that

Suffering can never be suppressed by statute. It is a law of nature, but as all other laws of nature, since it must be obeyed, let us at least submit as sons of God and co-heirs with Christ —not as beasts of burden and as those who believe that all labour is in vain.

CHAPTER 8

THE WICKED JESUIT AND COMPANY

FEW modern horror comics could equal in crudity, sadism, hysteria and blood-curdling violence the story of Jesuits in popular Victorian fiction. From the best-selling literature of the day we see that the Jesuit loomed large in Protestant imagination as a villain of the blackest dye, a spy, a secret agent, suave, supercilious and satanically unscrupulous, laying his cunning plots for the submission of England to "Jesuitocracy", wheedling rich widows, forcing his converts to change their wills in favour of his Order, to kneel in penitence almost naked for hours through chilly winter nights and to leave their families for life at a minute's notice. When frustrated in his knavish tricks he would frequently gnash his teeth, foam at the mouth and write frantic letters in cypher to his General. Even in the most serious religious fiction the Jesuit appears as a diabolical monster; Mrs. Sherwood, Miss Worboise and "Charlotte Elizabeth", all influential Protestant novelists of the time, did not hesitate to form their Jesuits on this traditional pattern and punish them at the conclusion of the story by a suitably sticky end.

For the Jesuits were, to the average Englishman, objects of suspicion, fear and hatred
throughout Queen Victoria's reign, and the disguised Jesuit (sometimes referred to as a "crypto-
Jesuit") occupied the same place in popular fiction of the nineteenth century as the Communist
spy in the fiction of today. The Oxford Movement, of course, increased the fear and hatred
enormously, Tractarianism being considered by
many Protestants as part of a devilish Jesuit plot
to convert England—Puseyism, Popery and
Jesuitism being to many unenlightened minds
synonymous terms. The flames of this hostility
were fanned to even greater heights by the appearance in France of Eugène Sue's *The Wandering Jew* (1844), which had several translations
into English in the forties and proved to be the
most popular anti-Jesuit novel in the world.
Readers of this amazing tale will remember how
the wicked Jesuit, having by trickery and intrigue ruined several people's lives and made
himself General of the Order, is punished by
poisoning and dies writhing in dreadful agony
in a dimly-lit crypt along with six corpses and a
mad woman shrieking with "maniac laughter".

Several of the more sensational and sadistic
features of Sue's tale are found in William
Sewell's *Hawkstone* (1845) already mentioned as
a cautionary tale for perplexed Anglicans. Intending to show the British public what a ghastly

mistake Newman had made in embracing the Scarlet Woman earlier that year, Sewell paints an abominable picture of Catholicism and makes his Jesuit villain a most loathsome character who foams at the mouth even more horribly than Mrs. Sherwood's Jesuits, and meets his death by being eaten alive by rats in a vault (full details given). Doubtless Sewell thought that Newman had been made to "pervert" by Jesuitical machinations (Newman, in *Loss and Gain*, speaks of Oxford's suspicion of "concealed Jesuits"), but then Sewell's anti-Jesuit obsession was almost pathological; he even suspected his fishmonger of being one of these gentlemen in disguise, and his novel is a revelation of a rot in his own mind rather than in the Society of Jesus.

All this was bad enough but worse was to follow. It was the restoration of the Hierarchy in 1850 that, provoking an extraordinary outburst of hysteria, fury and panic on the part of John Bull, whipped Protestant novelists up into a frenzy of rage and produced some of the most angry novels ever written, fulminating particularly against the "snakes", "pests", "poisonous microbes" and "emissaries of Satan", as the sons of Loyola were variously called. Let us examine for a moment the work of Miss Catherine Sinclair. Miss Sinclair was, like Sewell, a writer of education and cultured background (she 'was

the daughter of a baronet and sister of an archdeacon), and, like Sewell, she wrote "religious"
stories full of hatred, malice, spite and sheer
ignorance. (A deplorable insularity manifests itself in so many of these Victorian tales dealing
with the Catholic Church and written by novelists who, one feels, should have known better.)
Miss Sinclair's deficiency of charity is equalled
only by her deficiency of knowledge. Her most
famous novel, *Beatrice: or The Unknown Relatives* (1852), bursting with indignation against
"Papal Aggression", enjoyed great popularity in
England and "unprecedented success" in
America, where dozens of New York clergymen
recommended it from their pulpits and a hundred thousand copies were sold in less than a
month. This moral tale, purporting to show the
joys of Protestantism contrasted with the
miseries of Popery (including a special warning
to British fathers about the dangers of placing
their daughters in foreign convents for the sake
of "accomplishments"), features a vile Jesuit
with the usual "bland smile", "insinuating
voice", "diplomatic skill", "noiseless velvet step"
(Jesuits always "glide" through Victorian
novels), and habit of "emptying people's purses
with a face of brass and dividing their families
with a heart of steel". The story is full of vehe-
ment abuse against "blind obedience", "dolls

and idols" and the rest, interspersed with remarks such as these:

> The true Italian school of morality is now
> about to raise its head in Great Britain ...
> Those who value the existence of British insti-
> tutions, of moral worth, of natural conscience,
> of human virtue and of human feelings, must
> unite in Parliament as one man in resisting
> this onset of Jesuitism in England.

> Romish principles are as out of place in
> an English drawing-room as an Italian organ-
> boy would be in a palace.

"Romish principles" were also distasteful to
Charlotte Brontë (although despair once drove
her to the confessional), and in *Villette* (1853)
she excuses the Catholicism of her foreign hero
by emphasizing that "all Rome could not put
into him bigotry, nor the Propaganda itself make
him into a real Jesuit". He even tells his beloved
(British and of "pure faith") to "remain a
Protestant".

No such compromises were permitted in the
novels of Charles Kingsley: his "No-Popery" is
strident and his picture of the Jesuits—a historical one this time—in *Westward Ho!* (1855)
is as unsympathetic as it is inaccurate. We
are invited to believe that Jesuit missionaries
in the West Indies deliberately baptized and

then murdered savages, that both Father Campion and Father Parsons were bullies and rogues, and that the Penal Laws were never intended to be effective, with the "English martyrs" just skulking around in hiding places for the fun of it. Both Kingsley's descriptions and his comments seem unworthy of one who held a University Chair of History.

But even the Jesuit did not represent the very blackest depths of evil for these novelists; there was, as Miss Sinclair related in her novel, something "ten times worse" and that was "a Jesuitess". Often in these Victorian tales we come across the female of the species, usually a most unpleasant character, full of hypocrisy and gluttony. Mrs. Trollope, in *Father Eustace* (1847), tells of one of these creatures, sent to England with a Jesuit to convert a rich heiress. The greedy wretch, however, dies from eating too many walnuts. An even more repulsive creature comes in Jemima Luke's novel *The Female Jesuit* (1851). In order to win the sympathy of a wealthy family, this lady pretends to be consumptive, mixes bullock's blood with water, fills basins with it and lies in bed looking pale and pathetic while secretly gratifying her enormous appetite with private supplies of gooseberry tart from a nearby pastry-cook's.

Even in the second half of the Victorian age,

when one might have expected public opinion on the question of Catholic practices to have mellowed somewhat, the tradition of the wicked Jesuit still reigned supreme in popular fiction and we meet with the same old cloak-and-dagger types, crafty liars and plotters of "infernal suavity" in the stories of Wilkie Collins and Sheridan Le Fanu. Even the myth of "Mrs. Jesuit" still persisted, and in *John Drummond Fraser*, a novel that appeared as late as 1893, we hear of a "Jesuit chambermaid" and all the hoary old clichés about the Church of England being "honeycombed" with "Jesuit intriguers". Religious novelists, too, were still making use of Jesuits as villains in the eighteen-nineties and the Rev. Joseph Hocking, a Methodist minister, created a really nasty character in Father Ritzoom, a cigar-smoking, bowler-hatted Jesuit in disguise, who flits through the pages of Hocking's novels right on into the twentieth century. Assisted by a staff of Jesuits sporting tweed suits and false moustaches, Father Ritzoom is an expert in stopping renegade nuns from leaving their convents. He often uses such simple and drastic methods as shaking the ladder down which these unfortunate women try to escape by night from the windows of their cells. This may of course cripple them for life, but, as Father Ritzoom explains blandly, "With us the body is nothing, the soul is everything."

Such examples of the *Maria Monk* class of fiction need detain us no further; they smack of melodrama at its lowest level, and the popularity they enjoyed for so long reveals the shocking bigotry and ignorance of author and reader alike. Occasionally we find that Protestant novels made a distinction between the system and the individual, between the Order they so detested and its representatives. Thus the wicked Jesuit is sometimes replaced by the pitiful Jesuit, the victim of a cruel and inhuman bondage, who, disillusioned yet powerless, generally dies an untimely death full of remorse for his wasted life and misplaced faith. Grace Kennedy, in her intelligent and widely influential novel *Father Clement* (1823), had set the fashion for these tales of suffering Jesuits, and the vogue continued throughout the nineteenth century. Several women novelists piled the agonies on more thickly by making their Jesuits fall in love. This served the double purpose of harrowing the reader's feelings most excruciatingly and demonstrating what a dreadful thing celibacy was. (And how cruel was any law that forced an Englishman to forswear all the joys of cosy Victorian domesticity with "a lovely wife", "little pattering feet in the nursery", and "the pure, fresh kisses" of baby lips! See Miss Worboise's anti-Popery novels *passim* for sentiments such as these.) Mrs. Trollope's *Father Eustace* becomes enamoured of the heiress he is supposed to convert and dies in her arms lamenting his ruined life, and in Miss Worboise's *Father Fabian* (1875), a novel permitted for Sunday reading in many Protestant households, the hero, who has "a noble nature, warped and vitiated, *forced* . . . into uncongenial baseness", falls in love with the governess in the wealthy household into which he has insinuated himself. To him too is meted out an untimely and repentant deathbed. (He also has a female accomplice, a "Jesuitess" with false curls, a "horrid little laugh" and a habit of puttting emetic in people's cough-mixtures.) Much nonsense of this kind was written about "the reluctant Jesuit", the unhappy celibate sufferer, by women who allowed their imagination to take wings (and the female imagination in Victorian days was capable of the most extraordinary flights of fancy on the subject of celibacy), but for family reading sentimentality was preferred to abuse and the many novels intended to excite pity for the "victim" were probably far more effective as anti-Jesuit propaganda than the fierce and uncontrolled outbursts of more rabid writers.

The fact remains however that, whether composed in sorrow or in anger, the overwhelming majority of Victorian novels on this theme present a most unflattering portrait of the life and habits of the Jesuits. Where, one asks, can correctives be found? Catholic novelists had an extremely hard task to supply suitable tales of counter-propaganda, but they did their best to introduce into their novels pleasant and attractive Jesuits of virtue and integrity. A belated but clever "answer" to Grace Kennedy's story comes in *Father Oswald, a Genuine Catholic Story* (1842), where the Jesuit hero has "an open engaging countenance" and the arguments for the Catholic faith and for obedience to authority are set out with intelligence and sweet reasonableness—rare qualities for any theological novel in the controversial eighteen-forties.

In the eighteen-fifties the great Thackeray (who, it will be remembered, was at one point of his life on the brink of conversion to Catholicism) came to the rescue and daringly broke with tradition by introducing into fiction a Jesuit both sensible and likeable. Father Holt, in *The History of Henry Esmond* (1852), is a minor character but a delightful one. He is an excellent tutor to young Henry (the Jesuit genius for educating youth is at last given its due in fiction), a kindly and humorous man, learned but unaffected. He even blushes—a most unusual habit for a Jesuit in any Victorian novel!

This example doubtless encouraged Catholic women novelists to create increasing numbers of agreeable Jesuits in their religious tales. In F. M. Oxenham's *Edith Sydney* (1867), the ne'er-do-well of the family becomes a most angelic Jesuit, and in Agnes Stewart's *Father Cleveland* (1868), the Jesuit hero is the Squire's son (no foreign intriguer!), tall, dark and handsome, and devoted to faith and duty. In Frances Noble's *Gertrude Mannering* (1875) we have another noble young Jesuit who has a "boyish face, with a sweet heavenly expression", and a sister whose sceptical lover reforms and joins the sons of Loyola as "an ardent mortified Jesuit".

The Jesuit of the sixteenth century also stood in need of vindication, and answers to Charles Kingsley's historical caricatures appear in novels about the Elizabethan age by Lady Georgiana Fullerton, Mrs. Ogden Meeker and Thomas de Longueville, where the Jesuit martyrs are depicted with sympathy and the pictures of history are more balanced although less vivid and brilliant than Kingsley's. Lady Georgiana, who of all Victorian novelists was the one most closely associated with the Jesuits, was well able to describe their finer qualities in fiction, and in her novel *Laurentia* (1861), a tale of the Jesuit missionaries and martyrs in sixteenth-century Japan, she paints an admirable picture of heroism, suffering, disciplined dignity and devotion. (Fortitude, of course, is a great virtue of the Jesuits, and several Catholic novelists make their heroes and heroines, on renouncing their lovers, strengthen themselves by studying the *Spiritual Exercises* of St. Ignatius.)

The most famous religious novel of the century also gives us a favourable picture of the Jesuits—somewhat surprisingly, since its author considered the Catholic Church "an enemy of the human race". But Shorthouse, in his celebrated High Church novel *John Inglesant* (1880), gives the devil his due; his hero is educated by a splendid Jesuit, Father St. Clare (again the brilliance of the Jesuits as instructors of the young is recognized), and he later works for the Jesuits in Italy. In spite of the fact that he rejects Catholicism for Anglicanism, Inglesant expresses his lasting feelings of gratitude, reverence and affection towards the Society of Jesus. Father St. Clare and his superiors, although somewhat given to the traditional arts of plotting and intrigue, do talk and act intelligently and reasonably; they are neither monsters nor victims, and they state the Catholic position with trenchancy. To the hesitating hero, hankering after "spiritual freedom", the General of the Orders says:

> You are standing at this moment...at a point where you may choose one of two roads, which, joining here, will never meet again. The question is between individual licence

and obedience to authority; and upon the choice, though you may not think it, depends the very existence of Christianity in the world. Between unquestioning obedience to authority and absolute unbelief there is not a single permanent resting-place, though many temporary halts may be made. You will scarcely dispute this when you remember that every heretical sect admits it. They only differ as to what the authority is to which obedience is due. We, in Rome at least, cannot be expected to allow any authority save that of the Catholic Church, and indeed what other can you place instead of it—a Book? Do you think that those who have entered upon a path of inquiry will long submit to be fettered by the pages of dead languages? You know more of this probably than I do, from your acquaintance with the sceptics of other lands.

It was of course the Jesuit emphasis on "unquestioning obedience to authority", rejected by Inglesant, loathed by Shorthouse and cordially detested by the majority of non-Catholics, that was mainly responsible for so much violent anti-Jesuit feeling in Victorian England. A nation that could heartily applaud the military obedience of the Six Hundred—

> Theirs not to reason why,
> Theirs but to do and die

—could not tolerate such an attitude in the religious sphere, and the notion of "corpse-like" passivity and obedience to a "foreign" power, especially one that appeared to believe in ends justifying means, was bound to enrage John Bull. As a man who, in Kingsley's phrase, had commited "moral suicide", the Jesuit provided the perfect villain for fictional purposes. A compound of all the seven deadly sins (lust in moderation to satisfy the conventions of the Victorian reading public—even Miss Worboise's Father Fabian never gets much further than having his "whole being thrilled" by his lady-love—but pride, avarice and gluttony *in excelsis*), utterly unscrupulous in an age of profound moral scruples, and capable of every crime, large or small, under the sun (the Jesuits were even accused of tampering with the Italian translation of *Uncle Tom's Cabin* and substituting "the Church" for "Christ" throughout), the wicked Jesuit of the Victorian novel captured popular imagination in a way that few villains of fiction have ever done, and the apologists for St. Ignatius, however much they might protest against the damaging falsehoods and monstrous distortions of creed and character, could not, in fiction at least, compete against them with any great measure of popular success.

CHAPTER 9

SOME NONCONFORMIST NOVELS

IF the Jesuit was only too often a nasty piece of work in Victorian fiction, so also was the Dissenter. But whereas the Jesuit and his intrigues were at least clever, exotic and exciting, the Dissenter was usually shown as ignorant, drab, provincial and depressing. We have a familiar parade of these types in fiction: the Reverend Dismal Horror, author of *Groans from the Bottomless Pit to Awaken Sleeping Sinners*; or the coarse, odious, thin-lipped Mr. Snale, smirking horribly at "the leedies"; or Mr. Chadband with his flabby paws, fat smile and "general appearance of having a good deal of train oil in his system"; or the hard, cold Mr. Cartwright, occasionally dropping his biblical phraseology to quote his favourite lines:

> While thousands go down to the pit,
> *My* name in the Covenant stands!

or Alton Locke's harsh mother, bringing up her children in a religion dominated by "hell, the rod, the ten commandments and public opinion" and entertaining a variety of repulsive missionaries—"grim, dark, bilious" or "squat, red-faced, pig-eyed", with "sensuality, conceit and cunning marked on every feature". (The missionary in Victorian fiction fares very badly indeed; one recalls Dickens' immortal Mrs. Jellyby, whose dress never meets up the back and whose house and children are in a perpetual state of dirt and disorder while she devotes her life to her "African duties". "Never have a Mission, my dear child", says poor Mr. Jellyby to his daughter.) We have scores of satirical and hostile sketches and unfortunately, to offset them, we have very few religious novels describing the inner life of characters who find true faith in Dissent or who deepen and enrich their belief in any of the Free Churches. Too often it is the opposite that occurs; the Nonconformist pilgrim's regress is more common than his progress in Victorian fiction; novels about hypocritical, smug, bigoted and unlovely Dissenters far outnumber novels about good and attractive Dissenters, and the escaped Puritan is a much more usual subject for a religious novel than the convinced Puritan.

One reason for this is clear—the novel was not, among avowed Free Churchmen, the accepted medium for describing the life of the spirit. Like some of the stricter Evangelicals in the Church of England, they considered the novel to be the Devil's Bible, and the puritan conscience classed novel-reading with theatre-going and card-playing as worldly amusements sent by Satan to ensnare the soul. The writer Silas Hocking tells us how he lost caste when, as a Methodist minister, he wrote his first novel in 1878 to the shocked bewilderment of his congregation. "Novels and the theatre they placed in the same category", he wrote. "Both were agents of the devil. How could I preach the Gospel and at the same time write what was not true?" In spite of the fact that celebrated Dissenters like Joseph Sortain encouraged the idea of Nonconformist novels, maintaining that, through the parables of the New Testament, "Fiction has been consecrated, as a vehicle of Truth, by the Divine Founder and Teacher of the Christian Church", and although a copy of *The Pilgrim's Progress* stood beside the Bible in most Dissenting households, few Victorian Puritans followed the example of such great story-telling.

If spiritual adventures were to be related to the general public they could be conveyed through the sermon, and the thundering dramatic eloquence of eminent preachers such as Spurgeon or Dr. Cumming (whose speciality was The End of the World, with plenty of burning and gnashing of teeth) could prove more vivid and moving to the faithful than any forms of fiction. If written, the record of such experiences could take the form of biography, essays or tracts.

John Wesley, it will be remembered, although
he himself edited a novel, preferred direct accounts of religious experiences and encouraged
his preachers to contribute stories of their own
lives and conversions to his *Arminian Magazine*.

It was the tract, however, that proved to be
the most popular literary medium for Puritan
spirituality in the nineteenth century. Through
this form of literature, the strictest Nonconformist mothers (such as Edmund Gosse, for example,
possessed), who would never allow a novel in the
house and would not even tell their children
fairy tales, were able to indulge their talents
for fiction by writing all kinds of exciting stories.
Although some tracts adhered closely to the
truth (the Salvation Army's "Red-Hot Library",
for instance, recorded nothing but authentic experiences), others were fiction pure and undis-
guised, and the general Dissenting public were
thus enabled to enjoy, in the cause of religious
edification, all manner of romances and adventure stories. It was not surprising therefore that
"the track" became the staple literary diet of
many Victorian Nonconformists, who, being in
general on a low social and cultural level (the
vulgarity of Dissenters is continually stressed in
Victorian writings), found that this form of literature provided "a perfect miniature religious
library" and could mix sensationalism with sermonizing in attractive proportions. The tract

was thus the Puritan substitute for the novel in the nineteenth century.

The Free Church religious novel is therefore somewhat of a rarity. In the scanty crop of religious fiction that Victorian Nonconformity did harvest, Methodism seems to have reaped the largest yield. Being a religion of intense emotional force, Methodism infused greater passion into the novel, and had, indeed, a weird effect upon the love story in fiction. A Nonconformist writer of the time tells us that it was the custom among Dissenters to use the word "love" only in "a spiritual or theologic sense", and a genuine Methodist lover was one filled with passion for divine objects—sobbing, wailing, going into ecstatic trances and losing sleep and appetite for love of God. In the novel, however, such fanatical transports of delight were occasionally transferred to the worship of human objects, with extraordinary results. This dangerous transference was most successfully employed by Emily Brontë in *Wuthering Heights* (1847), where she appears, in the words of a critic, "to have translated the Methodist passion for the Divine Lover into the language of human love and to have affirmed that in essence the love is identical". Although Heathcliff's outlook and conduct are totally unchristian, he can yet talk with all the rapture of a Methodist ecstatic: "My soul's bliss kills my body," he cries, and the whole novel glows with the flame of an almost religious fervour, and testifies to Emily Brontë's eager reading of what her sister Charlotte described as "mad Methodist Magazines, full of miracles and apparitions and preternatural warnings, ominous dreams and frenzied fanaticisms". Such strange and powerful enthusiasms are not uncommon in Methodist novels; some of John Ackworth's heroes behave in a similar way, rolling about and groaning when slighted by the lady of their choice and then, finding their love returned, falling on their knees sobbing and shrieking in an agony of bliss: "Stay Thy Hand, O God! Stay Thy Hand! Thou wilt kill me! Kill me with joy!"

George Eliot's treatment of Methodist lovers is somewhat more sober, but she also sees an intimate connection between the two forms of love, and in *Adam Bede* (1859) she attempts to justify the emotions of those who "do the coortin' and the religion both together" and tells us that all "deep or worthy love . . . whether of woman or child, art or music" is "hardly distinguishable from religious feeling". *Adam Bede* is not, of course, primarily a religious novel; it is the work of an agnostic who considered Methodism as "rudimentary culture for the peasantry", but it was not with philosophic detachment but with "hot tears" that George Eliot wrote her heroine's sermons and she gives us a charming, idyllic, almost nostalgic picture of Methodism in English village life. Her deep sympathy with "the Methodies" sometimes even leads her into over-idealization. This is particularly noticeable in her heroine, Dinah, modelled on George Eliot's aunt, a Methodist preacher whom her niece afterwards described as "a truly religious soul", full of "the spirit of love which clings to the bad logic of Arminianism". (George Eliot in her youth passed through a phase of very stern Calvinism and used to argue at length with her aunt about predestination. Although she later became an unbeliever she never quite shook off her Calvinistic concepts of sin, and of all great English novelists she most clearly exemplifies the "Nonconformist conscience" at work, tracing for us in her novels the grim, inexorable consequences of sin, with all the Puritan emphasis on punishment for evil-doing and the inevitable reaping of what we have sown.) "Bad logic" though the Arminian Methodists may have had, yet George Eliot found their compassion "beautiful" and shows Dinah as a most saintly exponent of Methodism—perhaps too saintly.

Indeed, the tendency to make the heroine of a religious story a faultily faultless paragon of piety shows itself just as clearly in novels inspired by Nonconformity as in those inspired by

other forms of Christian faith in the nineteenth
century. The fate of these Puritan heroines is
generally more domestic than that of their Anglican or Catholic sisters—they almost always
marry the men they convert and the novel invariably closes by showing them in a state of
matrimonial and financial as well as spiritual
content. Lucy, in William Yates's *Nathaniel
Cartwright* (1889), is a typical example. Like
Dinah, she is an exemplary young woman and a
comfort to all around her. She even persuades
her snobbish Mamma to take up welfare work
among the poor. After converting her sceptical
lover she marries him, and this "saintly couple",
the author informs us, are happy and successful
"not only in the lower but in the higher sense".
The Hockings too—Joseph, Silas and their sister
Salome, who all wrote vigorous tales of Methodist life—tended to specialize in beautiful believers who converted and married the heroes,
the most extraordinary of all being Dorothy, the
angelic and intrepid missionary's daughter in
Joseph Hocking's *Elrad the Hic* (1890), who
tames, converts and marries a wild Arab, chief
of a strange Galilean tribe, and settles down with
him to a life of surprisingly happy domesticity
in Beyrout. (A distinct improvement on Mrs.
Jellyby.)

Heroines of tender years were popular too,

and several little girls exemplifying Nonconformist virtue in America crossed the Atlantic to
invade the Victorian nursery. The most famous
of these was Ellen in *The Wide Wide World*
(1851), a best-seller by the Presbyterian writer
Elizabeth Wetherell (Susan Warner). Victorian
maidens lapped up the story of Ellen's trials and
temptations, but amongst little boys it was not
quite so welcome. Lord Frederick Hamilton tells
us that "in my early youth I was given a book to
read about a tiresome little girl called Ellen
Montgomery, who apparently divided her time
between reading her pocket Bible and indulging
in paroxysms of tears." This tale, with its lively
scenes of American life and its continual exhortations to remember "our dear Saviour", "our
best Friend," "our Physician", was approved by
thousands of Protestant mothers, and Ellen's
popularity has survived to the extent of having
her story serialized on B.B.C. Children's Tele-
vision a hundred years later. Ellen was followed
a year afterwards by an even more virtuous little
heroine Fleda in *Queechy*, by the same author.
Here again we are shown piety and lacrimosity
in a delightfully vivid American setting, and
Fleda's faith and fortitude are at length rewarded by romance, riches and a stately home in
England.

Such studies in Puritan female virtue, however, tend to become somewhat tedious to the

modern adult reader, and it is a relief to turn from them and strike a richer vein of spiritual biography in stories of the sufferings of Dissenting ministers. A Nonconformist minister of the nineteenth century was very much a creature of his people and at the mercy of his congregation who, often smug, narrow and ignorant, imposed their will upon him on the principle that he who paid the piper called the tune. As a cynic in one of Joseph Hocking's novels expressed it, "There's more hypocrisy needed in a Dissenting Church than in the Established Church. A vicar can do pretty much what he likes; but the minister of a little Bethel belongs heart and soul to his flock. If he were to dare to tell them the truth, his bread and cheese would be gone."

This conflict in the mind of a young minister between the desire to serve God and the desire not to estrange the influential but stupid members of his local congregation formed the theme of several Nonconformist novels in the Victorian age. Often such a conflict resulted in the sufferer losing all faith in organized Christianity. The Hocking brothers wrote much about this (based on personal experience, for they both eventually resigned from the Methodist ministry). Perhaps the best-known story of such a clash is Mrs. Oliphant's *Salem Chapel* (1863). In this novel Mrs. Oliphant, influenced by the example of her own brother William's unhappy career as a minister, tells us of the unfortunate young man, Arthur Vincent, who, setting out from his theological college full of hope, ambition and enthusiasm, soon finds that, as minister in a small market town, he is at the mercy of "a limited and jealous coterie" and the victim of local gossips, scandal-mongers, and vulgar families with flirtatious daughters. He has the courage to resign and give his reasons to his flock. "I am," he tells them, "either your servant, responsible to you, or God's servant, responsible to Him. Which is it? I cannot tell, but no man can serve two masters, as you know." He retires in a state of disgust with Nonconformity and in a very misty spiritual condition altogether.

Mrs. Oliphant's many scenes of Nonconformist life are extremely entertaining, but from a religious point of view her novels lack depth. Like Trollope, she is interested in the social rather than the spiritual life of her ministers and their congregations. For a far more profound and penetrating study of spiritual conflict and desolation we must turn to William Hale White, whose treatment of the minister's dilemma, drawn from his own experience, is one of great power and pessimism. Who can read the opening chapters of *The Autobiography of Mark Rutherford* (1881) without a shudder at the infinitely gloomy picture it presents? Here is all the narrow dreariness of life among rigid Victorian Calvinistic Independents in a small Midland country town, with their excruciatingly boring Sabbaths, their mechanical deadness in the observances of religion, the hollowness and sham of the teaching of their theological colleges, the unsavoury, self-satisfied nature of so many of their supporters, demonstrating only too clearly the pride and cruelty that may be engendered by the conviction of being God's "elect". (Such studies in repulsive *superbia* abound in Hale White's novels; like W. B. Rand, he can skilfully dissect those specimens of bigotry whose notions of divine love are essentially that it is "distinguishing", "electing", "peculiar".) It forms, indeed, a sombre and melancholy account of the soul's sufferings under Nonconformity. George Macdonald too, as a Dissenting minister, experienced similar sorrows and frustrations at the hands of his congregation, and wrote of them in several novels. Such stories as these, however, are tales of orthodox faith lost rather than found, and must be relegated to another chapter, for in the novels of Mrs. Oliphant, Hale White and Macdonald alike Nonconformity, to the intelligent and sensitive pilgrim, appears not as the way to the Celestial City but only as the path to Doubting Castle and Giant Despair.

The same theme was tackled by John Ackworth, the Methodist novelist, and, as we might expect from this purveyor of the heady wine of revivalism, his hero in *The Minder* (1900) wails loudly and rolls about on the floor in agonies of doubt as to his vocation. Much of Ackworth's work is over-emotional and melodramatic, but occasionally we find that he can convey in fiction some of the burning intensity and sheer passion of devotion that characterized the early Methodists, and his best novel, *The Coming of the Preachers* (1901), gives us this in plenty. Here at last, at the very end of the Victorian age, we find a novel devoted to the study of one of the most interesting of all religious phenomena—a typical Puritan conversion in all its subtle and spectacular manifestations. The hero, Mark, a young hatter's assistant and "about as innocent of religion as any other young pagan", is at first revolted by the behaviour of the visiting Methodists and their adherents—the weird hysterical laughter of the women, the sobbing and wailing, the quarrels and riots that they cause—and he feels that Methodism is about the likeliest thing he can think of "for bringing Christianity into disrepute with all well-disposed persons". But, as with Charles Reding and Callista in Newman's novels, God is working on Mark's soul independently, and Mark soon becomes aware of this, feeling as if "some mysterious power were at work on behalf of these hated religionists". The

immediate cause of his conversion is a common
Puritan one—the hearing of an inspired
preacher—and the author describes how conviction of sin comes upon Mark, affecting him
physically as well as mentally and spiritually.
Listening to the impassioned Methodist sermon, Mark suddenly turns white as a sheet and
"a sense of utter and awful lostness" takes possession of him. This feeling produces the inevitable violent misery of the early stages of a
Puritan conversion: Mark sobs and cries "in a
pitiless, hopeless wail"; he groans all night, "God
ha' mercy!" and his "spiritual sorrow", utterly
incomprehensible to his bewildered sister,
renders him quite unfit for normal life.

The light does not break in at once, but the
interim period, while Mark is groping towards
"a personal relationship with the Deity", renders
him "querulous, absent-minded and deeply
melancholy". (One thinks again of Newman's
characters.) Mark reads his Bible, prays, and
spends sleepless nights in spiritual agony. The
last phase of his conversion comes when he meets
"a meek-looking little gentleman" who proves
to be John Wesley himself. After a talk with this
religious genius, Mark finds that, as the sun
breaks through fogs, so the face of Christ shows
itself to him. He has thus passed through the
three conventional stages of conversion and is

now "a servant of Christ". Although much of Ackworth's plot is unoriginal and the novel concludes with the usual happy marriage, there is a certain spiritual insight shown, a skilled knowledge of that "soul-surgery" for which Bunyan was so famous, and the power to portray with understanding and sympathy those fierce sweeping transports of emotion that are associated with Wesley and his followers.

In most of the novels we have mentioned the main characters have been those homely humble folk or impecunious struggling young ministers, and the appeal of the Free Churches to souls nurtured in an atmosphere of wealth, leisure or worldly culture has not been emphasized at all in fiction. Dissent and the novel of high life do not apparently go together. But in the stories of Miss Ellen Thorneycroft Fowler (Mrs. Felkin) we move in a more exalted sphere, and in such novels as *Concerning Isabel Carnaby* (1898) and *The Farringdons* (1900) the impact of Methodism is shown upon cultivated and aristocratic types. Some of her characters utter cynical remarks that would have pleased Disraeli—"It is always safe to pray for the inevitable . . . It strengthens prayer without incommoding Providence"—and her heroines, even when converted and repentant, still keep a sophisticated and half-flippant tone: "I intend to make a trustworthy step-ladder out of my dead selves to upper storeys." Miss Fowler, like her heroines, is intelligent and witty, and although she sees the weaknesses of Methodism and its deficiencies in regard to the beautiful ("I can never forgive the Puritans for eradicating the beauty from holiness", says one of her characters), she sees also its great strength and its singular power of "adapting religion to the needs and uses of everyday life, and of bringing the infinite into the region of the homely and commonplace", an aspect of its genius that so attracted George Eliot, and one that would have supplied a wealth of material for religious fiction had not the novel been looked upon with such suspicion by the majority of practising Methodists.

One thing, however, did succeed in breaking down the Nonconformist barriers of prejudice against fiction, and that was what was known as the "Condition of the People" question, embracing so many social, political and economic problems of the day. Nonconformist writers tackled these matters courageously in their fiction, and here the religious novel tends to ally itself with the social novel; a new variety of practical applied Christianity appears, theological controversy gives way to social controversy and we have the "novel with a purpose" written by Nonconformists fired by ardent philanthropical ideals.

In the eighteen-forties and fifties Miss Eliza Meteyard wrote stories of great vitality—temperance fiction drawing attention to the evils of "ACCURSED, BRUTALISING GIN" (she liked capital letters), and stories containing propaganda for vaccination, emigration to Australia (particularly favoured then as remedy for current social evils) and better manners, cooking and household management among the poor, the author being convinced that "half the miseries and the drinking usages of the working classes spring from the abominable temper of ill-trained women."

Miss Meteyard was a close friend of the indefatigable Howitts (William and Mary), who supported her belief that fiction could and should reflect "the *truest Christianity*" and produced during this time dozens of tales intended to encourage temperance, self-education, moral conduct and facilities for emigration among the working classes. The Howitts, both devout Christians, were once Quakers but had resigned from the Society of Friends, feeling that the majority of Friends lived too much in "the crippling spirit of sectarianism"; they contrive, however, to give some fair pictures of Quakers in their novels, perhaps the best being William's Rebecca Heritage, a middle-aged woman "of heroic piety and peace" in *Woodburn Grange* (1867).

Philanthropic fiction also flowed from the pen of Miss Harriet Martineau. Before finally discarding her Unitarian faith she wrote stories covering a large range of subjects, including taxes, tithes, slavery, strikes, factory conditions, Polish exiles in Siberia and a host of pressing contemporary political and economic matters. A good friend of Malthus, she even tackled in fiction the problem of birth-control, at that time a most daring and dangerous subject for anyone, particularly an unmarried woman, to write about. Her high-minded solution, that of "disinterested friendship" replacing marriage between men and women in order to avoid more little mouths to feed, is hardly a practicable one. Prominent in her fiction is the Unitarian emphasis on forgiveness. Among Nonconformist sects Unitarians were conspicuous, one might even say notorious, for their freedom from hell-fire doctrines; their creed was not one blazing with damnation and their tracts and tales did not follow the usual convention of dealing out heavy punishments for sin. Miss Martineau's *Deerbrook* (1837), a novel about a man who marries the sister of the woman he loves, has a heavily-pointed moral of overcoming evil with good—sound Christianity but poor romance, and Miss Martineau cannot cope with eternal triangles any more than she can with the Trinity. Her next novel, *The Hour*

and the Man (1840), deals with Toussaint
l'Ouverture (already celebrated in a famous son-
net by the poet Wordsworth, another friend of
Miss Martineau's). Here she preaches the same
message of forgiveness and love (but on safer
ground—political rather than romantic), with
some excellent anti-slavery propaganda and
Christian pacifism making its *début* in the Victorian religious novel. "The highest charity", she
tells us, is to do good to those that hate us, and
in the Negro race she sees this charity exemplified, for the negroes, she believes, have "the
generosity that can forgive offences seventy-
and-seven times renewed". Furthermore she
prophesies that "in this race will the spirit of
Christianity appear more fully than it has yet
shown itself among the proud whites".

Miss Martineau's sympathies with the Negro
were shared by another Nonconformist Harriet,
a fellow abolitionist and "crusader in crinoline"
who enjoyed great popularity in England—the
American Mrs. Beecher Stowe, author of the
world-famous anti-slavery novel *Uncle Tom's
Cabin* (1852). Here indeed is an inspired religious story—"The Lord Himself wrote it: I was
but an instrument in His hand", says the author
—a novel whose urgency of purpose overrode all
other considerations, for Mrs. Beecher Stowe, as
she tells us, "no more thought of style or literary

excellence than the mother who rushes into the street and cries for help to save her children from a burning house, thinks of the teachings of the rhetorician or the elocutionist". *Uncle Tom's Cabin* illustrates perfectly both the emotional force and the fearless practical idealism that formed the greatest strength of nineteenth-century Nonconformity, and it has probably done more for humanity than any other single work of fiction.

While visiting England Mrs. Beecher Stowe met the Unitarian novelist Mrs. Gaskell. The two ladies had read and admired each other's work. Indeed, Mrs. Stowe had cried over Mrs. Gaskell's stories. (A novel's power of drawing tears was in those days an important test of its value. George Eliot, Charlotte Brontë, Matthew Arnold and several Chartist families were also among those who wept over Mrs. Gaskell's fiction.) The success of Mrs. Stowe's story doubtless inspired Mrs. Gaskell to turn from the exquisite enchantments of Cranford to produce another explosive social novel, and in *Ruth* (1853) we have the "unmarried mother" problem treated on a Christian level—a level that shocked most of the Victorian reading public, in whose eyes the "fallen woman" deserved nothing but ostracism and death. (Even Catholic novelists who spared their Mary Magdalenes sent them straight into convents.) But Mrs. Gaskell makes her betrayed heroine Ruth recover, keep her child and rise to great heights of heroism, aided by a saintly Nonconformist minister, Mr. Benson, and opposed by a smug pompous pillar of the chapel, Mr. Bradshaw. The clash between these two men, representing the two faiths—enlightened, compassionate Christianity (showing the "highest charity" of which Miss Martineau wrote), and narrow rigid Pharisaical Nonconformity, makes this a most stimulating religious novel, although of course it was considered all very improper and unladylike by many Puritan readers —two members of Mr. Gaskell's congregation (he was a Unitarian minister) burnt their copies of *Ruth* and other Nonconformists sent her so many disapproving letters that she became ill and felt like "St. Sebastian tied to a tree to be shot at with arrows". (An experience shared by Mrs. Beecher Stowe, who, after the publication of *Uncle Tom's Cabin*, received dozens of letters "curiously compounded of blasphemy, cruelty and obscenity", and by Nathaniel Hawthorne, whose "hell-fired story" *The Scarlet Letter* (1850), showing the exaggerated Puritan horror of sexual sins, made him many enemies. "If I escape from the town without being tarred and feathered, I shall consider it good luck," he wrote.)

Mrs. Gaskell, however, rallied and clung to her unfashionable notions of Christianity as a religion of real forgiveness, and indeed this idea runs all through her work. In *The Sexton's Hero* (1855) we see traces of Christian pacifism, patriotic military leaders being pitied as having "a poor unchristian heroism, whose manifestation consists in injury to others". Even in that charming idyll *Cousin Phillis* (1864), a note of religious conflict arises over the question of forgiveness, and we are shown another clash between a narrow orthodox Dissenter and a less strict but more Christ-like soul. When his child Phillis has brain-fever, the good minister Mr. Holman is visited by his fellow-ministers, who, smug and stupid, bid him search his heart for the secret sins that must have caused this trial to come upon him. Mr. Holman answers, "I hold with Christ that afflictions are not sent by God in wrath as penalties for sin", a reply which displeases his brethren, who immediately demand, "Is that orthodox?" The situation is saved, however, by the old servant Betty (one of the nicest in the delightful Gaskell collection of servants), who says, "I'll do some ham and eggs and that'll rout 'em from worrying the minister. They're a deal quieter after they've had their victual."

Mrs. Gaskell, with her humour, intelligence and stress on Christianity as a creative rather than punitive power, was obviously not on the side of her more rigid Nonconformist brethren. Indeed, it is sad to find how very badly the strict Nonconformist is treated in most Victorian novels, and when we see that the adversaries have the field almost to themselves it is needful and salutary to remind ourselves that the greatest achievements of Nonconformity lie in life rather than literature, and that, in the words of Professor Dowden,

> Religious ideas and religious emotions, under the influence of the Puritan habit of mind, seek to realize themselves not in art, but without any intervening medium, in character, in conduct, in life. It is thus that the gulf between sense and spirit is bridged; not in marble or in colour is the invisible made visible, but in action, public and private.

It is clear that the Nonconformist religious novel did not come into its own in the Victorian age, partly because the Free Churches themselves did not produce apologists of adequate literary stature, and chiefly because, as we have tried to indicate, the Puritans' prejudice against novels and the novelists' prejudice against Puritans cancelled out all chances of great religious fiction inspired by Nonconformity in nineteenth-century England.

2

LOST FAITH

CHAPTER 10

THE TRAGEDY OF UNBELIEF

A LL conversion, as Newman found, is a matter of loss and gain, and if we were to examine all the novels written by Victorians who lost faith in one kind of religion to find it in another the material would be far too vast and varied for a single chapter. So, treating lost faith as lost orthodoxy, we shall concentrate on those novels devoted to studies of characters who have lost their orthodox beliefs, novels in which the emphasis is more on the loss than the subsequent gain, if any—novels that tell of the lives of the many "theological martyrs" of the nineteenth century, the victims of doubt, the tragic casualties in the battle of belief.

For, although scepticism and unbelief have always existed and found a voice in literature, the dethronement of orthodoxy in the Victorian age was a major event of far-reaching consequences, and the reverberations from this mighty crash were minutely and accurately recorded in contemporary writings. Never has any age in history produced such a detailed literature of lost faith, or so many great men and women of religious temperament standing outside organized religion. This loss of faith, with all its

different results and all the complicated tangle
of substitute values and individual religions that
it occasioned, is an important factor in judging
the nineteenth-century literary scene.

For the attack was indeed shattering. The
Oxford Movement, by not letting sleeping clergy
lie, and by showing that simple faith was not as
simple as the ordinary Anglican imagined, raised
a spectre of doubt, and although it quickened the
faith of some to a new birth it almost completely
destroyed the faith of others, while the conflicts
that arose between science and orthodoxy,
geology and Genesis, evolutionary theories and
accepted beliefs, caused those warriors whose
shield of faith was not very stout to find themselves miserably defeated, and in the face of
powerful enemy forces of Continental biblical
critics and treacherous stabs in the back by
Anglican bishops themselves, the situation
seemed very gloomy for the orthodox. It would
be interesting to compile a complete list of eminent Victorians who lost their faith in the fray,
or to enumerate the well-known figures of that
period who, having contemplated or been destined for a career in the ministry, were forced
by their changing convictions to renounce it.
(This latter group would include men so diverse
as Carlyle, Clough, Ruskin, Morris, Butler,
Pater, Hardy, Burne-Jones, Alfred Tennyson

and his brother Frederick, J. A. Froude, Hale White and even Charles Darwin himself.) Although it is sometimes difficult for us in the twentieth century to appreciate the full force and significance of the struggle with religious doubt, we cannot but recognize the fact that, to our Victorian forefathers, uncertainty about the literal truth of the Bible provided materials for a tragic conflict of the profoundest intensity and poignancy.

When such conflicts found their way into literature they found their fullest and most popular expression in the religious novel. Indeed, by the end of the century theologians were complaining that "it sometimes seems as though the man who has fresh light to throw upon the problems of orthodoxy will be compelled to write a novel to get himself listened to". The introduction of this element of perplexity and tragedy into religious fiction was a new development; side by side with the didactic religious novel we find the problem religious novel, and as well as the lives of orthodox saints and sinners in fiction we have the lives of spiritual melancholics, bewildered doubters, regretful unbelievers and tormented agnostics.

The development was, of course, gradual. At first the loss of orthodoxy was treated in the religious novel as an unmitigated tragedy with fatal effects. Then, in the hands of the women novelists, it came to be considered as a malady to be cured by the love of a devout believer, or the efforts of a competent clergyman. Finally, as unbelief became more and more widespread, the rejection of orthodoxy was regarded in so many novels as a necessity for all thinking men and women (and occasionally as a happy release from the bondage of bigotry and superstition), until in the last decades of the Victorian age we find the heroes and heroines of half the best-sellers busily, if regretfully, engaged in discarding the Hebrew old clothes that Teufelsdröckh had discarded even before Queen Victoria came to the throne. A brief survey of the novel of lost faith, tracing the spiritual biographies of these victims (as well as of those who contrived to live on the sunnier side of doubt) will reveal to us something of the very significant movement of mind in connection with the Christian belief of Victorian England.

In the religious fiction of the eighteen-forties doubters and freethinkers were, as we have seen, generally treated as sinners and almost invariably punished by madness or death. There must have been many at this time who felt that Strauss and others had demolished the biblical miracles and that Lyell and others had demolished the Mosaic cosmogony. (We have Disraeli's amusing description in *Tancred* (1847) of some of the seeds of scepticism sown by Chambers' *Vestiges of Creation* (1844). Lady Constance tells Tancred all about it: "First there was nothing, then there was something . . . and the next change there will be something very superior to us, something with wings. Ah, that's it: we were fishes, and I believe we shall be crows. But you must read it.") Yet, in spite of all the new and disturbing findings of scientific research, religious fiction is still dominated by the conventional view that condemns doubt and unbelief as sin. The author of *Enthusiasm not Religion* (1848) brings to a bad end all the followers of Guelph Frankenstein, the wicked German Rationalist. (In the popular drama of lost faith the villain of the piece was usually a German, infecting the feeble with the deadly doctrines of the Tübingen School.) In *Ernest Singleton* (1848), Robert Armitage makes Charles the freethinker fall a victim to the various "isms" of his day (Liberalism and Mesmerism being considered the most injurious) and end in the padded cell of Hanwell Asylum.

Two novels of the eighteen-forties stand out in protest against such an attitude—Geraldine Jewsbury's *Zoë* (1845) and J. A. Froude's *The Nemesis of Faith* (1849), both novels of doubt, both partly autobiographical and both inspired to a certain extent by Carlyle. Geraldine Jewsbury was an eccentric and ardent spirit who attached herself passionately to Mrs. Carlyle, smoked cigarettes, proposed marriage to men by letter and wrote most daring and over-heated novels that were strictly taboo for the orthodox. *Zoë* was her first novel and tells of the doubts in the soul of Everhard, a Catholic priest into whom, as Miss Jewsbury tells us, "I put *my own* religious botherations." After four years of theological study Everhard, like the later hero of a famous religious novel, *Robert Elsmere*, begins to have serious misgivings on the whole question of *testimony*, and feels that Christianity is slipping from his grasp. His attack of religious doubt is, however, distinguished less by its intellectual aspect than by its violent emotional accompaniments—groanings, swoonings, brain-fevers and agonies of speechless torment. He further complicates his situation by falling in love with Zoë, who is a married woman, and the author treats us to an ardent love scene which contemporary critics condemned as indelicate and offensive. But in the end he leaves both the Church and Zoë and, again foreshadowing Robert Elsmere, goes away to practise a kind of undogmatic religion of helpfulness among the poor, and dies an untimely death. Despite the very eccentric, defiant and over-emotional nature of the story, characteristic of the personality of its author, we do obtain some slight glimpse into the depths

of suffering undergone by a religious temperament attacked by religious doubt.

Froude's hero resembles Miss Jewsbury's in
ruining his life through loss of orthodoxy, and
Froude, too, is revolutionarily and shockingly
sympathetic in his attitude to the whole process.
Here again is the tale of the man who comes to
be "without dogma" and then finds that "the
most genuine emotion of his life" is love for a
married woman. Its author, however, is no
flamingly unconventional rebel standing completely outside the religious traditions of his
time, but rather a man of strong and earnest
theological and intellectual interests, whose
voice could certainly command a hearing in
orthodox circles. Froude not only introduced this
immoral tale (taken from "French novels", declared his enemies) into the theological fiction of
the eighteen-forties, but invested it with profoundly autobiographical touches (his hero
comes under Newman's spell and then grows
disillusioned with Tractarianism), so that the
story of the hero's downfall did not appear as a
dreadful warning to doubters, an awful history
of a sinner's crime and punishment, but a sincere and moving confession of unbelief and the
tragedies attendant on it. Small wonder, therefore, that this novel, marking a most dangerous
departure from the tradition that "religious fiction must be didactic", caused a sensation and

a scandal and was publicly burned at Oxford by the zealous William Sewell, who loathed sceptics nearly as much as Jesuits.

Another of these early victims, who dies from loss of faith brought on by the Oxford Movement, is the hero of *Oakfield; or, Fellowship in the East* (1853), a little-known novel by William Arnold, son of Dr. Arnold and brother of Matthew—his death is lamented by the poet in "A Southern Night" (1861). Arnold's hero is another young and sensitive idealist of "earnest spiritual interests" who had once assented to the *Credo in Newmannum* and then suffered disillusion. But, as we might expect from the hero of any novel by a son of Dr. Arnold, he turns for consolation not to women but to work—hard, practical, useful work, social reform and service with the Indian Army. Soon, however, he becomes as disillusioned in "the grand work of civilizing Asia" as he is in the Church of England, and the book throws an interesting, if unfavourable light on British rule in India in the mid-nineteenth century. The hero is attacked by terrible conflicts between "hermitizing" and "helpfulness", conflicts which seemed especially to trouble sons and pupils of Dr. Arnold, who had perhaps exaggerated the wickedness of the world to his young *alumni* and caused those with tender consciences to have the greatest difficulty in reconciling themselves to society in after-school life. We have the same problem stated for us in Clough's "Dipsychus" (1850) and in Matthew Arnold's "Obermann" poems (1852 and 1867). Indeed, this novel might gain considerably by detailed comparison with many of the ideas and questions raised in the poetry of Clough and Matthew Arnold. The hero, like Clough, never attains to any settled convictions as to belief or conduct, and returns home from India to die with all his mind still clouded with a doubt, convinced only that "the combination of worldly activity and godliness seems becoming more and more impossible". We are left with a sad and strangely haunting impression of the hero as a dutiful, "high soul'd" being, baffled and frustrated by the problems of life, one who, like Clough, never fulfilled the promise of his youth, one who had the flame of his faith extinguished by the Oxford Movement and who never afterwards regained sufficient light to live by.

Novels such as Froude's and Arnold's, in which the author is clearly identifying himself in many ways with his tragic hero, point the way to a new attitude to "infidelity" in religious fiction. During the next thirty years the citadels of orthodoxy were rapidly being stormed by men who, like Arnold's hero, were of unquestionable integrity and sincerity. Scientists and philosophers such as Darwin, Huxley and Leslie Stephen were clearly not posssessed of the wickedness of the Guelph-Frankenstein school and indeed, in more than one skirmish between the sceptic and the churchman, the character of the sceptic revealed itself in a more favourable light than that of his opponent. It became abundantly clear that unbelief did not always go hand in hand with evil-doing and it was no longer advisable to depict the unbeliever in fiction as a double-dyed villain who merited every iota of the heavy punishment meted out to him.

Accordingly, many women novelists sought to cope with this alarming new situation by accepting doubt as a pitiful affliction rather than a sin, and by treating it in their novels as a temporary spiritual disease that could fairly easily be cured, the best remedy lying in human affection. They give us the spiritual biographies of sceptics restored to faith by love for a devout and orthodox believer. Mrs. Craik's *Olive* (1850) is one of the earliest tales of these anguished doubters, lost, strayed and brought back to the fold by an angelic member of the opposite sex. Here the clergyman hero, Harold Gwynne, is ostensibly a model parson, but he has "a pallid restless look", for the demon of doubt has attacked him and in church, we are told, "his hands were not folded in prayer—they were clenched like those of a man writhing under some strong and secret agony." Mrs. Craik does not trouble to tell us the cause of Harold's doubts; she cares little whether Oxford, Germany or contemporary geological studies have shattered her hero's creed; her interest is merely in emphasizing the spiritual agony as much as possible, without reference to its origins. Fortunately Harold has what Froude's and Arnold's heroes lacked—a virtuous young churchwoman filled with anxiety "to lift the burden" from his soul. She soon succeeds, of course, and Harold, restored to health and orthodoxy, marries his fair rescuer at the end of the story.

Another feeble rescue story is Miss Skene's *Through the Shadows* (1856), where the hero is saved from scepticism, pessimism and suicide by a devoted young believer. (This novel, with its exaggerated descriptions of the hero's spiritual desolation, foreshadows some of Marie Corelli's highly-coloured accounts of lost faith, like the hero of *Ardath* writhing in anguish caused by "the poison of doubt" or staggering wildly under "the blighting blow of blank Atheism".) Even in those comparatively halcyon days of orthodoxy, before the *Origin of Species* (1859) and other monsters had reared their ugly heads, it seemed to the more thoughtful members of the reading public that the cure of scepticism by a good woman's love was too easy a way out of the difficulty, and discriminating readers soon tired of the "hero whose intellectual crotchets or delusions or blindness are to be entrusted for repairs to a fascinating heroine". "Sceptics are not plastic and obliging", declared one enraged critic. "Would to Heaven scepticism *could* be cured by bright eyes, dulcet tones and a novelist's art of love."

The stupendous popularity of *St. Elmo* (1867), a novel by Augusta Evans of Alabama, showed, however, that even in the eighteen-sixties the general reading public, in England and America alike, could still be captivated by stories of sceptics rescued by pure and lovely heroines. This novel tells of how the sweet prayerful Bible-reading orphan girl Edna converts St. Elmo Murray, a fierce, moody, unbelieving misanthrope of "Satanic pride". (The grand and gloomy hero, contrasted with the little orphaned heroine, was a very popular type in nineteenth-century fiction ever since *Jane Eyre* set the fashion.) In the end St. Elmo actually becomes ordained before marrying his Edna. This intertwining of the Cinderella theme with that of the Prodigal Son—a passionate mingling of romance and religion—proved quite irresistible to the public; towns, steamboats and hotels in the Southern States were named after St. Elmo, and on both sides of the Atlantic multitudes of readers, we are told, were reclaimed from vice and infidelity and became "trusting, praying Christians" through the influence of this novel.

When Miss Charlotte Yonge tackled the problem of doubt she determined to show that the sceptic's salvation lay not through the illusory charms of romance but through sound and sensible advice from a sound and sensible clergyman. Her novel *The Clever Woman of the Family* (1865) shows the career of a female doubter, a rare type in mid-Victorian fiction, where the woman's role was usually that of ministering angel to the doubts of man. Her heroine is intellectual, discontented, rebellious and sceptical, with careerist ambitions far beyond the "quiet Lady Bountiful duties" of the village. Like so many of the heroes and heroines of later fiction, she tries to compensate for loss of orthodoxy by plunging herself enthusiastically into social work, and she founds the F.U.E.E. (Female Union for Englishwomen's Employment), and busies herself with a school for lacemakers. The pattern of this story, showing the doubts of an intelligent and honest thinker and the transformation of a Christian believer into a kind of agnostic welfare-worker, was one that was destined to be repeated over and over again in the last two decades of Queen Victoria's reign.

Miss Yonge, however, as might be expected, writes not to approve but to condemn such a transformation. Her clever woman suffers from taking the path of sceptical revolt and finally returns to orthodoxy and to parish work with her doubts nicely settled for her by a "highly educated" clergyman, and her presumptuous ambitions, together with all the follies of "a woman's efforts at scepticism", gently but firmly snubbed by the author. Miss Yonge, like so many High Church novelists of the time, was particularly hard on rebellious young female intellects. The doubting daughter Janet in *Magnum Bonum* (1879) is another very clever and headstrong girl, whose intellectual career culminates in marriage to a suave and nasty foreign scientist with "neat little features" and a glib tongue. Needless to say, Janet ruins her life, and later repents and is brought back to faith by her sufferings and by a helpful clergyman. She serves to point a favourite moral of Miss Yonge's— that the weaker sex can be led along the road to Doubting Castle "by fashion and pride of intellect".

But unfortunately these well-meaning attempts by devoutly orthodox women novelists to stem the flood of scepticism were as ineffectual as a child's sand-barrier against the tide. The days were passing when doubts could be promptly and permanently removed by pretty girls or kindly clerics. A generation of readers that had passed through the storms raised by the *Origin of Species* (1859), *Essays and Reviews* (1860), *The Pentateuch and the Book of Joshua Critically Examined* (1862–79), was gradually beginning to realize that religious doubts did not admit of such facile solutions, and it is significant of the change in public opinion that in the most popular of all English religious novels showing the good sceptic's conversion to Christianity, Edna Lyall's best-seller *Donovan* (1882), the author's sympathies seemed dangerously on the side of the unbeliever, as *The Church Quarterly Review* was quick to notice. The good sceptic is moving rapidly to his position as undisputed hero of religious fiction, and the public's interest in the virtues and activities of unbelievers is beginning to oust interest in any subsequent conversions to orthodoxy.

It is indeed in this last quarter of the nineteenth century that we find the most valuable records of lost faith in the novel. The theme of doubt now reaches its greatest heights of popularity in fiction, and amidst the profuse outpourings of sceptics' confessions and agnostics' propaganda there is much that was written with the "heart's blood", as Mrs. Humphry Ward said of *Robert Elsmere* (1888), much that came *de profundis* from the novelist's own vivid and painful

experience. Religious fiction becomes partly sub-
merged in the wave of pessimism that sweeps
over much of English literature at this time—
"the 'religious novel' is the most irreligious of
all", complained a critic in 1899—but in this
very gloom it deepens in spirituality, in thought-
fulness and maturity.

Novels about lost faith in this period fall
naturally into two different groups. In the first
the heroes have lost their faith before the story
opens and the novel centres upon what we might
call their post-orthodox spiritual life, and in
the second the story is principally concerned
with the actual losing of faith, showing the hero
at the beginning as a devout believer and then
describing the sudden or gradual destruction of
his belief (frequently at the hands of bigoted
orthodox or highly cultured agnostics). These
two types of novels, the one showing chiefly the
result and the other the process of lost faith, were
both enormously popular towards the end of
Queen Victoria's reign, the second type being
slightly more in demand than the first, for the
late Victorian public, although keenly interested
in the plight of those unhappy beings forced to
live without faith in the supernatural, still
relished religious controversy in fiction and enjoyed most of all the spectacle of the last shreds
of orthodoxy being torn from the quivering and

helpless victim. "Give us the Agnostic who perverts the curate in twenty minutes", was the popular cry, and novelists were not slow to meet this demand. It will be useful, however, to examine some representatives of the first category before proceeding to the second.

In this group we find tales of men and women who, having been rendered spiritually forsaken and forlorn by loss of faith, try unsuccessfully to come to terms with themselves and with a universe that seems to hold no meaning for them. Their spiritual lives are tinged with varying hues of pessimism, and in their melancholy consciousness of the worthlessness of life without faith they continue the tradition of the religious fiction of Froude and Arnold. They are of the company of the Swiss professor Henri-Frédéric Amiel, whose *Journal Intime*, published in 1882 and translated by Mrs. Humphry Ward in 1885, shows the spiritual paralysis of the idealist sceptic, unable to find either the inward peace for which he craves or the motive power necessary for effectual decision and action. Perhaps their most outstanding representative in fiction is the hero of Henryk Sienkiewicz's famous novel *Without Dogma* (which appeared in 1891 and had its first translation from Polish into English in 1893), a man whose scepticism debars him from all firm convictions and leads him through a dreary life of failure to suicide. The soul of the reluctant unbeliever is laid bare in this brilliantly analytical novel, and Sienkiewicz's hero is unquestionably the leader of that unhappy band of spiritual cripples who yearn for the Celestial City but are unable to take a single step in its direction, men who have the will to believe but not the capacity, heroes of a painful spiritual drama, their tragic flaw being their powerlessness to believe the ancient dogma.

When a critic in 1895 called W. H. Mallock "one of the pioneers of the contemporary religious novel", he was referring to this type of fiction of lost faith, and although Mallock was in fact only following in the trail blazed thirty years previously by Froude (who was his uncle) and Arnold, his heroes are the most striking representatives in English fiction of the melancholy of intelligent unbelief. They are convinced that life without religion is an absurdity, but that is the sum total of their convictions. Deprived of all spiritual dynamic, yet completely unimpressed by all the various alternatives to Christian orthodoxy, they linger wistfully, as their author did, at the door of the Catholic Church. Wealthy, worldly, leisured, gifted, cultured men, they indulge in prolonged self-analysis of their unsettled states, writing journals and twenty-page letters and turning themselves inside out emotionally and spiritually. Vernon in *A Romance of the Nineteenth Century* (1881), Carew in *The Old Order Changes* (1886), Grenville in *A Human Document* (1892), Pole in *The Heart of Life* (1895), Lacy in *The Individualist* (1899) —all these men belong to the same frustrated company of those whose intellect rejects orthodoxy but whose emotions demand it—a characteristic Victorian predicament. For them the Christian religion is "nothing but a nursery dream", "a myth or fable", "a Penelope's web, which is woven by the soul in emotion, and which the mind unweaves in meditation", and with faith shattered before the story begins they pass their lives in discontented contemplation of their spiritual position and in unsatisfactory love affairs, usually with married women. The cultivated pessimist's *penchant* for other men's wives is very much in evidence in Mallock's novels, and serves to illustrate the author's conviction that human love is one of the chief things degraded by loss of faith.

> Belief or unbelief
> Bears upon life, determines its whole course,

wrote Robert Browning, and it is to Mallock's novels that we should turn to see how unbelief can make barren the life of a certain type of man, turning all good things to dead sea fruit and reducing him to the spiritual sterility of

A wandering sorrow in a world of dreams.

The nearest approach to Mallock's and Sienkiewicz's portrayals of the ineffectual sceptic is
Mrs. Humphry Ward's study of Langham in
Robert Elsmere (1888). Langham, although a
minor character, is a very carefully drawn portrait whose original is obviously Amiel. A brilliant, gifted, oversensitive idealist, Langham sees
faith in orthodoxy as "the passionate acceptance
of an exquisite fairy tale ... which at the first
honest challenge of the critical senses withers in
our grasp!" Like Mallock's heroes, he is quite
unmoved by any substitutes for this exquisite
fairy tale, and this absence of faith, combined
with his natural deficiency of will-power and
excess of self-analysis—the "curse of autovivi-
section", as Bernard Shaw called it—condemns
him to a solitary existence of failure, pessimistic
quietism and complete paralysis from *la maladie
de l'idéal*.

Another of these unhappy relics imprisoned
in the dungeons of Doubting Castle was the
novelist Robert Buchanan. His own spiritual
life was a genuine tragedy. He believed, like
Amiel and Mallock, that "a man must accept
Christianity all along the line, i.e. miracles and
all, or reject it altogether", but his own inability

either to accept or reject caused a lifelong conflict within him. We find him writing in middle
age to Leslie Stephen, "I know that I am struggling in deep waters and can land on neither
side—neither on the side of Orthodox Religion,
nor on that of outright Materialism", and at
the end of his life he confessed, "All my wish,
all my prayer, all my endeavour, has been to
believe certain things—and I have failed to do
so." His life is one of the saddest examples
of that most painful nineteenth-century malady,
regretful unbelief. Unlike Mallock, however,
Buchanan was a novelist of the trashily sensational school—we have already sampled some of
his melodrama in *Foxglove Manor*—and when
he came to write of his own spiritual experiences
he adorned his tale with all manner of adventures, moonlight trysts, villainous rivals, biga-
mous marriages, outrageous coincidences and
unrestrained passions. His characters lose their
tempers on almost every other page, and white
teeth flash, blood boils, frames shake with rage
and agitation and faces grow livid the whole
time; there is a kind of continuous thunderstorm
of emotions in progress throughout the story.
This is a pity, for *The New Abelard* (1884), be-
hind its cheap façade of tawdry exaggeration,
contains some valuable pieces of spiritual autobiography and raises the important question of

the sceptic's attitude to death and immortality. The hero, Ambrose, is convinced that there is "no *via media* between Christ's Christianity and Schopenhauer's pessimism; and these two religions, like the gods of good and evil, are just now preparing for a final struggle on the battlefield of European thought". He can, of course, accept neither, and when his beloved dies his loss is "awful, full of horror, too deep for words". (Robert Buchanan, having rejected all belief in a hereafter, passed through similar anguish on the death of his mother.) Although Ambrose is of the same stamp as most of Mallock's heroes, being "hopelessly biased against veracity" by "temperament and superstition" (both authors considering "veracity" as incompatible with Christianity), the atmosphere of his spiritual drama seems crude and childishly violent beside the subtle grey mists of Mallock's melancholy tragedies, and his final rushed and unexplained acceptance of Christianity in the last chapter is as inartistic as it is unconvincing.

The story of the female doubter now comes into its own with a spate of novels dealing with young women sceptics, perhaps the three most popular being Olive Schreiner's *The Story of an African Farm* (1883), "Rita's" *Sheba* (1889), and Mrs. Humphry Ward's *Helbeck of Bannisdale* (1898). The heroines of all three novels are

agnostics—rebellious, sceptical, impulsive, idealistic young girls—and they all meet with tragedy.
They are the clever women of the family, but
for them there is no returning to the fold. They
have all "outgrown" orthodoxy, but have nothing else to fall back on, no bedrock of dogma of
any kind on which to base their lives. They are
ill-equipped to fight the battle of life, and at the
mercy of themselves and their undisciplined
emotions, for, if we are to believe the novelists,
religious doubt in a woman does not paralyse the
will but rather unleashes the emotions, and loss
of faith does not make her life a pathetic and
negative failure but a vivid and positive disaster.

Lyndall, in *The Story of an African Farm*, a
novel which enjoyed a *succès de scandale* in
England, is one of the earliest of these "advanced" young women. She believes, with her
author, that "existence is a great pot, and the
old Fate who stirs it round cares nothing what
rises to the top and what goes down, and laughs
when the bubbles burst. And we do not care.
Let it boil about. Why should we trouble ourselves?" But this dismissal of religion does not
bring peace of mind to Lyndall—on the contrary.
Never was there such a self-tormented heroine
in fiction; like Mallock's heroes she examines
herself and her emotions on page after page,
but her self-analysis is more vituperative and

bitter than that of any cultivated pessimist, her disillusion more stormy and scornful—she is a fierce, seething mass of passionate discontent, perpetually tortured by the cruelty and purposelessness of life, by her scorn of the human mind, of human love and of her own longing. Sharing her author's cravings for maternity without marriage she has an illegitimate child which dies, while she herself dies shortly afterwards, the author moralizing over her end thus: "Had she found what she sought for—something to worship? Had she ceased from being? Who shall tell us? There is a veil of terrible mist over the face of the Hereafter." The combination of bitterness and passion in Lyndall's character is strikingly brought out, and the whole life of this untutored girl of the African veldt has the quality of a feverish and very vivid nightmare. Few novels have succeeded in giving the reader such a powerful impression of sustained mental and spiritual agony.

There seemed to be a world-wide epidemic of female doubt and in continent after continent is raised the voice of the rebellious and unhappy woman sceptic. From America comes the agonized voice of Helen Ward, heroine of Mrs. Deland's *John Ward, Preacher* (1888), whose refusal to believe the religious doctrines of her Presbyterian husband causes her the most terrible pain and persecution. Helen refuses to give the slightest hypocritical assent to orthodoxy, knowing that, like her author, she has outgrown it, "as a child outgrows Santa Claus". From Australia the heroine of *Sheba* by "Rita" (Mrs. D. Humphreys) cries out in protest against the "nursery stories of Christianity", and follows Lyndall in a career of headlong rebellion and disaster. She, too, has an illegitimate child that dies, and after being on the brink of suicide, she finally returns to her stupid widowed mother, still unsettled, lonely and bitterly conscious of the agony of existence: "What is there in the present? Only pain. What in the beyond? Only dreams."

In England, late Victorian fiction contains many of these rather terrifying lives of young, passionate and catastrophically sceptical women, so strikingly difficult from their saintly sisters of the orthodox religious novel. Hardy's Sue Bridehead in *Jude the Obscure* (1896) has something in common with Sheba, and a critic of *Jude* who wrote that Hardy's heroine was "the first delineation in fiction of the woman who was coming into notice in her thousands every year—the woman of the feminist movement—the slight pale 'bachelor' girl—the intellectualized emancipated bundle of nerves that modern conditions were producing" had overlooked these earlier stories of young women whose scepticism was part of their emancipation and who proved totally unable to control passion by principle.

The best portrait in all Victorian fiction of the tragic woman sceptic is that of Laura in Mrs. Humphry Ward's *Helbeck of Bannisdale* (1898). Laura, daughter of a free-thinker, is a defiant young agnostic who, like Lyndall, Sheba and Helen Ward, is obviously destined for disaster. Like these heroines, too, she falls in love with the most unsuitable man imaginable—in this case a pious, almost fanatical Catholic of the old school. The conflict between the faiths of the lovers, symbolizing "the eternal clash between the medieval and modern mind", and probably based on Mrs. Ward's relations with her father, is the chief interest of the novel. Laura cannot accept Catholicism; to her it is a hideous tyranny and in Helbeck's devout household she is "an alien and mocking spirit". The main tragedy of the story lies in the fact that Laura's wild and instinctive scepticism is a feeble thing beside the strength, scholarship and dignity of Helbeck's religion: "She had no tools, no weapons. The Catholic argument scandalized, exasperated her; but she could not meet it." Mrs. Ward, with her fine sense of spiritual drama, gives us a deeply moving account of Laura's conflicts, of her sincere efforts to understand Helbeck's faith, her decision to break off the engagement, her flight, her return, her reconciliation and her suicide, which is regarded as a kind of martyrdom, for she is the "blind witness to august things". The moral implicit in the story is that a woman's emotional, undisciplined and uneducated scepticism brings inevitable tragedy. ("Why do we leave our children's minds empty like this?" asks one of the characters. "If you believe, my good friend, Educate! And if you doubt, still more —Educate! Educate!") Laura is one of the finest examples in the novel of the turbulent female doubter, caught up in the blind forces of scepticism that claimed their victims from Australian bush and African veldt alike, the woman who "thinks with her heart", and whose refusal to be guided, sheltered and supported by accepted orthodox beliefs, although not reprehensible in the eyes of her author, is responsible for a tragic career and an early death, a spectacular martyrdom to the "rational life".

These late Victorian novels of doubt that we have been discussing all deal with the spiritual life of confirmed sceptics, and the process by which they became unbelievers is of no particular importance to the story—indeed, with Laura we have passed to a generation of born agnostics and the acceptance in fiction of "an agnostic temperament". But the majority of Victorian unbelievers were nurtured in the traditional faith and rejected it only after the most grievous struggles. For many the separation from the Christian religion was, in Mrs. Ward's words, like "the rending asunder of bones and marrow". It is this parting with the faith, the actual process of breaking away from Christian orthodoxy, that inspires some of the finest religious novels of the Victorian age. (As well, one must admit, as some of the most foolish and fantastic tales, for the weird and bizarre treatment of religious themes in fiction was becoming increasingly popular.)

Among the major Victorian novelists the name that immediately comes to mind in connection with tragic loss of orthodoxy is that of Thomas Hardy, who himself once contemplated a career in the Anglican ministry, but whose faith deserted him in his twenties, being replaced by that melancholy fatalism so powerfully expressed in his novels and about which so much has been written. *Jude the Obscure* (1896), which tells of the downfall of a young man desirous of taking Holy Orders, might well be expected to contain some illuminating flashes of spiritual autobiography. But when we come to examine the inner life of Jude we find that he has hardly any strength of Christian belief whatsoever. We are told that he is a believer, for "the deadly animosity of contemporary logic and vision towards so much of what he held in reverence was not yet revealed to him", and that his battle is "a deadly war waged between flesh and spirit", but we look in vain for indications of such a struggle in the story and find not even the faintest echo of those tumultuous conflicts of St. Augustine and others who fought so fiercely in the name of Christ to overcome their sexual temptations. Jude's orthodoxy is almost entirely non-combatant—it is a mere Aunt Sally to be knocked down, not by the scientists or the biblical critics, but by the forces of social setbacks and unrestrained fleshly lusts. Indeed, in *Jude the Obscure*, as in all Hardy's novels, orthodox religion is absurdly impotent and ineffectual and no match whatsoever for the forces of temptation. Jude's tragedy, in the eyes of his author, springs not from a life deprived of the supports of the Christian faith but from the very nature of life itself.

A more conventional and melodramatic story of lost faith comes from the pen of Winwood Reade, a freethinker, nephew of Charles Reade and author of the famous *Martyrdom of Man* (1872), a history of the world which breaks out into a passionate denunciation of Christianity in the last chapter. In his novel *The Outcast* (1875), Reade makes his sceptic a clergyman's

son whose doubts drive him into fits of madness.
During these fits, we are told, he

> ... dressed always in black, and said he was
> in mourning for mankind. The works of Mal-
> thus and Darwin, bound in sombre covers,
> were placed on a table in his room; the first
> was lettered outside, *The Book of Doubt*, and
> the second, *The Book of Despair*.

(Darwin is shown in so many of these novels as
the arch-enemy of belief and the champion faith-
destroyer; Malthus, Chambers, Lyell and Strauss
are all good runners-up.) The poor creature becomes completely insane and at last contrives to
hang himself in his padded cell.

Similar dramatic and horrific accompaniments to the losing of orthodoxy are recounted
by Mrs. Lynn Linton, particularly in her novel
The Autobiography of Christopher Kirkland
(1885). This is what happens when the hero, on
reading Greek myths, thinks to himself, "What
difference between the legends of old times and
the stories of Sara, Hannah, Elizabeth, and the
Virgin Mary?" As the thought of this last name
came, he tells us,

> ... a terrible faintness took hold of me. The
> perspiration streamed over my face like rain,
> and I trembled like a frightened horse. My
> heart, which for a few seconds had beaten like

a hammer, now seemed to cease altogether. The light grew dim; the earth was vapoury and unstable; and, overpowered by an awful dread, I fell back among the long grass where I was sitting, as if I had been struck down by an unseen hand.

It is emphasized in both Mrs. Linton's and Winwood Reade's novels that the process of rejecting orthodoxy is similar to an actual illness. It is a "spiritual disease which has to be gone through, like measles or small-pox", affecting the sufferer physically as well as mentally, spiritually and emotionally, and most of the novelists agree in regarding profuse perspiration, extreme faintness and cardiac disturbances as necessary accompaniments to the first shocks of scepticism. These symptoms are especially noticeable in fictional accounts of young children's attacks of scepticism. It is hard to believe that the demons of theological doubt and despair could claim their victims even in the nursery, and one would be inclined to dismiss the whole matter as a novelist's device for wringing an extra tear from the reading public, were it not for the existence of *bona fide* documents such as Elizabeth Sewell's autobiography to support the evidence. Juvenile doubt, like the juvenile deathbed, provided convenient opportunities for an orgy of the most lush and sickly sentimental writing, opportunities which such novelists as Mrs. Lynn Linton, "Rita" and Marie Corelli were not slow to seize. Even Olive Schreiner, whose studies of childhood are usually so sensitive and delicately penetrating, inclines to exaggeration in her descriptions of the struggles of Lyndall's little brother Waldo—his fierce night-terrors, his lonely hours of agony, his passionate sobbing, his "great beads of perspiration", as he torments himself with "adder-like thoughts" about the Bible and questions such as "Why did the women in Mark see only one angel and the women in Luke two? Could a story be told in opposite ways and both be true? Could it? Could it?" Novelists of the period, it seems, were quite incapable of keeping their heads when they came to describe the sufferings of the child sceptic.

To most of us today this nineteenth-century spiritual disease of doubt, whether manifested in adult or child, cannot but seem so dated in its appearance, so preposterous and exaggerated in its symptoms and so absurdly grave and far-reaching in its consequences that, even with a willing suspension of disbelief, the modern reader can find little interest or sympathy, still less enjoyment, in these faded records of such peculiar attacks and such ancient and incomprehensible battles. Only the greater works can

transcend the spirit of their age and make us
feel the real power and poignancy of such conflicts, and, happily for us, there are two Victorian
religious novels that have survived the acid test
of time and remain as classics in the literature of
lost faith. One is *The Autobiography of Mark
Rutherford* (1881) by William Hale White and
the other is *Robert Elsmere* (1888) by Mrs. Humphry Ward. Rutherford and Elsmere are the two
noblest in the noble army of theological martyrs
that the Victorian age produced, and these two
doubters deserve a chapter to themselves.

CHAPTER 11

TWO DISTINGUISHED DOUBTERS: MARK RUTHERFORD AND ROBERT ELSMERE

THE story of Mark Rutherford, told in *The Autobiography* and its sequel *The Deliverance* (1885), is the work of a man of over fifty, and it combines the simple, almost naïve self-revelations of a first attempt at fiction with the best qualities associated with maturity: mellowness and finish of style, emotional control and restraint, a certain gracious austerity, the fruit of a seasoned and philosophic mind. Its author, William Hale White, led a long, introspective and uneventful life. Brought up in provincial Dissent in Bedfordshire (we have already mentioned his contribution to the Nonconformist novel), and destined for the ministry, he was expelled from his theological college in 1851 on account of his heterodox biblical views. After that, we are told, not only White but his entire family broke off all connection with Dissent and gave up going to any place of worship at all. White obtained a post in the Admiralty, where he worked at routine tasks for the rest of his life. While holding this post he wrote for several newspapers and magazines, produced a very painstaking but unsuccessful book on Bunyan, and a mere handful of novels, each typical of his quiet and thoughtful personality and his concern with the life of the spirit, and none achieving great popularity in his lifetime, not being sufficiently dramatic, colourful and sensational to attract the reading public of the day.

In *The Autobiography*, Mark Rutherford's life is recorded in the first person, and later narrated by "Reuben Shapcott", a fictitious "friend" of the author and "editor" of his manuscripts. (Such careful anonymity was a fairly common device in Victorian confessional literature, and White was even more secretive than most authors on the subject of his intensely autobiographical novels.) The hero, Mark Rutherford, is brought up in an atmosphere of pious Independency in an East Midland town, and is designated to the ministry, but at college he is repelled by the unintelligent teaching of his professors and the lack of true Christian ideals among his fellow-students. Forced to resign from his first pastorate on account of the petty narrow-mindedness of his flock, he drifts into Unitarianism and, after some futile attempts to revive a stagnant Unitarian church, he loses all interest in theology and works at uncongenial employment in a London office to support his wife and stepdaughter until his sudden death in middle age.

This bare outline of the story can give very little idea of the power of the novel, for White's plots are always weak and poorly constructed; his genius lies in his gift for vivid portraiture, for the evocation of atmosphere and the revealing of the interior development of personality. The character of Mark Rutherford, which dominates the two books, is a fine and delicately-drawn self-portrait. Mark is a slightly morbid and second-rate sensitive mind for whom the time is out of joint—an almost stock character in this kind of fiction, and White, drawing heavily on his own experiences, plunges him into deeper waters of suffering than most doubters of fiction. He is, besides being a tormented sceptic, an intensely lonely figure, longing for kindred spirits and ideal friendships; he is disappointed in love, for the girl of his choice dies of consumption; like the Victorian poet James Thomson, he becomes a victim of melancholia and alcohol, and he suffers appallingly from his later routine of dreary office drudgery in a depressing atmosphere of poverty-stricken London squalor. White outdoes Gissing in his magnificent descriptions of hopeless gloom in the poorer quarters of the metropolis; his account of a Sunday afternoon spent in this mud-grey misery is one of the most effectively depressing pieces of writing in all fiction. Indeed, so masterly is his power of describing the dingy and the dreary that an American critic has declared that "no greater triumph of drabness has ever been achieved in English than this Autobiography." With equal facility he can paint not only the greyest but the blackest hues of life, and his account of the agonies of melancholia is another superb triumph of wretchedness. Certainly this is, as Matthew Arnold said of Amiel's *Journal*, "not a tonic book".

But, despite the author's genius for depicting the miseries of existence, Mark's life is not presented as a ghastly chronicle of unrelieved tragedy. On the contrary, it is presented as a story of adversities met and overcome, it is passionate emotion recollected in tranquillity, the grim and rather bleak tranquillity of Mark's later resignation. It is the tale of his storm-tossed youth by a man who has finally come to terms with life, and in describing his sufferings he never fails to describe immediately afterwards his deliverance from them, adding the comments of his wiser, maturer years. Mark overcomes his longings for perfect friendships, his author commenting thus:

> Sympathy or no sympathy, a man's love should no more fail towards his fellows than that love which spent itself on disciples who altogether misunderstood it, like the rain which falls on just and unjust alike.

Similarly, Mark conquers his melancholia to the best of his ability, overcomes his cravings for alcohol and gives advice to the reader on how to master these afflictions:

> Try the effect of eating and rest. Do not persist in a blind, obstinate wrestle. Simply take food, drink water, go to bed, and so conquer not by brute strength but by strategy.

He recovers, too, from the loss of his love, marries and learns to love his wife and even his stodgy little stepdaughter, love, he realizes, being an acquired art, involving the will as well as the emotions and demanding "that the two persons who love one another shall constantly present to one another what is best in them, and to accomplish this, deliberate purpose, and even struggle are necessary". He relieves his loathing of London squalor by frequent excursions to the country and the sea to observe the face of Nature (Nature, in White's novels, fulfils the Wordsworthian conception of a moral and religious influence: indeed, he emphasizes that a reading of the *Lyrical Ballads* at college "re-created" Mark's entire spiritual life), and he triumphs over his distaste for uncongenial office work by sheer force of habit:

> Habit, after a while, mitigated much of the bitterness of destiny. The hard points of the

flint became smoothed and worn away by perpetual tramping over them, so that they no longer wounded with their original sharpness; and the sole of the foot was in time provided with a merciful callosity.

Through this method of narrative interspersed with comment we are able to see the inner development of Mark Rutherford's character and its gradual toughening by the passage of time. The Victorian practice of moralizing in fiction over young people's strivings and sorrows was common enough, but White, in making his abundant comments spring from the character himself in his own middle age, transforms mere "sermonizing" into a subtle form of character-revelation, a thing of psychological value, a measure and indication of the mental, emotional and spiritual growth of the subject. Thus it is that he penetrates so deeply and delicately into the mysteries of the inner life.

Much might be written about the character of Mark Rutherford and the psychological skill of the author's presentation, but we are here concerned with its particular relation to religious matters, especially the discarding of orthodoxy. Although Mark is at first presented as an unquestioning believer it is a clear case of *fides delenda est*. Like Samuel Butler, White introduces the representatives of orthodoxy to us as narrow-minded and hypocritical characters, and, like Butler's hero and many others of religious fiction, Mark becomes disillusioned with Christians themselves before becoming disillusioned with the Bible. It is obvious from the author's presentation of the mouthpieces of Independency that they are not so likely to satisfy, still less inspire, the hero. Take, for instance, this portrait of the President of the seminary:

> I see him now, a gentleman with lightish hair, with a most mellifluous voice and a most pastoral manner, reading his prim little tracts to us directed against the "shallow infidel", who seemed to deny conclusions so obvious that we were certain he could not be sincere, and those of us who had never seen an infidel might well be pardoned for supposing that he must always be wickedly blind. About a dozen of these tracts settled the infidel and the whole mass of unbelief from the time of Celsus downwards. The President's task was all the easier because he knew nothing of German literature; and, indeed, the word "German" was a term of reproach signifying something very awful, although nobody knew exactly what it was.

The descriptions of Mark's fellow-students are equally vivid and illuminating. One remembers in particular the blond youth with "an eternal simper upon his face" and a weakness for "watery rhetoric". Nor were the members of Mark's first pastorate a great improvement on this. We have already made the acquaintance of the third deacon, Mr. Snale, smirking at "the leedies"; here is Mrs. Snale:

... large and full-faced, correct like Mr. Snale, a member of the church, a woman whom I never saw moved to any generosity, and cruel, not with the ferocity of the tiger, but with the dull insensibility of a cart-wheel, which will roll over a man's neck as easily as over a flint.

Indeed, the first part of this novel is distinguished by its magnificent portrait-gallery of repulsive Dissenters (all, it seems, drawn from life, for White, as he told his second wife, "never *created* a character, never sat down to write without having somebody before his mind's eye"). Small wonder, therefore, that the unhappy young pastor is delighted to make friends with a man called Mardon, whose appearance is agreeably different from that of the majority of Mark's flock. "There was in his face", Mark tells us, "a perfectly legible frankness, contrasting pleasantly with the doubtfulness of most of the faces I knew." (White consistently describes and regards the face as an index of character.) Mardon,

however, is a freethinker, and despite his congenial appearance and manner, Mark finds his
conviction of the mythical nature of Christianity
and his "remorseless criticism" of orthodoxy
most disturbing and begins to dread meeting
him for this reason. The inward conflicts have
now started in earnest.

"With me", Mark writes, "the struggle to re-
tain as much as I could of my creed was tremendous. The dissolution of Jesus into mythological
vapour was nothing less than the death of a
friend dearer to me than any other friend I
knew." Besides this feeling of personal loss come
also the full torments of uncertainty about a
future life. As with Robert Buchanan and so
many other sceptics, Mark's dawning unbelief
affects his hope of immortality most painfully.
"My hope began to fail", he tells us, "and I was
surprised to find myself incapable of living with
proper serenity if there was nothing but blank
darkness before me at the end of a few years."
The whole problem of life after death absorbs
him "even to the point of monomania". But as
usual he adds the comment of his riper years:

> I say nothing, now, for or against the doc-
> trine of immortality. All I say is, that men
> have been happy without it, even under the
> pressure of disaster, and that to make im-
> mortality a sole spring of action here is an

exaggeration of the folly which deludes us all through life with endless expectation, and leaves us at death without the thorough enjoyment of a single hour.

Although Mark shrinks from Mardon's company the "process of excavation" of his faith proceeds apace. The foundations are gradually undermined and, after a quarrel with the odious Mr. Snale, who accuses him of preaching a "German" Gospel, Mark resigns. (George Macdonald, the Scottish novelist, was forced to resign from the Congregational ministry for similar reasons.) Betaking himself to Unitarianism, Mark finds it "even more intolerable" and White's description of the chapel and the hospitality of provincial Unitarians is another masterpiece of the dreary and the drab. Mark's freethinking friend dies; we are shown the beautiful and dignified death and funeral of an unbeliever, whose last words to Mark are, "Learn not to be over-anxious about meeting troubles and solving difficulties which time will meet and solve for you." *The Autobiography* ends with Mark in a state of deep spiritual gloom, "entirely unorthodox" through "mere powerlessness to believe".

The Deliverance, as its title suggests, shows how Mark is rescued from his worst agonies and redeemed not by faith but by a sort of grim and courageous resignation to his own spiritual paralysis. He follows Mardon's advice, and the additional advice of the author given in the preface:

Don't bother yourselves with what is beyond you ... Metaphysics and theology, including all speculations on the why and the wherefore, optimism, pessimism, freedom, necessity, causality, and so forth, are not only for the most part loss of time, but frequently ruinous ... One fourth of life is intelligible, the other three fourths is unintelligible darkness; and our earliest duty is to cultivate the habit of not looking round the corner.

Having become adept in this habit of not looking round the corner, Mark resolves to "submit calmly and sometimes cheerfully to the Creator", and in this spirit he preaches contentment with one's lot to the slum population of Drury Lane and submits to a life of "infernal drudgery" in an office, never permitting himself to speak of his home life to his office associates and never thinking of talking of such things as orthodox faith, death and immortality. "I clapped a muzzle on my mouth", he tells us, and in spite of his frequent assurances that his misery is relieved by his love for wife and step-daughter (salvation through human love is the theme of several of White's novels), and by week-end excursions to the country, the reader is far from convinced that Mark has gained any true deliverance. Indeed, the metaphor of the muzzle seems far more appropriate than any metaphor of redemption or release. The one and only real deliverance seems to be through death, and in the description of Mark's end we have the author's laconic style at its best. Mark has a stroke in his office; he

> ... was seen to turn white and fall forward in his chair. It was all over! His body was taken to a hospital and thence sent home. The next morning his salary up to the day of his death came in an envelope to his widow, without a single word from his employers save a request for acknowledgment. Towards midday, his office coat, and a book found in his drawer, arrived in a brown paper parcel, carriage unpaid.

Stoicism, fatalism, determinism, pessimism—critics may differ in their interpretations of Mark Rutherford's "message", but it is clear that, as a spiritual biography of lost faith, the story shows with more sad lucidity and more dreary realism than any other novel in the language, the sufferings of the religious temperament unable to accept orthodox religion and yet incapable of reaching any other inspiring alternative of faith and hope. White, perhaps, like

Hardy, loads the dice a little too heavily against his hero, but Mark submits with a courage that contrasts favourably with the forlorn helplessness of so many of Hardy's characters. He is indeed the martyr without a cause, and exemplifies the type of virtue praised by a character in one of White's other novels, who tells us:

> The highest form of martyrdom ... is not even living for the sake of a cause, but living without one, merely because it is your duty to live. If you are called upon to testify to a great truth, it is easy to sing in flames. Yes, yes, Mr. George, the saints whom I would canonise are not martyrs for a cause, but those who have none.

As well as being a profound and sensitive study of a temperament *The Autobiography* also gives us valuable insight into many facets of nineteenth-century scepticism. A thoughtful Victorian clerical critic, R. E. Welsh, investigating the problem of religious doubt, suggested three principal causes: first, the "hypocrisy and cruelty" of so many orthodox Christians who present a "misshapen form of Christianity", which provokes and justifies scepticism as a rebellion from "a grim repulsive perversion of pure religion"; secondly, experience of the misfortunes of life, which drives many into the "deserts of unbelief"; and thirdly, infection caught from "an epidemic of doubt", clearly raging in England at this time, having previously visited this country during the latter part of the seventeenth century, and again of the eighteenth century. Mark Rutherford is obviously the victim of all three influences—the unpleasantness of his fellow Dissenters, the sorrow and disappointment of his own personal affairs and the subtle workings of the *Zeitgeist* with all the forces of "enlightened" denial. Intensely personal, completely sincere, and devastatingly sombre, *The Autobiography*, as a confession of doubt, stands supreme in English fiction.

The only other novel of lost faith comparable to White's as a work of art is Mrs. Humphry Ward's *Robert Elsmere*. Like Mark Rutherford, Mrs. Ward's hero is "infected" with doubt caught through contact with a highly intelligent and cultured unbeliever. But here the similarity ends. Infinitely more popular and provocative, this novel may be viewed as the first great Modernist tract in English fiction, and indeed it owes much of its widespread success to its associations with certain trends of Liberal thought. But although Mrs. Ward, a skilful mistress of the *roman à thèse*, makes her story serve as propaganda for the new faith, the accent in

Robert Elsmere is more on the loss than the gain, more on the death of the old creed than the birth of the new one, more on "the shaking off of old beliefs" than "the growth of a natural faith". It is, moreover, a piece of confessional literature, profoundly autobiographical and written not in a state of calm resignation and retrospect like *The Autobiography*, but with much sorrow and suffering, the author being frequently "shaken with tears" during its composition.

Mary Augusta Ward was born into a family distinguished by intense and unsatisfied spiritual cravings. Her father was Thomas Arnold, Dr. Arnold's favourite son, whose conversions to and reversions from Catholicism caused his family much pain as well as financial hardship, and her uncles included Matthew Arnold as well as the unhappy author of *Oakfield*. In fact there was, one might say, a certain spiritual melancholy and instability in the blood, which, in Mrs. Ward's case, hardly benefited from residence at Oxford in an atmosphere of religious controversy, with post-Tractarian Liberalism still "a living and combative force". Mrs. Ward followed White, Froude, Buchanan, Butler and so many chroniclers of lost faith in reacting strongly against the narrowness of certain orthodox Christians, especially in their condemnation of scepticism as wickedness, and her pamphlet *Unbelief and Sin* (1881), a vigorous protest against an attitude still persisting in University pulpits, was in fact the germ of *Robert Elsmere*.

Mrs. Ward's friendship with such men as Mark Pattison, T. H. Green and Edmond Scherer, and her translation of Amiel's *Journal Intime*, were all powerful influences in assisting her departure from orthodoxy, but the real uprooting of her faith came from her own researches into early Spanish and West Gothic Christianity in preparation for a contribution to *The Dictionary of Christian Biography*. The years 1879 to 1881, spent in these studies, aided at every step by German criticism and research, were, she tells us, "the determining years of life" for her. Her investigations into the great problem of the value of testimony as to historic facts resulted in her loss of all faith in the supernatural element of Christianity, a process that she has produced most faithfully in *Robert Elsmere*, where she maintains her claim that "the present collapse of English orthodoxy is due to one cause, as far as I can see, and one cause only—*the invasion of English by German thought.*" (Small wonder that German sceptics and a "German" Gospel were shown as anathema to the orthodox in so many novels.) A woman of wide reading, brilliant intellect and earnest endeavour (A. G. Gardiner wickedly calls her "a University Extension lecturer in disguise"),

Mrs. Ward is clearly at home in the Chair of Theology and in the world of religious controversy. We have already noticed in another chapter her fine account of an agnostic and Catholic clash in *Helbeck of Bannisdale*. Besides *Robert Elsmere* and *Helbeck* she wrote twelve other novels, most of them concerned with religious, social or political reform, and many lying outside our period. *Robert Elsmere* however, written when she was thirty-seven, was her own confession of lost orthodoxy, and her first, greatest and most sensational success. It was quoted in a thousand pulpits, it excited a spirited controversy with Mr. Gladstone, it was passionately denounced by Marie Corelli, it caused a *furore* in America and it was translated into dozens of foreign languages, a Swiss lady even being moved to write and publish a sequel to it. Few novels have ever attained so great a vogue.

Yet Mrs. Ward's presentation of religious doubts and difficulties is perhaps superior to her presentation of the leading character. Robert Elsmere is not drawn from life; he is, as Mrs. Ward tell us, "a figure of pure imagination", and although he suffers from the same conflicts that ravaged the conscience of his author and of countless other Victorians, he remains a somewhat over-idealized figure. Indeed, Mrs. Ward has made a striking departure from conventional portraits of the doubter in fiction; Robert is neither a wicked sinner nor a morbid, ineffectual weak-willed sceptic, but a balanced, manly and exemplary clergyman, resembling the heroes of earlier didactic religious fiction. The stories of Oakfield and Mark Rutherford leave the reader with the impression that if their lives had not been shipwrecked on the rocks of religious doubt they would probably have come to grief elsewhere—they were men born, in William James's expressive phrase, "close to the pain-threshold". But Robert Elsmere is no misfit, and in reading the opening chapters of Mrs. Ward's novel one is struck by the essential difference in this hero and his world. Robert is "frank, genial and open-hearted"; and at school he has been "bright, docile, popular, excellent at games". Although at Oxford he has been exposed to the teachings of the melancholy sceptic Langham (a portrait of Amiel) and the theist philosopher Grey (a character based on that of T. H. Green, to whom the book is dedicated), the fabric of his orthodoxy is untouched. He has a genuine "delight in living"; other people find him "sensible and nice and well-mannered", and indeed, in the first two books of the story (the novel is divided into seven books) he moves in a world as cosy and comfortable and secure as Jane Austen's or Charlotte Yonge's, a world of matchmaking

matrons, happy families, teasing younger sisters,
jolly family doctors and afternoon teas in pleasant vicarage gardens.

All this, of course, makes the drama of doubt
even more effective when it takes place. But
Mrs. Ward is in no hurry to raise the spectres
of unbelief; she indulges in some idyllic romanc-
ing and before making Robert an unhappy
doubter she makes him an impassioned lover, a
contented husband and a joyous father, settling
happily into his "world of loveliness" in a Surrey
rectory and completely at home in Holy Orders.
Although he is frequently occupied with "dirt,
drains and Darwin", the author is careful to
tell us that the *Origin of Species* has not shaken
his faith in the slightest and, despite arguments
at the dinner-table with the freethinking Squire
who, bony, shrivelled, Berlin-educated and
atrociously bad-mannered, harks back to the
Guelph-Frankenstein school of sceptics, Robert's
spiritual horizon remains quite unclouded, and
his happiness in his work is equalled only by
his happiness at home with Catherine and the
baby, in that "exquisite home-life of theirs, that
tender, triple bond of husband, wife and child"

Much too good to be true, thinks the reader,
tiring of the rose-coloured spectacles and of the
impossible perfection of the hero and his life.
But at last Robert's character quickens when the

author brings him down from the Celestial Mountain heights of his matrimonial and rectorial bliss and plunges him, a frightened and new-born doubter, into the depths of the Slough of Despond. Only then, when following in the same treacherous paths that Mrs. Ward trod, does Robert really begin to come to life.

His first doubts occur, as Mrs. Ward's did, through the study of history. Grey and Langham have advised him to pursue "the life of thought" as well as "the life of doing and feeling". (Mark Rutherford, of course, would have advised him most strongly to the contrary, for White and Mrs. Ward are fundamentally opposed in their views as to the importance of the intellect in the life of man.) He therefore devotes part of his day to historical studies, and one quiet evening, when his wife has gone to bed early, he decides to glance at *The Idols of the Market Place*, the Squire's monumental history of religion, which is at the same time a masterly attack on orthodoxy. His first attack of doubt is described thus:

Robert began to read vaguely at first, then to hurry on through page after page, still standing, seized at once by the bizarre power of the style, and the audacity and range of the treatment.

Not a sound in the house. Outside, the tossing, moaning December night; inside, the faintly crackling fire, the standing figure. Suddenly it was to Robert as though a cruel torturing hand were laid upon his inmost being. His breath failed him; the book slipped out of his grasp; he sank down upon his chair, his head in his hands. Oh, what a desolate, intolerable moment! Over the young idealist soul there swept a dry destroying whirlwind of thought. Elements gathered from all sources—from his own historical work, from the Squire's book, from the secret half-conscious recesses of his mind—entered into it, and as it passed it seemed to scorch the heart.

After this there is no peace. Night after night Robert is attacked by "phantom stabs of doubt", and when he becomes a close friend of the Squire the process of demolition proceeds rapidly—too rapidly perhaps, for Robert's orthodoxy collapses without any great show of resistance, and Mr. Gladstone, as well as many other critics, deplored the feebleness of Robert's defences. The Squire, too, is depicted not as an admirable and morally elevated freethinker like Mark Rutherford's friend, but rather as a cynical old villain, chuckling sarcastically over Robert's naïveté and taking a "cruel whimsical pleasure" in having Robert's soul "quivering and struggling in his grasp".

But Mrs. Ward has far too much intelligence,

religious sense and artistic skill to treat of lost faith merely as a silly melodrama in the manner of so many popular sensation novelists, and after these shaky opening scenes her touch becomes more sure and we are treated to some excellently analytical descriptions of all the various stages through which an honest doubter may pass. Robert pursues his researches, and he examines and compares the work of Anglican and German critics on the Book of Daniel. Unbelief deepens and the first new vision of "a purely human Christ" comes to him. This is followed by a temptation to crush his doubts. (Such was Miss Sewell's method of fighting unbelief and a common and recognized practice among perplexed spirits in the High Church and Catholic communions.) Robert conquers this temptation by remembering Grey's words, *"God is not wisely trusted when declared unintelligible"*, and decides that it would be easy but wrong to "mutilate and starve the rebellious intellect". Depression, irritability and intense weariness accompany the later phases of the struggle and the final defeat comes when, at a party, he listens, almost against his will, to an animated religious argument between the Squire and a young Catholic convert. He realizes that his sympathies are completely on the Squire's side and the convert's passionate defence of organized religion has aroused in him "no echo, no response".

Feeling "that old fierce temptation of Bunyan's" to sell Christ, Robert remembers the
words of St. Augustine: "Commend to the keeping of the Truth whatever the Truth hath given
thee, and thou shalt lose nothing!" He then
puts himself through "a desperate catechism"
to see what to him is the truth:

> *Do I believe in God?* Surely, surely!
> "Though he slay me yet will I trust in Him!"
> *Do I believe in Christ?* Yes—in the teacher,
> the martyr, the symbol to us Westerns of all
> things heavenly and abiding, the image and
> pledge of the invisible life of the Spirit,—with
> all my soul and mind!
>
> *But in the Man-God,* the Word from Eter-
> nity,—in a wonder-working Christ, in a risen
> and ascended Jesus, in the living Intercessor
> and Mediator for the lives of His doomed
> brethren?
>
> He waited, conscious that it was the crisis
> of his history, and there rose in him, as though
> articulated one by one by an audible voice,
> words of irrevocable meaning.
>
> "Every human soul, in which the voice of
> God makes itself felt, enjoys, equally with
> Jesus of Nazareth, the divine sonship, and
> *'miracles do not happen'*."

It was done. He felt for the moment as
Bunyan did after his lesser defeat . . . He moved

mechanically onward, and presently, after the first flutter of desolate terror had passed away, with a new inrushing sense which seemed to him a sense of liberty—of infinite expansion.

Such a "catechism" must have appealed tremendously to hundreds of earnest and soul-searching Victorians who had passed through similar crises in their histories and come to almost identical conclusions. One can almost hear Uncle Matthew applauding. The popular rejection of supernatural Christianity, the greatest religious phenomenon of late Victorian England, had found in *Robert Elsmere* its most vivid and intelligent expression in fiction. Mrs. Ward's research work is prominent throughout the book and she fits in with admirable dexterity innumerable extracts from books and discussions that weigh Christian evidences in the balance and find them wanting. Grey, Langham and the Squire, whatever their other deficiencies, are all presented as men of a high intellectual order (the Squire is, in fact, a partial portrait of Mark Pattison), and Mrs. Ward does ample justice to their intelligence in her records of their conversations and writings. This, of course, adds enormously to the strength of her case against orthodoxy, and *Robert Elsmere* is indeed, as Marie Corelli noticed with horror, a novel "calculated to disturb the mind, and arouse trouble in the heart of many an ardent believer". Mrs. Ward is the first Victorian novelist to present in fiction the arguments against Christianity in a serious, scholarly and detailed form, and Robert's struggle for belief presents a continual appeal to the reader's intellect as well as to his emotions.

The appeal to the emotions, however, as we have seen, is by no means lacking, and as well as Robert's own individual "thought-drama" we have the "bitterly human tragedy" of personal relationships to be played out, for Robert is not only a clergyman but also a husband, married to the incarnation of orthodoxy, "the Thirty-Nine Articles in the flesh". Domestic clashes resulting from changes of religious conviction were, of course, wildly popular themes in Victorian fiction, "Puseyism" or "Popery" being almost invariably the agents of marital discord. Mrs. Ward now shows us the repercussions of scepticism on the family circle and the impact of religious doubt on the husband-and-wife relationship. Robert's domestic miseries are as well described as his intellectual ones and indeed, his conflict seems to resolve itself into one between heart and head. His wife, as one critic noticed, is "purposely divested of all intellect, Langham and the Squire of all heart". Mrs. Ward, like White, tends to employ the device of argument from character, and in the final outcome of the struggle Robert follows the theist Grey, who alone combines the best qualities of head and heart, and rears his theistic temple on the ashes of a failing Christianity.

From thenceforth he becomes insufferably idealized again. What Henry James called "the high, oblique light" of the author's admiration for Robert begins to play on him in full dazzling radiance once more, and Robert Elsmere the founder and leader of the "New Brotherhood" is just yet another propaganda prig of didactic religious fiction. The reader is unmoved and unconvinced by Mrs. Ward's glowing accounts of his teaching and preaching, his personal magnetism, his zealous efforts among the poor and his untimely death through overworking for the cause. Mrs. Ward is at her most earnest during this last part of the novel, but, as in the early religious fiction of the eighteen-forties, propaganda ousts character study to the detriment of the novel, and Robert recovers from his loss of orthodoxy only to become the saintly and uninteresting exponent of Mrs. Ward's own personal Modernist creed.

In fact one may safely say that, as spiritual biography, the story of Robert Elsmere attains to strength and vividness of religious experience only in those parts concerned with loss of orthodoxy. Robert is at his weakest as a model Anglican clergyman at the beginning, and as the high priest of Mrs. Ward's new faith at the end. It is only in the middle that he comes to life, as a tortured sceptic, shaken to his very foundations by the overwhelming arguments of "Higher Criticism" against Christianity, and faced, not only with the loss of all belief in the supernatural, but with the ruin of his own happy home life. Mrs. Ward's own personal experience had given her this deep insight into the complex processes of intellectual ferment and the agonies of religious controversy within the home, and these she reproduces for us with a skill and a sympathy that make her novel, despite its unevenness and occasional lapses into melodrama, one of the finest examples of the fiction of lost faith.

Mark Rutherford and Robert Elsmere differ widely in background, circumstance and temperament, but they share this same painful religious experience, and their authors can communicate to us the reality and intensity of such experience more successfully than any other novelists of the time. Although we in the twentieth century may smile rather than weep at the extraordinary collection of Victorian doubters in fiction—the sobbing children, the passionate, rebellious young women, the morbid youths, tormented into the grave or the asylum—yet we may find, in the works of such authors as William Hale White and Mrs. Humphry Ward, the stories of "souls bereaved" that have power to move us still. As we read these novels we are touched with pity at the spectacle of a cruel and subtle spiritual suffering, we feel the depth and anguish of a genuine tragic conflict, and we listen sadly to the "long withdrawing melancholy roar" of the ebb tide of the sea of faith in the nineteenth century.

CHAPTER 12

ESCAPE TO HAPPINESS

NOT all lost orthodoxy was associated in Victorian fiction with tragedy and tears. For some the discarding of traditional belief was a joyous deliverance, and according to several novelists great and lasting happiness was to be found in escaping from bigoted sectarianism or ecclesiasticism and in exchanging the stifling forms of orthodox faith for the delights of benevolent theism or enthusiastic positivism or "ardent agnosticism". The novels in which interest is centred on the faith acquired by the character after loss of orthodoxy must be relegated to our next chapter, but, if only to correct the rather dismal impression of agonized conflict and fatal tragedy produced by most of the novels of lost faith previously mentioned, we must include here a few specimens of fiction that claim to show how separation from orthodox belief may well cause more pleasure than pain, more strength than weakness and more virtue than vice in the life of a character.

Winwood Reade, in *The Outcast* (1875), does in fact set before us in a single novel two types of sceptic—the one negative and pessimistic, the other positive and optimistic. After the tragic life of Arthur, whose doubts, as we have seen, lead him to the padded cell and suicide, Reade gives us the life of Edward, who has "climbed above theology as the Alpine mountaineer above the clouds". He has lost his faith through reading Lyell's *Principles of Geology*, and after the first few pangs of loss comes a feeling of shame that he "could ever have credited the many profane and ridiculous fables contained in the Bible". From that time onward his spiritual development proceeds apace towards "a pure and sublime Theism" and he assures us at the end of the book that if he were a young man he would adopt as his life's work "the diffusion of doubt", for, he declares, "doubt dissipates superstition, and softens the rancour of religious life. Without doubt there can be no tolerance, and the history of tolerance is the history of doubt." He has embraced the "Religion of Unselfishness" which he considers far more ennobling than any religion holding out hope of a celestial reward, and it is emphasized throughout the story that Edward's discarding of orthodox theology has brought him great happiness, perfect peace of mind and a considerable increase in spiritual power and stature.

A similar message is preached in the stories of George Macdonald, one of the most influential religious novelists of the nineteenth century. George Macdonald himself passed from Scottish

Congregationalism to a kind of benevolent theism, and most of the leading characters in his novels follow this course. The conflict of "stereotyped theology" with "the simple human aspiration towards the divine" is Macdonald's favourite theme in fiction, but the conflict is never bitter or tragic; the author's serene and genial optimism colours all his work and his heroes escape from hard dogmatic religions without permanent hurt or hatred. The few pangs of lost faith that they may have to endure are but a "birth agony"; doubt is "the hammer that breaks the windows clouded with human fancies and lets in the pure light", and the change from being a Christian who lives "by the clergy and their traditions" to one who lives "by the fresh spirit of God" is a necessary and salutary part of the spiritual progress of mankind. The heroes of *Robert Falconer* (1868) and *Thomas Wingfold, Curate* (1876) are two of his best-known characters who develop along these lines, but, as is usual in George Macdonald's novels, the accent is more on what they gain than on what they lose by freeing themselves from "a withered, starved, miserable death's head of Christianity" and their spiritual histories thus fall into the group of tales to be dealt with in our next chapter. Macdonald wrote of the honest doubter with sympathy and admiration; Ericson in *Robert Falconer* is an inspiring figure, and the sceptical hero of *Paul Faber, Surgeon* (1879) is contrasted favourably with several of the representatives of the traditional creeds.

Macdonald, too, has the distinction of being one of the few Victorian novelists who could write of the child sceptic without indulging in sentimentality or melodrama. All Macdonald's studies of childhood are excellent and he has a gift for describing children's spiritual growth, as *Robert Falconer* shows. Robert's boyhood is passed with a rigid Calvinist grandmother. She refuses to pray for her dead son, Robert's father, because she considers him damned (in her creed, the author says, "hell is the deepest truth, and love of God is not so deep as hell"), she opposes Robert's musical ambitions, burns his violin and clips all his youthful aspirations "with the shears of unsympathetic age and crabbed religion". Given such a situation, most religious novelists of the period would have wallowed in tear-jerking exaggerations of little Robert's miseries, but Macdonald's good humour and good sense prevail. He knows the resilience of childhood— "God makes children so that grief cannot cleave to them"—and Robert loves his grandmother in spite of her unlovable creed, although his secret sympathies are with Satan, for he thinks his grandmother's God "pompous, scarcely reasonable and somewhat revengeful". As a young man he quickly manages to escape from the shadows of this grim theology, yet without rancour or prejudice, but rather with continued love towards his grandmother and gratitude for the religious discipline in the life of prayer in which she has educated him. Robert, a healthy and sensible youth, can see the good in all religions, even the Puritan fanaticism from which he has extricated himself. From the eighteen-sixties onwards these happy, sane and good-tempered tales of escape from bigoted orthodoxy had an extraordinarily powerful influence: "No dogmatic theologian has had the widespread commanding authority in our day that Macdonald has exercised", wrote a critic in 1906, and Macdonald's novels brought to many of his readers a joyful spiritual deliverance from "the bondage of old-fashioned theology".

To mention the name of George Gissing in connection with the happiness of lost orthodoxy may at first seem startling, for this "chronicler of misery" is hardly to be associated with joy of any kind, and the pages of his novels breathe an atmosphere of drab and sordid gloom almost as depressing as that which surrounds Mark Rutherford. But when we come to examine the spiritual lives of his characters we find that for them, as for Gissing himself, the rejection of the authority of ecclesiastical dogma in favour of that of Strauss, Comte and others is like "the first ray of heavenly light piercing the darkness of a night of anguish and striving and woe unutterable". In *Workers in the Dawn* (1880) a vicar's daughter, disgusted with orthodoxy, turns to Strauss' *Leben Jesu* (a significant influence in the spiritual life of George Eliot and many other Victorians) and there she finds joy and solace,

> ... bending over the pages of him whose eyes saw with surpassing clearness through the mists of time and prejudice, whose spirit comes forth, like a ray of sunshine in winter, to greet those toiling painfully upwards to the temple of Truth.

Thus inspired, she actually goes to Tübingen to study, and then returns to help the poor in London, "her lovely features aglow with the fire of boundless benevolence". Her life serves to illustrate "the nobility of a faith dispensing with all we are accustomed to call religion". Similarly, Godwin Peak, in *Born in Exile* (1892), is a member of those enlightened folk who "take it for granted that a clear brain and religious orthodoxy are incompatible". Peak comes to regret his foolish simulation of orthodoxy (for motives of social ambition) and goes abroad to seek the company of "free, intellectual people—men who have done with the old conceptions". "Noble and generous freethinking" seems in fact, for Gissing, to be the one bright light in a world of darkness, meanness and sorrow.

The soul's happy release from orthodoxy is also recounted in the humorous story of *The Agnostic Island* (1891) by F. J. Gould. This tale tells of a party of distinguished Anglicans who set out as missionaries to convert the agnostics of a remote island, and find to their surprise that these agnostics are good, gentle, charming, charitable beings, in every way superior to themselves. The Rev. Philip Clerestory is quickly won over to the belief that the agnostic attitude is "a wiser, braver, happier attitude towards the problems of existence, and the conduct of life, than that which the Church teaches us to assume", and cheerfully resigns from the office of priest and the profession of Christianity to settle down to a blissful life of agnosticism on the island. This novel is as amusing in parts as W. H. Mallock's satiric picture of life on a positivist island in *The New Paul and Virginia* (1878), although the author is in complete sympathy with his island inhabitants (the satire is reserved for the Anglican missionaries) and anxious to show that the way of salvation lies through the abandonment of "perplexing creeds" and the adoption of this "most blessed religion" of agnosticism, which teaches people to be "pitiful and just and kind".

Much the same gospel had been preached in Beatrice Harraden's *Ships That Pass . in the Night* (1883), a best-selling novel that doubtless owed its extraordinary popularity to its mixture of agnostic propaganda with lush sentimentality. Its heroine goes about begging people to spread "a little kindness" in the world and consoles a dying man by telling him that, if there is a God, "he will understand better than ourselves that life is very hard and difficult, and he will be astonished *not because we are not better, but because we are not worse.*" (Optimistic kindness as a form of religion for agnostics and doubters was widely favoured, and was in fact closely related to the "social-welfare" versions of Christianity that we shall discuss in a later chapter.)

For the sheer delights of unbelief, however, we must turn to George du Maurier, whose characters are certainly the jolliest agnostics in all Victorian fiction. Most of them cannot be classed as those who have lost orthodoxy, for they have never really embraced it; they are "congenital agnostics" and their "profession of unfaith" is something very charitable and civilized. Their adventures, however sombre, are related in a gay, chatty style, and Peter Ibbetson, the hero of Du Maurier's first novel (1892), reveals, in spite of his melancholy experiences, that warm-hearted exuberance characteristic of his creator; he mocks gently and wittily at clergy of all denominations, just as his author did in the pages of *Punch*. Little Billee, in *Trilby* (1894), is another attractive agnostic. He describes himself as a man "whose only choice lay between Mr. Darwin and the Pope of Rome, and who has chosen once and for ever—and that long ago—before he'd even heard of Mr. Darwin's name", and his deathbed, far from revealing the weakness of agnosticism, shows its strength and shakes "the infallibility of a certain Vicar down to its very foundations". *Trilby* was published in the same year as *Jude the Obscure*;[1] both novels reveal a certain fatalist philosophy and in both orthodox religion is regarded as a totally ineffectual force in life, but no greater difference could possibly be found between the charming, effervescent Bohemian unbelievers of Du Maurier and the helpless, mournful, tragic figures of Hardy. Temperamental optimism and pessimism could clearly transfigure the spiritual lives of those who, standing outside all organized religion, lived devoid of either great faith or great hope.

The satiric masterpiece on the theme of departure from orthodoxy lay unpublished throughout these last years of Queen Victoria's

[1] *Jude* appeared in serial form in *Harper's Magazine* (1894–5), in book form in 1896.

reign and it was not until two years after the Queen's death that the horrified public were able to read *The Way of All Flesh*. Samuel Butler's novel is, as we have seen, an excellent satire on Broad-Church propaganda fiction; it is also a study of lost orthodoxy, for Ernest Pontifex discards his childhood beliefs, his Evangelical creed and his later High Church enthusiasms and becomes a dishonest doubter, practising cultured unbelief under the generous cloak of Broad Churchmanship. Butler's own loss of orthodoxy was, it must be remembered, a very real and important event in his life. He himself was destined for Holy Orders, and it was while acting as a kind of lay curate in London that he was attacked by doubts concerning biblical miracles and Anglican doctrines of infant baptism. These doubts, followed by years of careful study of theological writings and biblical criticism, and reinforced by his own natural revulsion from the Anglicanism exemplified by his parents, at length drove him far from orthodoxy into the adoption of an apparently cynical, tongue-in-the-cheek form of Christianity of very questionable sincerity.

In *The Way of All Flesh* Ernest's loss of orthodoxy is caused by the same two factors—disillusion with the spiritual integrity of actual practising Anglicans, and doubts as to the authenticity of the Bible. Such dissatisfaction, first with Christians themselves and then with their book, was a fairly common preliminary to loss of faith in the Victorian age—Mark Rutherford, it will be remembered, experienced this same double discontent. Indeed, it is interesting to compare the lives of Mark Rutherford and Ernest Pontifex. Both are brought up in a narrow faith and become ministers of religion. Both are possessed of extreme sensitivity and a naïveté which makes them easy victims of the unscrupulous and hypocritical orthodox. Both weigh their fellow Christians in the balance and find them wanting (Butler's portrait-gallery of unpleasant believers is as brilliant and devastating as White's), and both even agree to the extent of finding that people to whom the Christian faith means little or nothing are better-looking than their own associates in orthodoxy! (Mark Rutherford, as we have noticed, contrasts Mardon's face favourably with the rest of his flock, and Butler makes Ernest contrast his friend Towneley's face in the same way—"The faces of men like Towneley were open and kindly . . . the faces of Pryer [the curate] and his friends were not like this.") Both then doubt the truth of the Bible itself and, after conscientious study, reject orthodoxy, and both later come to distrust and disparage the intellect and all habits of metaphysical speculation, exalting in their place a kind of healthy commonsense indifference to such matters—clearly a reaction, in both cases, from the miseries of too much theological questioning and heart-searching. But whereas Mark Rutherford plods slowly on towards the Celestial City in pain and poverty, with Mr. Stand-fast as his only guide, Ernest is won over to the counsels of Mr. Money-Love and Mr. Worldly-Wiseman and cheerfully takes up his abode in Vanity Fair.

For—and this is an important difference—Ernest's loss of orthodoxy is not a parting with something valuable and irreplaceable, nor a separation from something outdated and outworn, but a deliberate rejection of something fundamentally fraudulent and harmful. The idea of Christianity as a lie, a humbug, a hoax and a cheat runs all through Butler's writings: he sees the older generation as the tricksters and the younger generation as the dupes. The lady who slept in John Pickard Owen's nursery when he was a child and said her prayers on the nights when she thought he was awake and omitted to say them on the nights when she thought he was asleep is, to Butler, typical of all practising Christians; their religion is a colossal piece of respectably organized deception calculated to ruin the lives of innocent young people. Thus Ernest's release from orthodoxy is viewed in the light of a young man's escape from a gang of swindlers, and such a liberation cannot be otherwise than beneficial in its effects. It is made clear that Ernest's rejection of orthodoxy (along with the rejection of his parents—"like giving up an aching but very loose and hollow tooth") brings him health, peace of mind, *"insouciance* and good humour". Darwin is now the ally and not the enemy: Ernest, we are told, "read Mr. Darwin's books as fast as they came out and adopted evolution as an article of faith", and money provides him with "the luxury of a quiet, unobtrusive life of self-indulgence"—a calm and pleasant existence in Vanity Fair.

The Way of All Flesh, in spite of its spiritually unsatisfying conclusions, indicates to a great extent that significant change of outlook towards "infidelity" in the nineteenth century. The doubter of orthodoxy in Victorian fiction has crept out from the condemned cell where, as a sinner and a criminal, he languished in misery like Dante's doubters in the clammy ooze of the Stygian marsh, and has now mounted his pedestal as the noble and praiseworthy hero to be generously rewarded and acclaimed. As we have seen, from the time of Froude's *Nemesis of Faith* onwards, the suspicion that men and women who questioned the truths of the Bible and the Churches were not necessarily monsters of wickedness was beginning to make itself felt in Victorian fiction, and with *The Way of All Flesh* the revolution is complete—the orthodox are the wicked and the doubters and deniers are the virtuous heroes to be crowned with health, wealth and happiness. The triumph of the sceptic is complete—his, indeed, is the success story of a great escape, and religious doubt, in the pages of the Victorian novel, has passed from its early and tentative presentation as an isolated evil, a tragedy or a pitiful disease, to reach its final glorification as the *sine qua non* of intelligent and enlightened humanity.

3

TOWARDS UNORTHODOX FAITH

CHAPTER 13

TOWARDS BEAUTY

THE relations between Christianity and the later Victorian novel are extremely complex. Although religious stories by orthodox writers continued to be produced throughout the century, novels of lost faith, as we have seen, became fashionable in the last decades of the Victorian age, and the best-sellers of later religious fiction were nearly all of the "up-to-date up-to-doubt class". Unbelief was in the air. According to the novelists, lords of the manor deplored the spread of infidelity in the village: " 'I'm an agnostic, Lord Clare'. That is what all the little girls say now ... and the boys, too, go about volunteering the quite unnecessary information that they know nothing." Thus complained Lord Clare in J. H. Shorthouse's novel *Sir Percival* (1886). Duchesses at the dinner-table, too, discussed the downfall of revealed religion: "Concerning Christianity, the poor system has been so belaboured of late with hard blows, that it is almost a wonder it still breathes", declared the Duchess de la Santoisie in Marie Corelli's *Ardath* (1889).

The "poor system", however, as well as continuing to have its orthodox adherents, had also

large numbers of supporters desirous of transforming it into something acceptable to the "enlightened" contemporary mind, supporters who,
refusing to take refuge in spiritualism, esoteric
Buddhism or any other of the religious cults
that became popular features of late Victorian
society, felt that the hope of the world still lay
in Christianity, but a Christianity shorn of many
of its traditional characteristics, a Christianity
purged, purified and transfigured. "La transformation graduelle du christianisme", was what
Taine, in writing to Mrs. Ward on the subject of *Robert Elsmere*, called "un des deux
problèmes capitaux du siècle."

Efforts at a kind of adaptation of Christianity
to special and individual requirements began
therefore to be made by certain writers and
thinkers. Mr. T. S. Eliot interprets the process
thus:

> The dissolution of thought in that age, the
> isolation of art, philosophy, religion, ethics
> and literature, is interrupted by various chi-
> merical attempts to effect imperfect syntheses.
> Religion became morals, religion became art,
> religion became science or philosophy; various
> blundering attempts were made at alliances
> between various branches of thought. Each
> half-prophet believed that he had the whole
> truth. The alliances were as detrimental all
> round as the separations.

In religious fiction especially we find tendencies by various novelists to mistake the part for the whole and to glorify isolated Christian virtues as a kind of religion in themselves. It is as if they had picked up pieces from the scattered mosaic of revealed religion and were holding out the broken fragments to us as complete and perfect pictures of the Christian ideal.

These "Christian deviations", as they have been styled, are numerous and of great interest in reflecting the spiritual needs and aspirations of the age. Three principal varieties of this "reduced" or "adapted" Christianity are traceable in the novels of the period: Christianity as the religion of beauty, Christianity as the religion of social helpfulness, and Christianity as the religion of the direct inspiration of Christ with no intervening media. From the first category emerges the story of the Christian as a worshipper of beauty, from the second the story of the Christian as a welfare worker, and from the third the story of the Christian as one directly influenced by Christ appearing himself as a character in the book. We may perhaps regard these beliefs and their fictional embodiments as the extensions of certain tendencies of High, Broad and Low Church respectively, or we may consider them with reference to the three absolute values of beauty, goodness and truth, and say that, for those Victorian novelists seeking to remould Christianity who were chiefly concerned with beauty, the ideal Christian becomes an aesthete, for those chiefly concerned with goodness, the ideal Christian becomes a social reformer, and for those chiefly concerned with truth, the ideal Christian becomes one who has direct contact with a divine Being. A glance at some representative novels of each type may help to make clearer these three separate approaches to the task of transforming Christianity and reveal the essential differences in the varieties of religious experience through which their leading characters pass.

When in the hands of the aesthetes religion becomes art, a mere department of the beautiful, the Christian hero is portrayed in their fiction as a well-bred hedonist whose sense of artistic rightness is more highly-developed than his sense of sin and whose religious experiences are in the nature of exquisite sensations and fastidious ecclesiastical pleasures. He is a spiritual voluptuary, who exalts beauty before truth, culture before charity and leisure before work. He is, of course, somewhat of a *rara avis* in religious fiction, for the majority of aesthetes did not write novels, still less religious novels in the accepted sense of the epithet. They were chiefly concerned with making a religion of art, not an art of religion, and, in general, valued orthodox

Christianity only in proportion to its power of satisfying, in the words of Dorian Gray, their "search for sensations that would be at once new and delightful, and possess that element of strangeness that is so essential to romance". Religious activity for most of them signified the occasional spectatorship of elaborate High-Church or Catholic ceremonial, and the usual attitude of the aesthetes and their followers to orthodoxy is perhaps best expressed by the hero of G. S. Street's satiric novel, *The Autobiography of a Boy* (1894), when he says:

> From a purely aesthetic point of view, there is much that is acceptable in the Church's ritual and surroundings. Why trouble about the import of her teachings? I never listen to them, or merely smile when some fragment of quaint dogmatism breaks in on my repose. But I love to sit in some old cathedral and fancy myself a knight of the middle ages, ready to die—dear foolish fellow!—for his simple faith.

But there were those who were seriously concerned with the idea of transforming Christianity into a faith compatible with certain contemporary aesthetic ideals, and who wrote fiction inspired by the earnest desire to "reconcile the artistic with the spiritual aspect of life". In their endeavour to adapt the Christian faith to their own needs as a kind of fine art and ingredient of culture they produced for us the spiritual biography of the aesthete in didactic religious fiction. Walter Pater is usually regarded as the innovator of this new species of religious novel, but in fact J. H. Shorthouse had already created the aesthete type in fiction five years before *Marius the Epicurean* was published. We have seen how *John Inglesant* (1880) was written as propaganda for the Anglican Church as opposed to the Catholic. It was also intended, as the author himself tells us, as "a protest on behalf of culture", written "to exalt the unpopular doctrine that the end of existence is not the good of one's neighbour but one's own culture". With this great article of the aesthetic *credo* Shorthouse occupied himself for many years, even to the extent of sending long and vague letters to Matthew Arnold on the subject, urging him to write a book on this new type of religion. (To which the apostle of culture politely but briefly replied that school-inspecting left him little time for such things.)

John Inglesant is the embodiment of Shorthouse's theories on art and religion, and its hero is the new type of saint in religious fiction—the well-dressed, well-groomed, gentlemanly connoisseur of the arts. Inglesant, feeble though his character is, can yet be distinguished by invariable sartorial elegance, a passion for the fine arts and a fondness for leisure and slumber as insatiable as that of Walter Pater himself. He dallies with philosophy after philosophy and his deepest spiritual experiences always take place amid scenes of surpassing beauty. Stained-glass windows, copes and candles and "exquisite music" all seem to be essential for his "spiritual visions". At Little Gidding it is the "exquisite strains of music" (Shorthouse overworks the word "exquisite" even more than Pater) and the "antique glass" in the East Window that cause him to be "lost in a sense of rapture". By Mary Collet's deathbed it is the "heavenly" sunshine and "the perfume of the hawthorn" that help to bring about his trance. His soul apparently can only lose itself and lie "silent and passive on the Divine" amid atmospheres rich with clouds of incense, twilit with the glimmer of sacred tapers in shaded chapels, or splendid with the delights of sunsets and glorious landscapes. All his religious experiences do in fact depend for their existence on the enjoyment of sensuous beauty, and without the aid of lovely lights, colours, scents and sounds he is unable to gain any form of contact with the divine. He favours Christianity in general and Anglicanism in particular because they provide excellent facilities for the enjoyment of such beauty and for the pursuit of this mysterious but invaluable thing, "culture". (Shorthouse uses the term in an even looser way than Matthew Arnold does.) A self-confessed epicure of his own emotions, Shorthouse associates religion, in *John Inglesant* at least, far too closely with culture, sunsets and gorgeous ceremonial. Reacting sharply from his Quaker upbringing, he seeks to ally the practice of Christianity with unlimited indulgence in the pleasures of intellectual and sensuous enjoyment. (He even recommended that agnostics should receive Holy Communion because of the "thrill" they would get out of it.) "In a perfectly good and prosperous world", he wrote to Lady Welby, "*enjoyment* would seem the only possible *occupation*. Therefore it would seem that enjoyment must be the end of all (*real*) existence. So far as this is true is it not a truth which has been too much overlooked by religious teachers and thinkers?"

In addition to *John Inglesant* Shorthouse wrote a "spiritual romance" to show the importance of reconciling art with religion, and the Prince, in *The Little Schoolmaster Mark* (1883–4), is another handsome, leisured, aristocratic hero, rejoicing in silk-embroidered clothes, priceless lace and a taste for "assorted colour and sweet sound and delicate pottery". In a later novel, *The Countess Eve* (1888), De Brie, the hero, is held up to us by Shorthouse as an ideal Christian youth, but his only motives for church-going seem to be his love of music and his enjoyment of "something that left the spirit better and more refined than before". ("Refined" is another dearly beloved word in the aesthetic vocabulary.) For him the safeguard and asylum "from all the attacks of Satan and of doubt" is not the existence of Christ and his Church but "the existence of beauty". De Brie and Robert Elsmere appeared in the same year; one could wish to hear these two heroes in argument together! De Brie, indeed, verges occasionally on the ridiculous and bears a dangerous resemblance to those aesthetic *précieux* so well parodied by *Punch* and Gilbert and Sullivan. But Shorthouse was in deadly earnest, and wrestled unceasingly with his problems of aestheticizing Christianity. "Is religion always to be a stranger and alien from Life's Feast?" he complained to Canon Carpenter, and again to Canon Ainger, "May not religion be conceived as a fine art?"

Canon Ainger's reply to this latter plea is not recorded, but the best answer, the classic response to such a question is provided by *Marius the Epicurean* (1885). Pater's masterpiece marks the full and glorious flowering of aesthetic romanticism in fiction, but it must not be forgotten that the author's whole purpose in writing his book was to show "the necessity of religion" and it thus lays claim to our consideration as a didactic religious novel.

Pater, like Shorthouse, was deeply interested in reconciling the artistic life with the life of religion and in showing an "individual mental pilgrimage" through the medium of the historical novel. To choose a period of Early Christian history as the setting for the spiritual biography of an aesthete might at first appear extremely foolish, for Christianity in the days of Fabiola, Callista and Hypatia was associated, in fiction if not in fact, with heroism rather than hedonism, with a life of sanguinary adventure, cruel persecution and most unaesthetic martyrdom rather than with a life of passive and cultured appreciation. But Pater hastens to justify his choice by claiming that this particular period in the Church's history (second-century Rome under the Antonines) was one when the "elegance of sanctity" and "aesthetic charm" of Christianity were being developed. He emphasizes this point more than once during the story.

> The ideal of asceticism [he writes] represents moral effort as essentially a sacrifice, the sacrifice of one part of human nature to another, that it may live the more completely in what survives of it; while the ideal of culture represents it as a harmonious development of all the parts of human nature, in just proportion to each other. It was to the latter order of

ideas that the Church, and especially the Church of Rome in the age of the Antonines, freely lent herself . . . For a little while at least, there was no forced opposition between the soul and the body, the world and the spirit, and the grace of graciousness itself was pre-eminently with the people of Christ.

The reader may be pardoned for showing slight scepticism here and a suspicion of historical distortions as biased—in a totally different direction—as Charles Kingsley's, but Pater is determined to subordinate the ascetic and militant character of early Christianity to its "serene, blithe and debonair" aspect, and, fitting style to content, he transforms that hardy annual, the "Early Christian novel" into a thing of surpassing beauty, an elaborate and carefully-wrought work of art, a triumph of highly finished and polished poetical prose, beside which the hastily-written *Fabiolas* and *Hypatias* seem mere crude adventure stories. Andrew Lang declared that although novels about the Early Church had always attracted the "intellectual middle classes", by the end of the century "not only the public but *les raffinés*" were addicted to them, and this extension of appeal can be traced directly back to Pater, who was the first to grace the Early Christian novel with a rare loveliness, a delicate, mystic and haunting beauty.

As a historical picture, of course, *Marius the Epicurean* is hardly accurate; too many uglinesses are carefully smoothed over by the rich cosmetics from the beauty-box of Pater's imagination. As propaganda, too, for "the necessity of religion" it has obvious weaknesses. But as an aesthete's apology, and an account of Pater's own spiritual rovings, it is splendidly rewarding. For the hero Marius (supposedly based on the character of Richard Jackson, a High Church cleric and friend of Pater's) emerges from the story as a self-portrait of the author. Most of Pater's heroes are reflections of the author's own personality—Florian, Sebastian von Storck, Gaston de Latour are all sensitive and sensuous idealists—and Marius is no exception. He is endowed with all Pater's "correctness of taste", his passion for visible beauty (that "lust of the eyes" that marked the true aesthete), his fondness for sleep, his sympathy with animals (excluding snakes), his love of ceremonial and ornate ritual, his "almost diseased sensibility to the spectacle of suffering" and his morbidity in matters of death, especially the death and burial of young children. Like Pater he has lost his father at an early age; he loses, too, his childhood beliefs and the interest of the novel, following a well-worn tradition of Victorian religious fiction, lies in his youthful quest for faith.

To pursue the comparison further we must give a short sketch of Pater's own religious history. In his youth he passed from fervent Ritualism (with a passion for organizing "little processional pomps") into the wilderness of unbelief, where he renounced all serious plans of ordination and indulged in offensive sneers against Christianity, retaining, however, his habit of churchgoing, which he regarded, in the true decadent aesthetic spirit, as a fruitful source of exquisite sensation. During this time he became absorbed in the study of different systems of Greek philosophy, particularly Epicureanism, and promulgated many of his famous teachings on the value of aesthetic experience—"not the fruit of experience, but experience itself, is the end"—and on the importance of "maintaining ecstasies", getting "as many pulsations as possible" out of life, and all those magic and memorable doctrines of the cult of beauty, a new and dangerously exciting goddess for Victorian youth to worship.

But in the eighteen-eighties, partly through the influence of Plato, the idea of discipline rather than pleasure began to take possession of Pater's mind and from that time onwards, his biographer tells us, "we find him crying, not 'Enjoy yourself', but 'Exercise Restraint'. . . One word was continually slipping from his mouth or his pen—the word *ascêsis*, an ecclesiastical term meaning 'restraint'—the restraint imposed upon himself by a monk". Towards the end of his life he drew nearer and nearer to the High-Church fold, becoming a regular communicant and reading "little else but the Bible, the Prayer Book and the Breviary", but, in spite of this apparent profession of faith, Richard Jackson, who probably knew more of the mysteries of Pater's inner life than anyone else, declared that his friend "could never truthfully be said to have become a Christian". Pater in fact never progressed very far beyond his conviction, expressed to Father Nugee some years before the writing of *Marius*, that the Church meant nothing to him "apart from its ornate services".

The hero of Pater's novel has, very broadly speaking, a similar spiritual history. We first see Marius as we first see Pater—absorbed in elaborate ceremonial and the prospect of priesthood. Marius is the devout acolyte of heathen mysteries, intending to become a priest of the religion of Numa. He then passes through a period of doubt and experiment. He has learned from pagan ceremony the idea of "a sort of hieratic beauty and order in the conduct of life"; he learns from Aesculapianism "a diligent promotion of the capacity of the eye" and from Aristippus and the new Cyrenaicism "a healthfully sensuous wisdom", an appreciation of "experience, concrete and direct". But he outgrows this last belief, and Pater, "sermonizing" in the true tradition of Victorian religious fiction, gives us some very earnest and persuasive preaching on the limitations of Cyrenaicism, a sermon which cannot fail to strike the reader as a recantation of Pater's previous ideas promulgated in the conclusion to his studies of the Renaissance.

Marius' conversion from faith in pleasure to faith in *ascêsis*, parallel to Pater's own, takes place when he goes to Rome and becomes a kind of amanuensis to the Emperor Marcus Aurelius. Here the Stoic philosopher convinces him that the will, even more than the eye, can be "an organ of knowledge, of vision", and that "flawless serenity" can be "better than the most pleasurable excitement". Here for the first time Marius learns the true value of discipline and control. Stoicism, however, does not content him; he finds it "gray and depressing". He dislikes the "melancholy intellectual attitude" of the Stoics and craves for something more satisfying and cheering. While still comparatively ignorant of Christianity, he feels the need for a Great Ideal pesonified, a friendly and companionable Creator, and his experience in the olive garden is perhaps the turning-point in his spiritual life. Pondering on the Emperor's words, " 'Tis in thy power to think as thou wilt", and pleasantly indulging in his fancy that he has had an unseen companion by his side all his life, Marius now suddenly feels for the first time the genuine presence of a "divine companion", an "unfailing 'assistant', without whose inspiration and concurrence he could not breathe or see, instrumenting his bodily senses, rounding, supporting his imperfect thoughts". This vivid realization, this new sense of "a friendly hand laid upon him amid the shadows of the world", makes for Marius this one particular hour "a marked point in life never to be forgotten". He has experienced, in the Augustinian sense, a true moment of understanding, and after this the outer world, we are told, becomes for him less real and "weaker in its hold". It was "as if he viewed it through a diminishing glass".

Had Pater only ended his novel here the meaning of it might have been less obscure and the spiritual biography of greater worth and integrity. It would have been the story of aestheticism outgrown, of the progress of the soul towards a realization of the presence and power of the Unseen. "Did Pater intend to tell us in his subdued way that he had exchanged the religion of sense for that of the spirit?" asked Dr. Barry. Marius' experience in the olive garden would suggest this, and the reader is led to expect that the hero's subsequent contact with Christianity will strengthen and confirm his new leanings towards the religion of the spirit rather than that of sense.

But unfortunately Christianity is introduced to Marius as a kind of intoxicant, enchanting the eye and ear with its lovely and decorative effects and bringing him back again to the exquisite enjoyment of a religion of the senses. Doubtless, Pater is here trying to show us that Christianity combines the best of Epicureanism with the best of Stoicism and is in fact an improvement on all that Marius—and Pater himself—had found attractive in other forms of religion and philosophy, but the impact of the Faith on Marius is described too overwhelmingly in terms of sensuous beauty.

What draws Marius to Cornelius, his first Christian friend, is his beautiful face and lovely hymn-singing. (Cornelius, rather than Marius, resembles Richard Jackson, who was distinguished for his handsome looks and the hymns that he composed.) Cornelius' physical attractiveness is heavily emphasized, and although Pater is at pains to tell us that Cornelius also possesses "an exquisite correctness of spirit" (whatever that may mean: such terms sound vaguely out of place when applied to a Roman soldier of the second century), Marius seems drawn to him

most of all by the beauty of his personal appearance, especially his face, which Pater compares
in detail to those in Renaissance paintings.
(Marius, unfortunately, cannot make such com-
parisons, but Pater is unable to resist them.)

Similarly Cecilia, the first Christian lady of
Marius' acquaintance, attracts the youth because
of her "virginal beauty". (This despite the fact
that she is a widow with several children. One
is reminded of one of Pater's earliest poems, "St.
Elizabeth of Hungary", a glorification of vir-
ginity, Pater's youthful enthusiasm for this state
leading him to ignore the fact that St. Elizabeth
had three children.) Cecilia reminds Marius of
"the best female statuary in Greece", and in her
house he revels in the "quiet signs of wealth and
taste" and particularly enjoys attending religious
services there. Pater gives us a lavish description
of Mass in the richly-decorated chapel of Cecilia's
house, and Marius, like a true aesthete, finds the
celebration of the Mass "a wonderful spectacle".

In death as well as life the decorative powers
of Christianity are a source of satisfaction to
Marius and the family burial place of the Cecilii,
full of "incense, light and flowers", with the
children's tombs charmingly decked with little
toys and tokens, contrasts favourably in his mind
with his own family resting place, all dark, dusty
and neglected, where chipped and fractured old

coffins occasionally reveal "a protruding baby hand" and the mouldering remains within. A Christian's death, for Marius, is not associated with any eschatological doctrines of the Faith but merely with the delights of an exquisitely adorned tomb in an aesthetically satisfying burial place.

This devotion to externals, this stress on certain accidents of religion at the expense of its essentials, tends to vitiate all Marius' dealings with Christianity. As Oscar Wilde noticed, Marius is "too much occupied with the comeliness of the benches of the sanctuary" to notice the real significance of the sanctuary and the message of its Founder. Similarly Marius' death, although "in the nature of a martyrdom", has little of the heroic and horrific elements in it. For an Early Christian martyr Marius is let off lightly, and although he has faced discomfort and fatigue and the possibility of torture, his final end is a martyrdom between the sheets, with the victim carefully tended and enjoying the happiness of "that great blessedness of physical slumber", the sweetness of being nourished with "mystic bread" (the Sacrament?) and the pleasant sensation of being gently massaged with medicinable oil.

It would perhaps be unfair to dismiss Pater's spiritual teachings along with Shorthouse's as

mere perversions of Christianity into a religion
of the senses. Pater's exceptional powers of "appreciation" and "passionate contemplation" enabled him to penetrate further into the profound
"mysticity" of the Christian religion than
Shorthouse ever did, and Marius, in his subtle
and delicate way, seems somehow nearer to the
Church than John Inglesant. But, in spite of
this, the shadow of distorted Ritualism and *fin-
de-siècle* decadence hangs over Marius just as it
does over Inglesant; both heroes associate the
Christian religion too exclusively with "strange
colours, and curious odours, or the work of the
artist's hands, or the face of one's friend," and
value it less for its call to redemption and
righteousness than for its strange and splendid
power of stirring the senses.

CHAPTER 14

TOWARDS GOODNESS

THESE aesthetes, toying with Christianity, indicate one line of development in Victorian religious fiction. Another and more popular tendency lay in a wholly different direction. With the decay of dogmatic religion many, to whom the thought of the enjoyment of beauty as the *summum bonum* was fundamentally unsound, followed the humanitarian and philanthropic ideals of the age and consoled themselves by thinking that what really mattered was to live a Christian life and do good to others rather than wallow in sensuous beauty or engage in fruitless theological controversies. They regarded a true Christian life as one spent, not in contemplation or argument, but in active and ceaseless labour for one's fellow-creatures, especially among the poor.

This ideal of social helpfulness, with its roots in the Christian ethical tradition, in nineteenth-century Evangelical philanthropy and in certain tendencies of Christian Socialism, proved more congenial to the average Victorian than the ideals of the aesthetes, and the Religion of Duty inspired many more souls and novels than the Religion of Beauty. "The worship of Deities has passed into the service of man", wrote Cotter Morison triumphantly in his once-famous essay "Towards the Religion of the Future", and already in the Victorian age Divine Service was becoming for many "human service". At that time, of course, social and economic conditions, especially in the large towns, were such that the reforming urge was common to most thinking men and women, whatever their creed. Social work, as well as playing a large part in the lives of zealous Anglicans, Catholics and Nonconformists, was one of the principal concerns of the Comtists and became, too, the refuge of the agnostics and the doubters. Not only do the young clerical heroes of later Victorian fiction tackle the task of slum reform (Father Adderley's Stephen Remarx and Hall Caine's John Storm lead this valiant group) but the unsatisfied sceptics in the novels of Hale White and Gissing also plunge themselves into good works in the poorer quarters of London. The ancient sage's advice:

Let be thy wail and help thy fellow men,

is taken by countless heroes and heroines of widely differing faiths in later Victorian religious novels.

To many of them, however, this kind of work is neither an act of charity commanded by their Church nor a relief from their own burden of doubt and despair, but a complete expression of Christian faith in itself. Christianity is portrayed as little more than an agency for social reform, and the leading characters, having once contacted this agency, become instantly transformed into the most energetic and saintly welfare workers. For them religion means conduct— Christ is an example to follow (chiefly on account of his dealings with the poor and the sick) rather than a God to worship, and conversion means a conviction of the necessity of social redemptive work and is usually effected by the realization, either through study, conversation or first-hand experience, of the horrors of city slums. Sin is chiefly associated in their minds with such conditions rather than with any interior state (Mrs. Humphry Ward, it will be remembered, believed firmly in the connection of sin with "physical and social and therefore *removable* conditions") and theology, dogma and church-going are frequently regarded as unimportant forms of bewilderment. A simplified version of the New Testament (emphasizing the Sermon on the Mount and the parables of the Good Samaritan and the Prodigal Son) is their Bible; their conscience is the guilty social conscience of Victorian England, the spirit of zeal is their most sought-after spiritual gift and their supreme virtue is the virtue of social activity.

All this, of course, is partly a reaction from the overdose of theological perplexities and soul-searchings brought on by the Oxford Movement and again by the "sceptic movement" (a great many people got the double dose), and characters no longer spend most of the story arguing about the finer niceties of baptismal regeneration or the historic value of testimony but, embracing the "new gospel" enthusiastically after a miserable period of existence as orthodox bigots or indifferent Christians or unhappy doubters, rush out into the slums of London, rescuing fallen women, tearing shirts off their backs to clothe the ragged, saving would-be suicides from the river's brink, selling their waistcoats to give breakfast to the starving, founding societies or brotherhoods of their own, preaching to crowds of working men in disused warehouses, studying the writings of the Booths and F. D. Maurice, and nearly always dying an untimely death from overwork, or from fever caught through nursing the sick in some squalid hovel, or from persecution by the enemy; a martyr's death in the cause of "social endeavour".

Fiction might be expected to benefit from this emphasis on action rather than argument, but only too frequently propaganda for the new faith rather spoils the narrative, as can be seen in the novels of George Macdonald, which show

us some of the earliest representatives in Victorian fiction of this new type of philanthropic
hero. In *David Elginbrod* (1863) we are introduced to the noble Robert Falconer, who
embodies Macdonald's ideas of what a true Christian should be. "It was not often that Falconer
went to church" we are told (only, in fact, when
F. D. Maurice was preaching), and he pities foolish people who think that theology must be like
a map with plenty of lines on it, for he knows
that God draws only "pure lines, without
breadth and consequently invisible to mortal
eyes". But he practises brotherly love, feeding
the hungry and assisting the sick and desperate,
even to the extent of providing them with
twenty-pound notes and first-class railway fares
to Scotland! His life story is told in full in a
later novel, *Robert Falconer* (1868). We have
already mentioned its valuable study of a child
sceptic. But when Robert comes to maturity,
settles in London and joins the "brotherhood in
Christ" among the poor of the city, as his name-
sake in Mrs. Ward's novel does twenty years
later, he loses much of his individuality and
vitality and becomes just another over-idealized
social-worker hero. His actual conversion is
brought about through his contact with the poor,
and particularly through his discovery of his own
father, a broken-down victim of alcohol and

opium, in a most sordid quarter of the metropolis, and his religious convictions may be seen from his conversation with an interested enquirer:

"Do you lay claim to no epithet of any sort?" [asks the enquirer.]

"We are a church if you like. There!" [replies Falconer.]

"Who is your clergyman?"

"Nobody."

"Where do you meet?"

"Nowhere."

"What are your rules, then?"

"We have none."

"What makes you a church?"

"Divine Service."

"What do you mean by that?"

"The sort of thing you have seen tonight. [i.e., rescue work among the poor.]

"What is your creed?"

"Christ Jesus."

Most of George Macdonald's heroes end up with this kind of creed. In *Thomas Wingfold, Curate* (1876), an Anglican cleric loses his faith and then comes to realize that the only "true and genuine" Divine Service is "helpfulness", and in the sequel to this novel, *Paul Faber, Surgeon* (1879), he converts a sceptical medical man

to this point of view. It is not made clear to the
reader whether the surgeon has conquered his
religious doubts caused by the conflict between
science and orthodoxy—"he would not say he
was a believer in the supernal", says his author
cautiously—but he believes in the power of good
works, which, for Macdonald is all-sufficing. Conduct, for Macdonald and for all his characters
who see the light, has become three-fourths of
life or more, and conduct must be primarily
directed towards the amelioration of the lot of
the suffering poor. This message Macdonald
preaches in almost all his novels, and although
he confesses to a "monotony of theme", he
attempts to justify this by declaring that, having
been deprived of his pulpit by the Congregational Church, he is using the novel as a substitute medium for the dissemination of his religious
convictions. Thus in his novels he rather regret-
tably subordinates his delightful poetic imagination, his mystical religious fervour, his dry and
subtle Scottish wit and his deep understanding
of childhood (so prominent in his verse and his
juvenile fiction) to the ends of propaganda for
the cause of practical social helpfulness, and
busies himself with spiritual biographies of the
Christian as social worker that are the most
monotonous and the least inspiring of all his
creations.

In the eighteen-seventies Mrs. Lynn Linton also began to preach a similar message in the novel and her hero in *The True History of Joshua Davidson* (1872) is a young man who, disgusted with the clergy, decides to follow the life of Jesus "literally, in simple exactness, and as we find it set before us in the gospels". This decision takes him to the East End of London, where he starts a night school for the working classes and teaches morality and good cooking to thieves, drunkards and lost women. Killed in riots organized by a hostile vicar, he is a martyr to what his author calls "true Christian communism". Mrs. Lynn Linton's sentimentality, her uncontrolled anti-clerical outbursts and her complete inability to describe the inner life of her characters make this rather an exasperating novel, but the whole theme of the book and the extraordinary popularity of its reception indicate the new trend of religious thought in the Victorian age, the movement of mind away from the Churches and nearer to suffering mankind, the "abandonment of the dead mystical for the living real", the growing confusion between Divine Service and human service, the increasing rejection of dogma in favour of duty, of theory in favour of practice, or churchmanship in favour of neighbourliness, processes of thought that were to prepare the way for *Robert*

Elsmere sixteen years later and make it the most
fashionable religious novel of the century.

Mrs. Ward, of course, is gifted with far greater
intellectual and spiritual discernment than Mrs.
Linton, and does not falsify religious issues by
oversimplification. Her heroes do not merely
turn their backs on the Churches, open the New
Testament and then fly to the slums, as Mrs.
Linton's and George Macdonald's tend to do.
She sees more clearly the conflicts, the lapses of
all those who have lost faith in traditional Christianity and are trying so earnestly to "reconceive
in Christ". Yet for all her spiritual insight she
ruins the later Elsmere, as we have seen, by
idealizing him too much, and having launched
him into "the full stream of religion-making"
she turns him into a propaganda prig as faultless
and dull as any of the priggish clerical heroes in
the theological novels of the eighteen-forties.

Nor is David Grieve, the hero of Mrs. Ward's
next novel on the subject (*The History of David
Grieve*, 1892), a great improvement. He rejects
orthodoxy but writes New Testament tracts,
runs a bookshop on philanthropic lines and
works for the "sick and unfortunate". But the
account of his spiritual travels, his long and
weary journey towards "the Christianity of the
future", is very muddled and lacks the vivid
moments and clearcut divisions that mark Robert Elsmere's spiritual history. He has none of

the dynamic enthusiasm of Elsmere or the "kindled mind" of Mrs. Ward's later Modernist hero, Richard Meynell, and his acceptance of the "new Christianity" does not entirely satisfy him. He still craves for "the last glow, the certainties, the *vision* of faith", and realizes, as Mrs. Ward herself, in her less sanguine moments, realized, the limitations of the new religion and the joys denied to those for whom Christianity has become "a system of practical conduct, based on faith in God and on the inspiring memory of a great teacher, rather than a system of dogma based on a unique revelation".

Such misgivings about their new faith, however, were not common to the majority of philanthropic heroes in later Victorian fiction; most of them continue the tradition of George Macdonald's heroes and radiate joyous, confident energy in their new-found vocation. Conversion gives them enormous happiness, enthusiasm and certainty and they become "instinct with all the burning fire of brotherliness", as W. H. Mallock described them in his brilliant and wicked satire on this "religion of social endeavour" in *The Individualist* (1899). Novels that could mingle the excitements of reform and romance in sufficiently thrilling proportions were sure to become best-sellers, as the stories of Edna Lyall and Hall Caine showed. Edna Lyall's rather surprising statement, "I should call all lovers of humanity Christians whether they are consciously followers of Christ or not", was considered a very beautiful sentiment, particularly suitable for late Victorian Birthday Books, and the public was quite taken by John Storm, Hall Caine's romantic slum-reforming hero in *The Christian* (1897), who, like Carlyle, believed in the "glorious gospel" of work, but who, unlike Carlyle, enjoyed aristocratic charm and a glamorous love affair with an actress while working out his "new social application" of the Christian creed.

Highly popular, too, were the stories written by the Hocking brothers, which tell of similar humanitarian enthusiasms. In *For Light and Liberty* (1892), a novel by Silas Hocking (himself an ardent disciple of George Macdonald), the hero, brought up by a cynical uncle who laughs "softly and contemptuously" at Christianity, is converted to the new faith by an American, Mr. Short. (America produced many enthusiasts for the "do-good" religion.) Radiant with belief, the hero studies the New Testament and declares:

> The more I read the gospels the more I feel this, that conduct is three parts of life. It seems to matter precious little what we believe unless we live up to it. I think I shall never wrangle, Mr. Short, about creeds and ecclesiasticism. Such things may have their place but

they do not impress me. They do not feed the hungry or heal the sick, and that was what Jesus Christ was always doing.

With these convictions the hero immediately begins work among the poor, and the practical fruits of his conversion are seen in the founding of a wood-carving school for labourers and the transformation of his manor-house into "a home of rest for sick and poor and deserving people".

In *One in Charity* (1893) by the same author, the controversy and bitterness that grow out of "gloomy dogmas" are forgotten when an outbreak of fever comes to the village and those of differing creeds become "one in charity" and join together in nursing the sick. Several characters learn from this the importance of social work and the love of one's neighbour. "He ain't got no theology to boast of, but he's charity, an' that's better than argiments", say the village people of the Vicar, who is presented as the ideal type of Christian. In *God's Outcast* (1898) a young minister loses faith and finds it only through "social and philanthropic schemes", and in *The Awakening of Anthony Weir* (1901) another young minister follows a similar course. The joy of conversion to such belief is greatly stressed here and the awakened Anthony Weir loses all his melancholy and becomes a lover of "mirth and music and laughter and all manly games". The philanthropist hero, we are assured, is "no moping, tearful saint". Spiritual progress, for Silas Hocking, means growing out of any dependence on dogmatic theology, so unsatisfactory, so conducive to controversy and misery, and finding happiness and inspiration in relieving the lot of suffering mankind. Religion is tending towards "anthropolatry", as Cotter Morison indicated.

Silas' brother Joseph was possessed of similar convictions, perhaps best expressed in his novel *All Men are Liars* (1891). His hero, disillusioned and pessimistic, takes to drink and gambling and tries to commit suicide, but is saved by his friend, a doctor practising in the slums of Battersea. The doctor's preaching of the new, non-ecclesiastical and socially redemptive Christianity, his revelation of the horrors of life in Battersea (some vivid pictures here) and his efforts to impress upon the hero the need for rescue work there, all combine to bring about a conversion and the hero comes to see that "Jesus Christ is the world's hope—in spite of the sneers of the times". Dynamic practical helpfulness now replaces self-torment and the hero's joy is crowned by his marriage to a fallen woman whom he himself has saved. (This new religion gives its novelists good opportunities for breaking conventions and permitting a happy marriage

to a woman with an "evil past".) Throughout the story the author repeatedly tells us that
there is little else but "bigotry, narrowness, caste
and hollow formalism" in organized Christianity,
and that the only true Christians are those who
go out into the highways and byways and help
their needy fellow-creatures.

In the same year appeared an equally earnest
and vigorous manifesto of "this religion of
human help": W. J. Dawson's *The Redemption
of Edward Strahan* (1891). Edward, sickened by
the hypocrisy of Church and Chapel alike—
"Christianity in London appears to be bankrupt"—is converted to the religion of social
helpfulness by a virtuous young girl Alice and
her sister Mary, who assure him that "every
Church is, after all, a commercial establishment",
and confess that "human kindness is about the
only form of religion we hunger and thirst for".
(Propaganda for "kindness" as a species of religion had been most successfully employed by
Beatrice Harraden in her best-selling novel
Ships that Pass in the Night (1883).) These two
saintly sisters inspire the hero with the "enthusiasm of humanity". He meets members of the
Salvation Army and declares that "they have laid
hold of the two most potent forces in the world,
and know how to use them: they believe in
Hope and Brotherhood." In his "newborn

humanitarian passion" Edward follows in the footsteps of Robert Elsmere, goes to Shoreditch, rents a disused warehouse and runs there a reading-room, a gymnasium and a canteen which sells a good cup of coffee for a halfpenny. He catches fever while nursing a sick barmaid, but recovers to marry Mary and give the story a happy ending. This is a lively and readable book, with plenty of realistic touches, but the hero becomes even more priggish than Robert Elsmere and his spiritual progress is painfully crude and at times even comic in its improbability.

This crudeness and lack of subtlety are apparent in nearly all the novels dealing with such characters: a logical consequence, perhaps, of the treatment of Christianity purely as a system of conduct. The Christian as a social worker, a single-minded man of action, fighting shy of creed, dogma and controversy and concentrating exclusively on clearcut practical everyday affairs, must inevitably be a stranger to the world of finer and more complex spiritual problems, and this distinctly altruistic brand of Christianity, however popular it may have been among those Victorians who, having lost faith in the supernatural part of Christianity, still clung to those lofty conceptions of duty that characterized the period, yet has definite limitations in the

spiritual sphere. With the advent of the Welfare
State in England the modern reader is made
acutely aware of these limitations, but even
those Victorians unacquainted with the benefits
of any National Health Services realized that
something important was lacking in this ardent
exaltation of philanthropy as a complete expression of Christian belief. Canon Scott Holland's
criticism of this religion may well be applied to
the religious novels it inspired. Condemning
W. T. Stead's *Church of the Future* (1891)—one
of several attempts at this time to promote a
Church "with the sole motto, to do good"—Scott
Holland wrote:

> Everyone can whoop, and throw up his hat
> and cry, "Come and do good! all of you, what-
> ever your creed or system! Come along!" So
> easy it is, till we touch the next question.
> "How can I do good? I can't, I don't want to,
> or I have the wish and not the will. I want to
> do good, and lo! I do evil. I do the thing
> which I hate. I cannot do the thing that I
> would."
>
> It is only at this point the hitch begins. The
> division between men begins at the point
> where the question arises, "Can I do good at
> all? Only Christ can do it" ... Mr. Stead
> leaves off before the difficulties of the Churches
> begin.

Similarly, we may say that these novels all leave off before the difficulties of real religious development begin. They are probably of more value as social than spiritual documents, for although they give us some interesting portraits of high-minded and public-spirited people, they give us more insight into the seamy side of late Victorian England than into any particular individual, and their authors are for the most part more concerned with laying bare the horrors of the hovel, the gin-palace and the gambling den than with exploring and revealing the workings of the human soul. A purely "do-good" religion has strikingly obvious defects, although, as these novels show, it supplied the dynamic for a full and active life of charity and hope to so many God-seeking Victorians for whom faith in orthodoxy was a thing of the past.

CHAPTER 15

TOWARDS TRUTH

THE aesthetes who went to church for transports of sensuous delight and the social enthusiasts who left the Church to move nearer to the slums indicate two paths taken by late Victorian pilgrims in search of the Christian faith. A third path led, like the second, away from the Church, but to Holy Lands rather than hovels, to realms dominated by the suffering figure of Christ himself rather than by suffering mankind, to regions where the divine presence shone full and clear in glory and majesty, even though such a pilgrim's progress might necessitate space travel. Perplexed and wearied by the battles of the Churches, sickened by the conflicts between the scientists and the orthodox, an ever-increasing number of souls in late Victorian England thirsted for some simple and direct inspiration from Christ himself, or from a divine source.

It was Disraeli, in *Tancred* (1847), who really introduced this theme into the Victorian religious novel, forty years before it was to become more generally popular. Readers of *Tancred* will remember that the young hero, "born in an age and in a country divided between infidelity on

one side and on anarchy of creeds on the other",
craves for direct and divine guidance on matters
of faith and duty. "It is time," he says, "to re-
store and renovate our communications with the
Most High", and for this purpose he goes to
Palestine (the alternative title of the novel is
The New Crusade), and here he has visions and
listens to a "voice from heaven" preaching to
him.

Tancred, in his impatience with organized religion and his demand to be instructed at first
hand by heavenly messengers, anticipates a later
trend of Victorian thought, and his wish to see
an angel rather than a bishop at Manchester
was probably shared by many as the century
advanced, many who regretted, as Tennyson did,
that God appeared only as

> a cloud and a smoke who was once a
>   pillar of fire,
> The guess of a worm in the dust and the
>   shadow of its desire.

People were longing, as George Eliot expressed
it, for "perfectly clear messages" from "the se-
raphs of unfailing wing and piercing vision",
and lamenting, as Florence Kingsley the American novelist lamented, that "in these hard grey
days there is no glory that shines, no voice that
speaks, no ecstatic vision of the Son of Man

standing at the right hand of power". This
hunger for vivid and marvellous experience of
the divine, the miraculous and the unseen is
associated, too, with the revival of interest in the
occult which spread over England in the eighteen-eighties and nineties. Visionaries and mystics such as Swedenborg, Buddha and Madame
Blavatsky, the spiritualist celebrity, all became
fashionable teachers, while theosophical societies,
psychical research and "miracle clubs" (often
imported from America) flourished abundantly,
as those who felt that Christianity was almost
bankrupt turned eagerly to the study of Eastern
philosophies and to the exploration of occult
forces of all kinds.

The demand by so many Doubting Thomases
to see the truth for themselves was met in fiction
by the spiritual biographies of those who received direct inspiration from supernatural
heavenly influences and who were converted not
by Bibles or clergy or Churches or Christians or
the sight of human suffering, but by Christ
himself appearing in person in the story. This
daring innovation, the portrayal of Christ in the
religious novel, is first revealed in the body of
"New Testament fiction" that grew up towards
the end of the nineteenth century, itself a development of the Early Christian novel, which
as we have seen, rose to heights of great popularity in the Victorian age. But until the last

decades of Queen Victoria's reign few Early
Christian novels had ever ventured to deal with
the actual lifetime of Christ on earth—they
usually stopped short at St. Paul or Rome in the
first century of the Christian era. "The Christian
world would never tolerate a novel with Jesus
Christ as its hero", thought General Lew Wallace—quite mistakenly, as it proved, for the
overwhelming success of his *Ben Hur* (1880) in
England as well as America showed that the time
was ripe for the presentation of scenes from the
Gospels in fiction, and by 1898 Andrew Lang
was complaining that "the modern novelist...
makes his raids on the New Testament. Here he
finds plots and characters ready made", although
he rather grudgingly admitted the value of such
novels:

> They exactly answer in our day, and grant-
> ing our social conditions, to the old dramas in
> which Biblical History was acted in Miracle
> and Mystery plays, they fill up the space which
> the imagination leaves vacant and show the
> characters in real dresses and properties.

Many of these religious novels lie outside our
limits of time and place, for it was on American
soil that this New Testament fiction flourished
most exceedingly, and until the appearance of
George Moore's *The Brook Kerith* (1916) English fiction had nothing to compare with the

stories of Florence Kingsley or W. F. Cooley or
E. S. Brooks on the other side of the Atlantic.
America took to "Gospel novels" as a duck takes
to water; stories of Judas Iscariot and Mary
Magdalene were widespread and tremendously
popular—and despite some occasional lapses into
shockingly bad taste, nineteenth-century American novelists soon succeeded in accustoming the
reading public to the idea of Christ in fiction,
not only through New Testament novels but also
through the "what would Jesus do?" type of
fiction (stories of contemporary life showing
Christ revealing true religion to weak and sinful
moderns). It was in fact a visiting English
journalist, W. T. Stead, who first inspired this
latter kind of novel by his sensational and provocative work *If Christ came to Chicago* (1894),
but England never developed the theme in her
fiction as America did and never produced any
novel as influential as, for example, C. M. Sheldon's *In His Steps* (1896). But let us look at the
English contribution to these particular literary
fields, meagre though it may be.

One of the first Victorian novelists to attempt
the story of someone influenced by Christ himself as a character in the novel was Dr. E. A.
Abbott in his *Philochristus, Memoirs of a Disciple of the Lord* (1878). Dr. Abbott holds to the
view of Christianity expressed in one of his later

novels: "It has been said that the religion of the Christians is a person—and nothing more. I should prefer to say the same thing differently. Our religion is a person—and nothing *less*." But the difficulties of portraying Christ in a story loom large. Dr. Abbott is cautious, anticipating Lew Wallace's decision to be "religiously careful that every word He uttered should be a literal quotation from one of His sainted biographies", and depicting Christ by showing his effect on others rather than by any purely personal description, the "lineaments of the countenance of Christ" being seen "as by reflexion, in the life of one that loved him". Although Dr. Abbott brings to the task great reverence and profound scholarship, the novel is a tedious one; its archaic English is badly suited to fiction and at times the story degenerates into a mere pedantic and stodgy biblical commentary. Matthew Arnold called it "neither quite a work of art nor quite a direct treatment of its subject, but something betwixt and between", which sums it up perfectly.

A slightly less timid and academic effort at this kind of fiction was made by J. Jacobs in his novel *As Others Saw Him* (1895), an attempt to tell of the influence of Christ on an imaginary Jewish Scribe, a member of the Sanhedrim. Jacobs, more than Dr. Abbott, succeeds in describing something of the great joy and enchantment of those personally influenced by Christ, although at the risk of putting his own words into the mouth of Christ. This jars slightly, and the patchiness of the story and the inartistic intrusion of rather dull propaganda at the end jar even more.

This scanty yield might have represented Victorian England's main contribution to this type of religious novel, had not Marie Corelli saved the situation by rushing in where more learned novelists feared to tread. Not only did she popularize New Testament fiction in England, but she rescued the religious novel from the somewhat depressing rut of practical rationalism and pessimism into which it had fallen and exalted it into the glorious, miraculous and often very dizzy heights of a most vivid and extraordinary Christocentric supernaturalism. "You certainly tell of marvellous things in a marvellous way", said Oscar Wilde to Marie Corelli, and no religious novel from this amazing pen is complete without a series of swoons, trances, psychic experiences, visitations of angels and aerial spirits, and generally an ecstatic vision of Christ himself to crown the day. In spite of the very glaring defects and limitations of Marie Corelli's sensational approach and style it is an undeniable fact that she brought zest, vitality, vision and imagination to Victorian religious fiction at a time when it most needed them. Queen Victoria, Gladstone, Tennyson, and Anglican and Catholic clergy alike, were quick to praise her colourful efforts to uphold the cause of Christianity in fiction at a time when it was fashionable to decry it, to write enthusiastically of the supernatural as a Christian rather than as a spiritualist or a theosophist, and to accept the findings of contemporary science as a confirmation rather than a denial of the divine order.

Marie Corelli's first novel, *A Romance of Two Worlds* (1886), is one of the most entertaining stories of religious conversion ever written. It is unashamedly propagandist—Marie Corelli expounds in detail her extraordinary theories of the "electric principle" of Christianity—but it has a vivacity and a bold imaginative appeal denied to most propaganda fiction of the nineteenth century. Although its author is, in Rebecca West's phrase, riding the "tosh-horse" at full gallop, the story is still exciting and even gripping in an age when so many accounts of conversion in Victorian fiction are quite unreadable. The young heroine, *"one of the rare few with whom the Soul is everything"* (italics the author's), wishes, like so many late Victorians, "to prove . . . the truth and necessity of religion". Her desperate longings "to be certain of the truth of Christianity" must have been shared by many of her readers, but few of them were lucky enough to be helped in their quest for faith as she was by a Chaldean "physical electrician" named Heliobas, who believed that "God's cable is laid between us and His Heaven in the person of Christ". (The first public electricity supply stations were just being developed in England at this time—Marie Corelli's religion was always in line with current events.) Heliobas, by his supernatural electric powers, sends her wandering through space accompanied by an angelic guide named Azul. The descriptions of the young girl's journey through the universe, surrounded by whirling planets and burning comets and waves of fire and light, is a genuine triumph of the imagination. It anticipates much modern space-travel fiction and combines the pseudo-scientific detail of such stories with the fervent religious marvelling reminiscent of St. John's revelations and the ecstasies of the mystics. The girl visits Venus, Saturn and Jupiter; she sees rays of light slanting in the form of a cross, and in the centre of the innermost "electric circle" she is permitted to see Christ himself. The fiery waves of light part and there approaches her "that supreme Figure, upon whose broad brows rested the faint semblance of a Crown of Thorns". He addresses her in a voice "penetratingly sweet"; he even touches her. "I felt a touch upon me like a scorching flame", she tells us, "a thrill rushed through my being." Here at last is the ultimate certainty, the direct contact with the divine that so many Victorians, appalled by the rise and power of agnosticism, were yearning for!

After leaving Christ "standing serene and smiling between the retiring waves of radiance", she comes down to earth again, and as a result of this unforgettable experience she is completely transformed and becomes "as plump and pink as a peach". (Marie Corelli's heroines, unlike Newman's, invariably find that religious conversion restores them to health and youthfulness and increases their physical attractiveness tenfold.) Not only does the heroine amaze her friends by her radiant beauty, she also surprises them by her knowledge and perspicuity; for she can now "perceive with almost cruel suddenness the true characters of all those" whom she meets. She urges others to cultivate the electric force within them, as Heliobas helped her to do, and the story ends with an impassioned appeal to all readers to forsake their materialism and lust of gain and believe in true Christianity.

After this remarkable work Marie Corelli did not bring Christ into her fiction for some time, although in *Ardath* (1889) the "electric Christian" Heliobas, now a monk, brings about the

conversion of an agnostic and despairing poet by
sending him on the most extraordinary journeys
through space and time. (Marie Corelli here has
much to say about contemporary scepticism and
the "poison of doubt". She cites St. Paul, Andrew
Lang and Mrs. Humphry Ward as enemies of
true Christianity—St. Paul apparently having
ruined the beautiful simplicity of the faith by
his preaching! She also disposes of the conflict
between science and religion thus: "Evolution
from what? . . . From one atom? What atom?
And *from whence* came the atom? And why the
Necessity of any atom?") The poet does not
actually see Christ, but angelic spirits and celestial forms surround him and Edris, a particularly
attractive female spirit, soon restores him to
faith. He returns to earth and fills his worldly
friends with "unmitigated amazement" at his
good looks (he is now sunburnt, magnetic and
"more than handsome") and still more at his
declaration, "I am a Christian", although he
hastens to explain that his is a Christianity
"without any church-dogma" and "set forth in
a 'new vehicle and vesture' to keep pace with the
advancing enquiry and scientific research of
man". The reward for his conversion is marriage
to Edris, for this beautiful female spirit has now
most conveniently become human and after a
series of shocks, thrills, shudders, agonized en-
trancements and ecstasies of passionate awe and

rapture, the poet (despite his dislike of churches) is united to this marvellous creature with "Christ's most holy blessing" in Cologne Cathedral.

It is not surprising that, with this talent for the weird and the wonderful, Marie Corelli's excursion into New Testament fiction should be slightly different from that of Jacobs and Dr. Abbott. If their tales smell of the lamp hers reek of the most powerful and pungent of exotic perfumes, and although in *Barabbas* (1893) she exercises reverential care in depicting the figure of Christ, she surrounds the central episode of the Crucifixion with a dazzling display of angels, thunderstorms, whirlwinds, visions, stabbings, swoonings, ecstatic trances and lovers' meetings. Barabbas the Robber is intended to represent "a type of human Doubt aspiring unto Truth"; he is converted by the sight of Christ, after which, like all Marie Corelli's converts, he becomes more attractive—"a great beauty illumined his dark features"—and while cast into prison he sees Christ again and is drawn upwards into heaven by him. Thus he dies, having indulged even more than any other Corellian hero or heroine in the wildest excesses of violent sensations and passionate feelings, his spiritual experiences having frequently caused his blood to freeze, his tongue to cleave to the roof of his mouth and his entire being to be seized with fits of shuddering or states of "transcendent ecstasy" or "stupefied, fascinated amazement". The whole novel, a passion play in more senses than one, leaves the reader astonished and not a little exhausted by the imaginative audacities of the author and the exaggerated emotional responses of Barabbas the Robber. Never has any spiritual ascent from "doubt" to "truth" been accompanied by so many thrills, ecstasies and raptures.

In *The Master-Christian* (1900), Marie Corelli essays something slightly different—a study in human saintliness, and in this novel she makes Christ appear to a holy and devout man, a noble Christian whose pure soul, spotless character and beautiful looks seem in no need of reform. Cardinal Felix Bonpré is well portrayed as a model cleric, but his good deeds shine in a very naughty world, for the rest of the Roman clergy, from the Pope downwards, receive the fiercest lashes of Marie Corelli's disapproval, and the Cardinal's problem and indeed the *Leitmotiv* of the novel, is "Christ or the Church? Which must I follow to be an honest man?" Here again we have stated for us in fiction a problem that must have agitated thousands of sincere Victorians, reluctantly tending towards Tennyson's pessimistic verdict that "the churches have killed their Christ". To settle this problem Marie Corelli, as usual, resorts to an actual *Deus ex machina*, for the waif Manuel, whom the Cardinal finds and befriends, is really Christ in disguise and he helps the Cardinal to perform miracles and to look beyond the Church, as so many Victorians were trying to do. Marie Corelli's rabid anti-clericalism weakens the story considerably and her *penchant* for swoonings and stabbings is very much in evidence here; the whole novel is in fact the usual Corellian mixture of high idealistic vision and low melodrama.

It is perhaps this daring and dazzling blending of the human and the divine, the seen and the unseen, that gives Marie Corelli's stories their unique appeal. Her success as a best-selling religious novelist too lies partly in her triumphant treatment of science as the handmaid of religion —few theological novelists of the time bothered themselves with electricity and atoms as she did —and partly in her genius for combining the most colourful sensationalism with the most sincere and genuine reverence and faith. She had her finger on so many of the most urgent religious problems of the day, and in a period of widespread spiritual perplexity her novels provided not only lively entertainment but a genuine help and inspiration to many people "groping after lost Christianity", as she expressed it. If today we find it impossible to take the spiritual content of these novels seriously, deeming it eccentric, fantastic and occasionally blasphemous, it is probably because the whole

subject of Christ in fiction is such an extremely
delicate and difficult one, and these stories of
men and women restored to faith and happiness
by direct visions of Christ, or guided through the
maze of contemporary religious problems by the
companionship of Christ in person are unquestionably the hardest types of spiritual biography
to record both convincingly and reverently
through the medium of the novel. For those who
hunger after new forms of Christianity with the
accent on truth rather than on beauty or goodness, fiction is not quite likely to satisfy the
appetite. As an American critic wrote:

> A sister art like painting may interpret, but
> literary art knows its limitations. It will be
> boldest in the forms of poetry and the drama,
> but fiction turns away. There is one subject
> before which great fiction, with all its mirror-
> like power, drops its eyes, and that is Truth
> Incarnate.

CONCLUSION

THUS the reign of Queen Victoria drew to its close, with Christianity being aestheticized, extroverted and even "electrified", and Marie Corelli and Mrs. Humphry Ward in undisputed sway as rulers of the religious novel, both commanding an enormous reading public and sales beyond the dreams of earlier novelists. (Marie Corelli's *The Sorrows of Satan* (1895) had an initial sale greater than that of any previous English novel.) Gresley and Paget, the fathers of Victorian theological fiction, would have been extremely shocked at the thought of such staggering influence allied to such staggering doctrines, for Miss Corelli's eccentric revellings in supernatural fantasy and Mrs. Ward's earnest efforts on the other side to cope with "the crumbling of the Christian mythology" testify alike to the dissolution of traditional belief. The nemesis of a faith had at last received its popular recognition and acclamation, and the religious novel, the most influential ethical teacher of the time, fed the hungry sheep of late Victorian England with spiritual fare that differed considerably from the popular brands of nourishment offered fifty years earlier. Septuagenarian Oxford Movement novelists deplored the "shallow creeds which

now mingle with novel-writers' visions of romance"; Charlotte Yonge thought *Barabbas* a
"horrid book" and wrote a tart letter of rebuke
to the *Church Illustrated* for joining in the
general approbation of Marie Corelli.

Miss Yonge died in the same year as Queen
Victoria, lamenting to the last the "shocking
irreverence" of contemporary religious fiction;
Miss Corelli died in 1924, her novels quite out-
moded and herself regarded more as an old
curiosity than as a serious author, and Mrs. Ward
in 1920, wishing shortly before her death that
she could write a good detective story. The desire
is not without significance. The sixty or more
years that separate us from the end of Queen
Victoria's reign have witnessed such great
changes in literary taste and religious atmosphere that the majority of Victorian fictional
sources of spiritual illumination, whether orthodox or unorthodox, Puseyite or Corellian, "infidel" or "perverted", are now condemned to
oblivion by the common reader of today, who
neither understands nor appreciates the complicated theological traditions of his forefathers,
and who generally finds crime more exciting
than religion in fiction.

But to the Victorian common reader, as we
have seen, religion was an intensely exciting and

absorbing affair. Even the religious novels least capable of communicating this excitement, three-deckers full of heavy didactic stodge with leading characters that are mere insipid "moral portraitures", stiff, clumsy and lifeless (Paget's pew was not the only "wooden hero" of a Victorian tale)—even these novels partly atone for their failure as fiction by demonstrating their authors' deep concern with the Christian faith and by helping us to untangle some of the complex skeins of thought and belief in the Victorian age. The greater novels—stories from the pen of a Newman or a Mrs. Craigie, a Miss Yonge or a Miss Sewell, a William Hale White or a Mrs. Humphry Ward—may well survive as works of art and inspiring records of religious experience in fiction, but so many of the lesser novels, written, as one novelist put it, "for explanation not for decoration", have a documentary rather than an artistic value.

So, in our brief glimpse of these novels we have perhaps recaptured a little of the history of the spirit during those times of momentous change and crisis. We have seen the struggle of High, Broad and Low fought out on a dozen different fronts; we have seen the rise of Tractarianism with its many developments and its gradual establishment as a religious power in

the life of the nation; we have seen the growth
of religious Liberalism and its fruits; we have
seen the Nonconformist barriers against fiction
being slowly broken down; we have seen the
revival of Catholicism on English soil and all
the aspirations and sufferings of the "perverts"
in the Victorian age, and we have seen, perhaps
the most saddening spectacle of all, the warfare
of science with theology in the nineteenth century and the many tragic casualties rendered

... most hopeless, who had once most hope,
And most beliefless, that had most believed.

We have also seen that, despite the strength of
his weapons, the sceptic was not left in full possession of the field at the close of the century,
many of the most popular religious novels re-
sponding to the sceptic's challenge with courageous, if curious, efforts at a reinterpretation of
the traditional faith.

From the beginning of the Queen's reign to
the end the religious novel thus mirrored faithfully the Victorian "transformation of theology"
and provided, on widely differing levels of intelligence, spirituality and artistic skill, a multitude
of answers to Tancred's burning questions, questions that indeed burnt themselves into the
hearts of countless Victorians, and questions that
may yet occur to the twentieth century with a

renewed fire of urgency: "What is DUTY and what is FAITH?—what ought I to DO, and what ought I to BELIEVE?"

BIBLIOGRAPHY

BIBLIOGRAPHY

A complete list of religious novels published in England during the reign of Queen Victoria would prove much longer than the text of this book. I have therefore selected only those that form a definite part of this study or its background. Limits of time and place have occasionally been transgressed to include certain novels (especially American ones) that were widely read by the Victorians and influenced their religious fiction.

Unless otherwise stated the place of publication is London. The first date given is that of the first publication in book form. (Several of these novels originally appeared in serial form, but details of this are not noted, unless of particular relevance.)

ABBOTT, Edwin A., *Philochristus, Memoirs of a Disciple of the Lord*, 1878.
—— *Onesimus, Memoirs of a Disciple of St. Paul*, 1882.
ACKWORTH, John, *The Minder: the story of the Courtship, Call and Conflicts of John Ledger, Minder and Minister*, 1900.
—— *The Coming of the Preachers; a Tale of the Rise of Methodism*, 1901.
ADDERLEY, James G., *Stephen Remarx, The Story of a Venture into Ethics*, 1893.
AGNEW, Emily C., *Geraldine, a Tale of Conscience*, 1837–9.
—— *Rome and the Abbey*, 1849.
—— *The Merchant Prince and His Heir; or, the Triumphs of Duty*, Dublin, 1863.
AIKIN, Berkeley (Fanny Kortright), *The Dean; or, The Popular Preacher*, 1859.
Alfred Lennox; or, Puseyism Unveiled, A Tale for the Times, 1851.
ANDERDON, William H., *Antoine de Bonneval*, 1858.

ANLEY, Charlotte, *Earlswood; or Lights and Shadows of the Anglican Church*, 1852.

ARMITAGE, Robert, *Doctor Hookwell; or, The Anglo-Catholic Family*, 1842.

—— *Ernest Singleton*, 1848.

ARNOLD, William, *Oakfield; or, Fellowship in the East*, 1853.

BAGOT, Robert, *Casting of Nets*, 1901.

BARRY, William F., *The New Antigone*, 1887.

—— *The Two Standards*, 1898.

BARTON, Annie M., *The Minister of Ebenezer Chapel*, 1887.

BESANT, Sir Walter, *In Deacon's Orders*, 1895.

BISHOP, Maria C., *Elizabeth Eden*, 1878.

BROOKS, E. S., *A Son of Issachar*, New York, 1890.

BUCHANAN, Robert, *Foxglove Manor*, 1884.

—— *The New Abelard*, 1884.

—— *Father Anthony*, 1898.

BURNAND, Sir Francis C., *My Time and What I've Done with it*, 1874.

BUTLER, Samuel, *The Fair Haven*, 1873.

—— *The Way of All Flesh*, 1903.

C —, M.A., *Enthusiasm not Religion*, 1848.

CADDELL, Cecilia M., *Blind Agnese*, Dublin, 1855.

—— *Home and the Homeless*, 1858.

—— *Never Forgotten*, 1871.

—— *Wild Times*, 1872.

CAINE, Sir Thomas H. H., *The Christian*, 1897.

CARMICHAEL, Montgomery, *The Life of John William Walshe*, 1902.

CHARLES, Elizabeth, *The Cripple of Antioch*, 1856.

—— *Chronicles of the Schönberg-Cotta Family*, 1862.

—— *Diary of Mrs. Kitty Trevylyan*, 1865.

—— *The Victory of the Vanquished*, 1871.

—— *The Bertram Family*, 1876.

—— *Conquering and to Conquer*, 1876.

—— *Lapsed but not Lost*, 1877.

—— *Joan the Maid*, 1879.

CHARLOTTE ELIZABETH (Mrs. Phelan, afterwards Tonna), *The Deserter*, Glasgow, 1836.

—— *Falsehood and Truth*, 1841.

—— *Conformity*, 1841.

—— *Judah's Lion*, 1843.

CHOLMONDELEY, Mary, *Red Pottage*, 1899.

—— *The Converts; A Tale of the Nineteenth Century*, 1837.

CONYBEARE, William J., *Perversion; or, The Causes and Consequences of Infidelity*, 1856.

CORELLI, Marie, *A Romance of Two Worlds*, 1886.

—— *Ardath, the Story of a Dead Self*, 1889.

—— *The Soul of Lilith*, 1892.

—— *Barabbas: A dream of the World's Tragedy*, 1893.

—— *The Sorrows of Satan*, 1895.

—— *The Master Christian*, 1900.

CRAIK, Dinah, *Olive*, 1850.

—— *Agatha's Husband*, 1853.

—— *John Halifax, Gentleman*, 1856.

CREED, Sybil, *The Vicar of St. Luke's*, 1901.

CYRIL (Canon Henry Dennehy), *Alethea: At the Parting of the Ways*, 1898.

—— *A Flower of Asia*, 1901.

DAVIES, C. Maurice, *Philip Paternoster, a Tractarian Love Story*, 1858.

—— *Broad Church*, 1875.

—— *Verts; or, the Three Creeds*, 1876.

DAWSON, William J., *The Redemption of Edward Strahan*, 1891.

DELAND, Margaret, *John Ward, Preacher*, Boston and New York, 1888.

DENHAM, Michael, *The Massingers; or the Evils of Mixed Marriages*, 1862.

DERING, Edward H., *Florence Danby*, 1868.

—— *Sherborne*, 1875.

—— *Freville Chase*, 1880.

—— *The Ban of Maplethorpe*, 1894.

DISRAELI, Benjamin, *Contarini Fleming, a Psychological Autobiography*, 1832.

—— *Sybil, or, The Two Nations*, 1845.

—— *Tancred; or, The New Crusade*, 1847.

—— *Lothair*, 1870.

—— *Endymion*, 1880.

DOUGLAS (afterwards Stock), Lady Gertrude, *Linked Lives*, 1876.

—— *Nature's Nursling*, 1885.

DU MAURIER, George L. P. B., *Peter Ibbetson*, 1892.

—— *Trilby*, 1894.

EDGAR, A. H., *John Bull and the Papists; or, Passages in the Life of an Anglican Rector*, 1846.

ELIOT, George (Mary Ann Evans), *Scenes of Clerical Life*, Edinburgh, 1858.

—— *Adam Bede*, Edinburgh, 1859.

—— *Romola*, 1863.

EVANS (afterwards WILSON), Augusta J., *St. Elmo*, New York, 1867.

FARRAR, Frederic W., *Eric, or Little by Little*, Edinburgh, 1858.

—— *Darkness and Dawn, or, Scenes in The Days of Nero*, 1891.

—— *Gathering Clouds*, 1895.

Father Oswald, a Genuine Catholic Story, 1842.

FLINDERS, Anne, *Felix de Lisle, an Autobiography*, 1840.

FOWLER, Ellen T. (Mrs. Felkin), *Concerning Isabel Carnaby*, 1898.

—— *A Double Thread*, 1899.

—— *The Farringdons*, 1900.

FRANCIS, M. E. (Mary Blundell), *Whither?* 1892.

—— *A Daughter of the Soil*, 1895.

—— *The Duenna of a Genius*, 1898.

FRASER, John D., *Philalethes, a Story of Jesuit Intrigue in the Church of England*, 1893.

FROUDE, James A., *Shadows of the Clouds*, 1847.

—— *The Nemesis of Faith*, 1849.

FULLERTON, Lady Georgiana, *Ellen Middleton*, 1844.
—— *Grantley Manor*, 1847.
—— *Lady-Bird*, 1853.
—— *Seven Stories*, 1855.
—— *Laurentia: A Tale of Japan*, 1861.
—— *Constance Sherwood*, 1865.
—— *Mrs. Gerald's Niece*, 1869.
GASKELL, Elizabeth C., *Ruth*, 1853.
—— *North and South*, 1855.
—— *The Sexton's Hero; and Christmas Storms and Sunshine*, 1855.
—— *Cousin Phillis*, New York, 1864. (In serial form in the *Cornhill Magazine*, 1863–4).
GERARD, Dorothea, *Orthodox*, 1888.
—— *Etelka's Vow*, 1892.
—— *A Forgotten Sin*, 1898.
GISSING, George, *Workers in the Dawn*, 1880.
—— *Born in Exile*, 1892.
GOULD, Frederick J., *The Agnostic Island*, 1891.
GRESLEY, William, *Portrait of an English Churchman*, 1838.
—— *Clement Walton; or, The English Citizen*, 1840.
—— *Charles Lever; or, The Man of the Nineteenth Century*, 1841.
—— *Bernard Leslie; or, a Tale of the Last Ten Years*, 1842.
—— *Church-Clavering; or, The Schoolmaster*, 1843.
—— *Colton Green, a Tale of the Black Country*, 1846.
—— *Frank's First Trip to the Continent*, 1845.
—— *Bernard Leslie, Second Part*, 1859.
HAMER, Selina S., *Phyllis Raymond*, 1887.
HARDY, Thomas, *Jude the Obscure*, 1896. (In serial form in Harper's *New Monthly Magazine*, Dec., 1894–Nov. 1895).
HARLAND, Henry, *Mea Culpa, a Woman's Last Word*, 1891.
—— *The Cardinal's Snuff Box*, 1900.
HARRADEN, Beatrice, *Ships that Pass in the Night*, 1883.

HARRIS, Elizabeth F. S., *From Oxford to Rome; and How It Fared with Some who Lately Made the Journey*, 1847.
—— *Rest in The Church*, 1848.

HARTE, Bret, *Lothaw, or the Adventures of a Young Gentleman in Search of Religion*, 1871.

HAWTHORNE, Nathaniel, *The Scarlet Letter: A Romance*, Boston, Mass., 1850.

HEYGATE, William E., *Godfrey Davenant, a Tale of School Life*, 1847.
—— *William Blake, or The English Farmer*, 1848.
—— *Godfrey Davenant at College*, 1849.
—— *Ellen Meyrick*, 1851.

HEYWOOD, J. C., *How Will It End?*, Philadelphia, 1872.
—— *Lady Merton, A Tale of The Eternal City*, 1891.

HOBBES, John Oliver, (Mrs. Pearl M.-T. Craigie), *Some Emotions and a Moral*, 1891.
—— *The Sinner's Comedy*, 1892.
—— *A Study in Temptations*, 1893.
—— *The Herb-Moon, a Fantasia*, 1896.
—— *The School for Saints*, 1897.
—— *Robert Orange*, 1900.
—— *The Serious Wooing*, 1901.
—— *Love and the Soul Hunters*, 1902.
—— *The Dream and the Business*, 1906.

HOCKING, Joseph, *Gideon Strong, Plebeian*, 1888.
—— *Elrad the Hic*, 1890.
—— *All Men are Liars*, 1895.
—— *The Scarlet Woman*, 1899.

HOCKING, Salome, *Chronicles of a Quiet Family*, 1889.

HOCKING, Silas, *Reedyford; or, Creed and Character*, 1890.
—— *For Light and Liberty*, 1892.
—— *One in Charity*, 1893.
—— *The Heart of Man*, 1895.
—— *God's Outcast*, 1898.
—— *The Awakening of Anthony Weir*, 1901.

HOLT, Emily, *Lady Sybil's Choice*, 1879.

HOWARD, Anne, *Mary Spencer, a Tale for the Times*, 1844.

—— *Ridley Seldon, or The Way to Keep Lent*, 1845.

HOWARD, Mary M., *Brampton Rectory; or, The Lesson of Life*, 1849.

—— *Compton Merivale: Another Leaf from the Lesson of Life*, 1850.

HOWITT, William, *Woodburn Grange*, 1867.

HUGHES, Thomas, *Tom Brown's Schooldays*, Cambridge, 1857.

—— *Tom Brown at Oxford*, Cambridge, 1861.

HUTTON, Edward, *Frederic Uvedale, A Romance*, 1901.

INCHBALD, Elizabeth, *A Simple Story*, 1891.

INGLELOW, Jean, *Allerton and Dreux; or, The War of Opinion*, 1851.

IOTA (Mrs. Kathleen Caffyn), *From Darkness to Light*, 1870.

—— *The Adventures of a Protestant in Search of a Religion*, 1873.

IRON, Ralph (Olive Schreiner), *The Story of an African Farm*, 1883.

JACOBS, Joseph, *As Others Saw Him*, 1895.

JENNER, Stephen, *Steepleton; or High Church and Low Church*, 1847.

JEWSBURY, Geraldine, *Zoë, The History of Two Lives*, 1845.

—— *Right or Wrong*, 1859.

KAVANAGH, Julia, *Madeleine*, 1848.

—— *Nathalie*, 1850.

—— *Rachel Gray*, 1856.

—— *John Dorrien*, 1875.

KENNEDY, Grace, *Father Clement*, Edinburgh, 1823.

KINGSLEY, Charles, *Alton Locke, Tailor and Poet*, 1850.

—— *Yeast, A Problem*, 1851. (In serial form in *Fraser's Magazine*, July–Dec., 1848).

KINGSLEY, Charles, *Hypatia; or New Foes with an Old Face*, 1853.

(In serial form in *Fraser's Magazine*, Jan.–Dec. 1852).

—— *Westward Ho! or, The Voyages of Sir Amyas Leigh Knt. in The Reign of Queen Elizabeth*, Cambridge, 1855.

—— *Two Years Ago*, Cambridge, 1857.

—— *The Water-Babies. A Fairy Tale for a Land Baby*, 1863.

—— *Hereward the Wake*, 1866. (In serial form in *Good Words*, Jan.–Dec., 1865.)

KINGSLEY, Florence M., *Titus: a Comrade of the Cross*, Philadelphia, 1895.

—— *Stephen, a Soldier of the Cross*, Philadelphia, 1896.

—— *The Cross Triumphant*, New York, 1900.

KINGSLEY, Henry, *Ravenshoe*, 1862.

LEITH, M. C. J., *The Chorister Brothers*, 1857.

LINTON, Mrs. Eliza Lynn, *Grasp Your Nettle*, 1865.

—— *The True History of Joshua Davidson*, 1872.

—— *Under Which Lord?* 1879.

—— *The Autobiography of Christopher Kirkland*, 1885.

LONG, Lady Catherine, *Sir Roland Ashton: a Tale of the Times*, 1844.

LONGUEVILLE, Thomas de, *The Life of a Prig*, 1885.

—— *How to Make a Saint*, 1887.

—— *Romance of the Recusants*, 1888.

—— *The Churgress*, 1888.

—— *Black is White*, 1890.

—— *Poor Dear Ann*, 1900.

LORD, M. L., *An Obstinate Parish*, 1899.

LUKE, Jemima, *The Female Jesuit*, 1851.

LYALL, Edna (Ada E. Bayly), *Donovan*, 1882.

—— *We Two*, 1884.

MABERLEY, Kate C., *The Lady and the Priest*, 1851.

MacCabe, William, *Bertha, a Romance of the Dark Ages*, 1851.
—— *Florine, Princess of Burgundy*, 1855
—— *Adelaide, Queen of Italy*, 1856.
Macdonald, George, *David Elginbrod*, 1863.
—— *Alec Forbes of Howglen*, 1865.
—— *Robert Falconer*, 1868.
—— *Ranald Bannerman's Boyhood*, 1871.
—— *Wilfrid Cumbermede*, 1872.
—— *Thomas Wingfield, Curate*, 1876.
—— *The Vicar's Daughter*, 1876.
—— *Paul Faber, Surgeon*, 1879.
—— *Donal Grant*, 1883.
Malet, Lucas (Mary Kingsley, afterwards Harrison), *The Far Horizon*, 1906.
Mallock, William H., *The New Republic, or Culture, Faith and Philosophy in an English Country House,* 1877.
—— *A Romance of the Nineteenth Century*, 1881.
—— *The Old Order Changes*, 1886.
—— *A Human Document*, 1892.
—— *The Heart of Life*, 1895.
—— *The Individualist*, 1899.
Marsh, Anne, *Father Darcy*, 1846.
Martineau, Harriet, *Deerbrook*, 1837.
—— *The Hour and the Man*, 1840.
Mayne, Fanny, *Jane Rutherford; or The Miner's Strike,* 1854.
Meeker, Mrs. Ogden, *Alice Sherwin*, 1857.
—— *Fortune's Football*, 1864.
Meteyard, Eliza, *Struggles for Fame*, 1845.
—— *The Doctor's Little Daughter*, 1850.
—— *A Glass of Gin*, 1850.
—— *Mainstone's Housekeeper*, 1860.
Monk, Maria, *Awful Disclosures of Maria Monk*, New York, 1836.
Moore, George, *Evelyn Innes*, 1898.
—— *Sister Teresa*, 1901.

MORE, Hannah, *Coelebs in Search of a Wife*, 1808.

MOZLEY, Harriett, *The Fairy Bower or The History of a Month*, 1841.

—— *The Lost Brooch, or The History of Another Month*, 1842.

—— *Louisa, or, The Bride*, 1842.

NEALE, John M., *Ayton Priory*, 1843.

—— *Theodora Phranza, or The Fall of Constantinople*, 1857.

NEWMAN, John H., *Loss and Gain: The Story of a Convert*, 1848.

—— *Callista, a Sketch of the Third Century*, 1856.

NEWTON, Emma, *The Modern Unbeliever*, 1847.

NOBLE, Frances, *Gertrude Mannering, a Tale of Sacrifice*, 1875.

OLIPHANT, Margaret W., *The Rector, and the Doctor's Family* (*Chronicles of Carlingford*), 1863.

—— *Salem Chapel* (*Chronicles of Carlingford*), 1863.

—— *The Perpetual Curate* (*Chronicles of Carlingford*), 1864.

—— *Miss Marjoribanks* (*Chronicles of Carlingford*), 1866.

OXENHAM, Frances M., *Edith Sydney*, 1867.

PAGET, Francis E., *Caleb Kniveton, The Incendiary*, Oxford 1833.

—— *St. Antholin's; or, Old Churches and New. A Tale for the Times*, 1841.

—— *Milford Malvoisin; or Pews and Pewholders*, 1842.

—— *The Warden of Berkingholt, or Rich and Poor*, Oxford, 1843.

—— *Luke Sharp, or Knowledge without Religion*, 1845.

—— *Lucretia; or The Heroine of the Nineteenth Century*, 1868.

PALEY, Frederick A., *The Church Restorers*, 1844.

PARSONS, Gertrude, *Thornberry Abbey, a Tale of the Established Church*, 1846.

—— *Avice Arden, The Old Man's Romance*, 1870.

PARSONS, Gertrude, *Sun and Shade*, 1871.
—— *The Story of Fordington Hall*, 1873.
—— *Wrecked and Saved*, 1878.
PATER, Walter H., *Marius the Epicurean*, 1885.
PHELPS, E. S. and WARD, H. D., *Come Forth*, New York, 1890.
RANDOLPH, Edmund, *One of Us*, 1882.
—— *Mostly Fools*, 1886.
—— *The New Eve*, 1889.
RANDS, William B., *Henry Holbeach, Student in Life and Philosophy*, 1865.
—— *Shoemaker's Village*, 1871.
READE, Charles, *The Cloister and the Hearth; a Tale of the Middle Ages*, 1861.
    (Earliest version—*A Good Fight*, in serial form in *Once a Week*, July–October, 1859.)
READE, Winwood W., *The Outcast*, 1875.
RICHMOND, Legh, *The Dairyman's Daughter: an authentic narrative*, 1810.
RITA (Mrs. D. Humphreys), *Sheba*, 1889.
ROBINS, Arthur, *Miriam May*, 1860.
—— *Crispin Ken*, 1861.
ROBINSON, Frederick W., *High Church*, 1860.
—— *No Church*, 1861.
—— *Church and Chapel*, 1863.
—— *Beyond the Church*, 1866.
ROCKSTRO, William S., *Abbey Lands*, 1857.
RUTHERFORD, Mark (William Hale White), *The Autobiography of Mark Rutherford*, 1881.
—— *Mark Rutherford's Deliverance*, 1885.
—— *The Revolution in Tanner's Lane*, 1887.
—— *Miriam's Schooling*, 1890.
—— *Catherine Furze*, 1893.
—— *Clara Hopgood*, 1896.
SCOTT, Lady Caroline, *The Old Grey Church*, 1856.
SERGEANT, E. F. Adeline, *No Saint*, 1886.
—— *Esther Denison*, 1889.
—— *The Story of a Penitent Soul*, 1892.

SEWELL, Elizabeth M., *Amy Herbert*, 1844.
—— *Gertrude*, 1845.
—— *Margaret Percival*, 1847.
—— *The Experience of Life, or, Aunt Sarah*, 1852.
—— *Cleve Hall*, 1855.
—— *Ivors*, 1856.
—— *Ursula, a Tale of Country Life*, 1858.
—— *A Glimpse of the World*, 1863.
—— *The Journal of a Home Life*, 1889.
SEWELL, William, *Hawkstone: a Tale of and for England in 184–*, 1845.
SHEEHAN, Patrick A., *Geoffrey Austin, Student*, 1898.
—— *The Triumph of Failure*, 1899.
SHELDON, Charles M., *In His Steps*, New York, 1896.
SHERWOOD, Mary M., *The History of the Fairchild Family, or The Child's Manual*, 1818–47.
—— *The Monk of Cimiès*, 1839.
SHORTHOUSE, Joseph H., *John Inglesant*, Birmingham, 1880.
—— *The Little Schoolmaster Mark. A Spiritual Romance*. 1883–4.
—— *Sir Percival, a Story of the Past and the Present*, 1886.
—— *The Countess Eve*, 1888.
—— *Blanche, Lady Falaise*, 1891.
SIENKIEWICZ, Henryk (tr. Iza Young), *Without Dogma*, 1893.
SINCLAIR, Catherine, *Holiday House*, 1839.
—— *Beatrice; or, The Unknown Relatives*, 1852.
—— *London Homes*, 1853.
SKENE, Felicia M. F., *Use and Abuse*, 1849.
—— *St. Alban's; or The Prisoners of Hope*, 1853.
—— *Through the Shadows*, 1856.
—— *Hidden Depths*, 1866.
—— *A Strange Inheritance*, 1886.
—— *The Lesters*, 1887.
—— *Scenes from a Silent World*, 1889.

SMITH, Eliza, *Clarendon*, 1848.

SORTAIN, Joseph, *Hildebrand*, 1851.

STEWART, Agnes M., *The Cousins, or, Pride and Vanity*, 1849.

—— *The World and the Cloister*, 1852.

—— *Eustace; or, Self-Devotion*, 1860.

—— *Father Cleveland, or, The Jesuit*, 1868.

STOWE, Harriet E. B., *Uncle Tom's Cabin, or Life among the Lowly*, Boston, Mass., 1852.

STRETTON, Hesba (Sarah Smith), *Jessica's First Prayer*, 1866.

—— *The King's Servants*, 1873.

—— *The Highway of Sorrow*, 1894.

TAYLER, Charles B., *Margaret, or The Pearl*, 1844.

—— *Mark Wilton, The Merchant's Clerk*, 1848.

THOMPSON, Harriet D., *The Wyndham Family, A Story of Modern Life*, 1876.

Trevor; or, The New St. Francis, a Tale for the Times, 1847.

TROLLOPE, Frances M., *The Vicar of Wrexhill*, 1837.

—— *Father Eustace: A Tale of the Jesuits*, 1847.

Truth Without Fiction, 1837.

WALLACE, Lew, *Ben-Hur*, New York, 1880.

WARD, Josephine Mary (Mrs. Wilfrid Ward), *One Poor Scruple*, 1899.

—— *Out of Due Time*, 1906.

WARD, Mary Augusta (Mrs. Humphry Ward), *Robert Elsmere*, 1888.

—— *The History of David Grieve*, 1892.

—— *Helbeck of Bannisdale*, 1898.

—— *The Case of Richard Meynell*, 1911.

WETHERELL, Elizabeth (Susan Warner), *The Wide Wide World*, New York, 1851.

—— *Queechy*, New York, 1852.

WHATELY, Elizabeth J., *Cousin Mabel's Experiences of Ritualism*, 1867.

WILKINSON, William F., *The Rector in Search of a Curate*, 1843.

—— *The Parish Rescued: or Laymen's Duties, Rights and Dangers*, 1845.

WISEMAN, Nicholas P. C., *Fabiola, or, The Church of the Catacombs*, 1854.

WORBOISE, Emma J. (Mrs. Guyton), *Amy Wilton, or lights and shades of Christian Life*, Bath, 1852.

—— *Helen Bury, or The Errors of my early life*, Bath, 1852.

—— *The Wife's Trials, or Lilian Grey*, 1858.

—— *Millicent Kendrick, or The Search after happiness*, 1862.

—— *Married Life*, 1863.

—— *Thorneycroft Hall: its owners and its heirs*, 1863.

—— *Overdale, or, The Story of a Pervert*, 1869.

—— *Canonbury Holt; a life's problem stated*, 1872.

—— *Husbands and Wives*, 1873.

—— *Father Fabian, The Monk of Malham Tower*, 1875.

—— *A Woman's Patience*, 1879.

—— *Esther Wynne*, 1885.

YATES, William, *Nathaniel Cartwright*, 1889.

YONGE, Charlotte M., *Abbeychurch, or Self-Control and Self-Conceit*, 1844.

—— *The Heir of Redclyffe*, 1853.

—— *Heartsease, or The Brother's Wife*, 1854.

—— *The Castle-Builders, or The Deferred Confirmation*, 1854.

—— *Hopes and Fears, or Scenes from the Life of a Spinster*, 1860.

—— *The Clever Woman of the Family*, 1865.

—— *The Pillars of the House, or Under Wode Under Rode*, 1873.

—— *The Three Brides*, 1876.

—— *Magnum Bonum, or Mother Carey's Brood*, 1879.

—— *Chantry House*, 1886.